Priming: Programming the Mind for Habit Change & Success

Also by Clifton Mitchell, Ph.D.

Effective Techniques for Dealing with Highly Resistant Clients

Priming:
Programming the Mind for Habit Change and Success

Clifton Mitchell, Ph.D.

Mind Management Publishing
Johnson City, Tennessee

Printed in the United States of America
10 9 8 7 6 5 4 3 2 1

For permission to use material from the work contact:
Clifton Mitchell
3328 Berkshire Circle
Johnson City, Tennessee 37604
United States
Email: cliftmitch@comcast.net
423-854-9211

Website: www.cliftonmitchell.com

Cover Graphics: In2Wit.com

ISBN 0-9760656-2-2

Contents

Don't Read This

The purpose of this book is to present current scientific research regarding how the mind works and to demonstrate how the findings can be used for habit control and self-improvement. I have been speaking on the topics in this book since 1988 and have received many requests from seminar attendees for more information regarding priming and dominant thought theory, and how to apply these concepts to their life. I am pleased to finally offer this information in this book.

More specifically, this book is about words.

It is about the amazing power that words have on everyone's life and how to use that power to improve your life. Ultimately, this book will explain how to use words to program your mind to create the habits that accomplish your desires.

As noted, this book offers a method of change based on robust scientific evidence. It appears that over the last 40 years researchers have attached scientific labels to the concepts that philosophical, motivational, self-help authors have been writing about for decades. These same researchers have also confirmed and refined what was previously conjecture. Thus, this book offers what I consider to be a much needed scientifically-based refinement to the self-help literature.

This book is not hyperbole and it does not promise success without consistent effort. I offer no voodoo, no magical fixes, no miraculous affirmations, and no reliance on the universe or the gods to mystically do anything for you. You have to chart your course, follow the path, and do the work. I provide the method and technique. You have to decide what you want and you alone must do the mental programming to achieve your desires. In the end, personal change is always an inside job.

Accordingly, this book was written for those who are genuinely serious about changing their habits and their life. It is a guide to effective mental programming which is at the root of all success and personal control. And while there are no claims that the process is effortless and does not require an absolute commitment to consistent thinking, I believe this book offers the simplest and most direct path to personal change available.

On a personal note, I have always had an appreciation of self-help books, particularly those that teach based on research. During my twenties I went through a period where I was lost in determining what direction to take in life. I was struggling to "find myself" and was clearly off course. During this time I read and listened to a lot of self-help material and I am certain it was helpful in guiding me toward a more meaningful life. I still today recall the lessons and ideas of those whom I read and listened.

Mind you, I learned not to set my sights too high regarding the books I read. I am fully aware that much self-help material is excessively optimistic, pie-in-the-sky gibberish. Many authors too often made it all seem just too easy. It is never as easy as they make it sound. Yet, within every self-help book or tape were jewels of knowledge that were of great benefit to me, sometimes just one line or two, sometimes much more. At the time, you could buy a book for $4.00 to $6.00. My personal rule was, if I gleaned one bit of information that was worth $4.00 to me, I felt I got my money's worth. I always got my money's worth.

Almost without question, the most common theme throughout the self-help world is that you must get your mind in the proper state for success. The authors who write about success always talk about the psychology behind success, the importance of "believing in yourself" so to speak. No other theme is more common in the success-accomplishment writings. You might look at this book as a more precise approach to this commonly alluded to cliché. This is the "how-to" book of mental programming that shows you how to get your head in the *precisely correct* place to reach your goals—the how-to book on believing in yourself. I sincerely hope you can glean a few dollars' worth from this material.

There is a considerable amount of information to discuss. There is so much that I have had an enormous struggle in organizing the material in a way that provides some continuity in presentation and makes it understandable. So, please bear with me as I make the initial points. Ultimately, the points will come together and support a simple axiom that you can use to guide your thinking. If the material appears disjointed or unrelated at times, please keep reading as everything written is moving toward a singular, summarizing principle.

Much Thanks and Gratitude

I have been very fortunate to have been provided a worthy band of proofreaders and editors who have been indispensable in making this book readable. Thanks goes out to David Franklin, John Greer, Jane Hilt, Tammy Moody, and Scot Price for their superb work in spotting all those writing errors my mind would robotically misread by way of subconscious auto-correction. Most importantly, I want to thank my wife and best friend, Linda, for her many consultations, proofreading, patience, and support as I have pursued what has certainly appeared to be a never-ending endeavor.

Important Note Regarding References

The purpose of this book is to make this knowledge accessible and understandable to the general public. Hence, this is a self-help book. It was never intended to provide details of every single scientific study, or to be a scholarly scientific treatise that labors in minutia. I often feel as if I am merely skimming the surface of the research available and I am forever grateful to the researchers who have worked to produce the evidence I present. They are the backbone of this book and much more capable than I.

For those seeking detailed scientific study into the concepts presented, references are provided. For each concept presented there are typically numerous studies supporting the findings and many of these findings are confirmed in a multitude of contexts. I do not provide every reference available supporting primary findings and I do not always provide primary sources and citations.

Because of the abundance of scientific research supporting the concepts presented, I most often reference a few key summary articles and chapters of edited texts which review and summarize numerous relevant studies. Subsequently, secondary sources are used frequently and references are referred to by the less formal term "notes." While not as formal, in many ways this is more practical for those readers desiring deeper study as these references provide a wealth of information in one place. Readers seeking detailed study of the concepts can efficiently proceed from the references provided. You can read about the topics for years if you like. Many of the specific scientific studies can be found on the internet. Mind you, be prepared to read a writing style that is tedious and exasperating.

By the way, what you have just read is the preface. Most people never read the preface. Rather than fight this I just tell them not to read the preface. Sometimes it works and they read the preface. Wonder why? Read on.

"*You are the magician in your own life.*
You are the agent of transformation,
your own transformation."
Eugene Burger
Magician, Philosopher, Historian

Chapter One

Priming: Why Did I Do That?

"There are mental activations of which we are unaware and environmental cues to which we are not consciously attending that have a profound effect on our behavior and that help explain the complex puzzle of human motivation and actions that are seemingly inexplicable, even to the individual performing the actions."[1]

Denise C. Park (p. 461)

The Hidden Guidance System that Influences Everyone

In the mid-nineties researchers Bargh, Chen, and Burrows[2] at New York University conducted a most fascinating experiment. Students from an introductory psychology class were asked to construct a grammatically correct four-word sentence using five words presented in a scrambled order. This is referred to as the Scrambled Sentence Test. Obviously, one of the words is discarded in the process. The students were instructed to do this as quickly as possible. You can try this yourself with the example words below. With the following five words construct a logical sentence using only four of the words.

he, it, hides, finds, instantly

If you said, "He hides it instantly," or "He finds it instantly," or "Instantly, he hides it," or "Instantly, he finds it," or a similar sentence, you have correctly completed the task.

However, the participants' skills at completing this task had nothing to do with what the experimenters were trying to determine.

There were two groups of subjects. Unbeknownst to one group of participants, the words provided to construct sentences were commonly associated with the elderly. This association had been substantiated by previous research. These were words such as *Florida, old, wrinkles, Bingo, sentimental, gray,* to name a few. Another group of participants were provided words for sentence construction that were deemed neutral as in the example above. That is, this set of words had no particular association with any one specific group or thing.

Now for the conclusion and the kicker.

Upon leaving the experiment, researchers used a stop watch to carefully time how long it took the participants to walk down a precisely measured stretch of hallway. The researchers doing the timing had no idea which participants had worked with the neutral words or which participants had worked with the words associated with the elderly. Can you guess the results?

As you may already suspect, the group of subjects that constructed sentences with words associated with the elderly walked significantly slower than those who constructed sentences with neutral words. For those scientific types reading this, the walking speed differences were significant at the $p < .01$ level. The findings were very strong. (Level of significance numbers will be presented for those interested. If you are unfamiliar with the use of such numbers, never mind. Just remember that all of the results presented in this book were scientifically significant. In lay terms, the results were impressive and consequential.)

In addition, subjects were tested to see if they had any awareness that words associated with the elderly were being used. Only 1 out of 19 subjects had any awareness that the words were associated with the elderly. Still, the subject who recognized the association had no idea how that association might have been related to the outcome measure of the study, which was walking speed.

The implications of this experiment are undeniably mesmerizing. These researchers demonstrated that physical behavior (walking speed in this instance) can be influenced by simply reading and bringing into the mind certain words. More importantly, people do not have to be consciously aware that words brought to mind are influencing them. That is, in some circumstances, people's behavior can be changed by bringing to mind certain words *and* this can be done without any awareness of it happening.(see footnote 1)

This study confirmed previous research that demonstrated that humans are frequently controlled by a hidden guidance system—an automatic pilot that directs behavior.[3,4] Further, this automatic pilot is often controlled by outside input to the brain of which we are not aware. In the above experiment the outside input was words. Studies such as this substantiate the idea that words have more influence on our behavior than we are typically aware.

These experimenters were investigating the influence of what is called *priming.* Priming research tries to determine the influence of arousing certain associations in someone's mind. Typically, the bringing to mind of these associations is done indirectly, without subjects knowing what is being stimulated or triggered in their brain. That is, people are primed without conscious awareness; they have no idea priming is happening and changing their behavior. Once priming occurs, a sort of automatic pilot kicks in and directs their behavior.

Priming has been defined in many ways. The dictionary states that priming means "...to prepare or make ready for a particular purpose or operation." The most common uses of the word usually involve priming a pump with water in order to make the pump work or priming a carburetor with gas in order to start an engine. In these instances, we are readying the pump or carburetor to do their functions.

Priming occurs when something that is presented to you—such as a word, image, fragrance, or object—influences something you do later. Stated a bit more scientifically, priming occurs when an "earlier stimulus" influences later behavior. From a formal scientific perspective, priming is defined as an increased sensitivity to certain stimuli due to prior stimuli. Wow, can scientists make things sound complicated? Yet again, the basic process is easy to understand: Something that you see, hear, smell, taste, or touch results in you doing something. It just so happens that this is occurring almost constantly in your everyday life. Various things are constantly triggering the behaviors you do.

More importantly, priming can be accomplished unconsciously, without you knowing it has happened. However, it can also be stimulated consciously with full awareness of what is being done and the intended outcome.[5] Most research on the subject is interested in unconscious priming. That is, "implanting" or triggering a thought in someone's mind and changing their behavior without them knowing what has occurred. The above experiment is an example of this and the results of similar research are equally astounding.

The basics of the underlying process are straightforward. Scientists have long recognized that priming triggers preparatory thoughts—thoughts that prepare us to take action. You see, actions do not just magically occur. They are always preceded by thinking. Everything you do has a momentary thought that triggers it. Even the most minute movement you do—such as stroking your hair, scratching an itch, or blinking your eye—has a momentary thought that causes it to happen. While these thoughts can be conscious and you can be fully aware of what you are planning, most of the time they happen instantaneously, without any awareness that they have occurred. Whether you are aware of the thought or not has nothing to do with it. The research has demonstrated that priming stimulates the momentary thinking we do before we take action regardless of awareness of the thoughts. After being primed, almost instantly your automatic pilot kicks in and you are on your way to doing something without even knowing what prompted you to do it.

In the study above, one group of participants was primed with words associated with the elderly—*Florida, old, wrinkles, bingo, sentimental, gray,* etc. These words were the "earlier stimulus" and the priming was accomplished by having the subjects do a task using these words. Although subjects were not aware that they had been primed with things associated with the elderly, the priming influenced the later behavior which was the speed that they walked down a hallway. The priming occurred at an unconscious level. The influence on the later behavior (i.e., walking speed) was remarkable and easily measured.

It is also important to understand that, while preparatory thoughts stimulated by priming are fairly easily implanted, they do not always result in changing actions. You can intercept a known primed thought with your own thoughts and block the action triggered.[2,4] Hence, you use your own reasoning to override the primed thought. Philosophically speaking, this is the use of free will. Years ago I quit smoking. During the struggle to quit, I was primed by a multitude of stimuli and the urge to smoke was triggered. Yet, I used my own thoughts and, thus, my free will to overrule and countermand the smoking desires triggered. It was not easy, but it was doable. However, if one is unaware that they have been primed, as in the experiment above, it can be more difficult to block the action triggered by the priming thoughts. These points will be discussed at length later.

As pointed out, you can also be consciously primed.[5] Conscious priming occurs when you are very aware of the thing that has been presented to you and aware of the purpose; yet, behavior is influenced nonetheless. A common example of conscious priming occurs when you order a burger at McDonald's and you are asked, "Would you like fries with that?" When cashiers at McDonald's were asked to prompt with this priming question, about 50% of the customers said, "Yes."[6] This question stimulates and triggers your desire for french fries and has resulted in millions of additional french fry sales. How many times have you ordered the fries when you were not originally planning to eat them? (Check yourself now, are you thinking about french fries?)

Similarly, Amazon reports that 35% of their sales come from suggesting related items.[7] Have you noticed that no book on Amazon is listed without an additional list of books on the same page and the prompt, "Customers who viewed this item also viewed…." Note that the prompt includes the word "viewed" which will likely trigger the idea to look at the other books. You are not told to do anything which is a "soft sell" approach; Amazon merely points out that others *"also viewed"* similar books. I am sure you are consciously aware that Amazon is trying to increase sales. Yet, the words and the pictures of similar books result in 35% of people buying additional books. (By the way, is it really true that others viewed similar titles or does Amazon simply list books about related subjects and plant a seed in your mind?)

The research on priming is absolutely compelling. There have been a multitude of studies that have substantiated the influence of priming on a variety of behaviors. Let's review a few studies and findings.

Can Words Prime Good Manners?

In a similar style experiment to the one above, the same researchers used the same Scrambled Sentence Test to prime subjects with certain words.[2] This time there were three groups of subjects and priming conditions. One group was primed with words associated with *rudeness* such as *aggressively, rude, intrude, interrupt, brazen, infringe,* etc. A second group was primed with words associated with *politeness* such as *considerate, respect, cordially, polite, courteous,* etc. A third group was primed with neutral words that had no association with one specific theme.

After the Scrambled Sentence Test was completed and each group of subjects was primed with the themed words, subjects were instructed to ask a researcher for directions as to how to complete the next aspect of the experiment. As the subjects approached the researcher for guidance, another person began asking questions first and dominated the conversation not allowing the subject the opportunity to ask for instructions. This "other person" was actually another experimenter posing as a subject. In scientific experiments a researcher posing as a fake subject is termed a "confederate" because they are not an actual subject. In this experiment, the confederate recorded how much time passed before the real subject interrupted the conversation and asked for guidance as to what to do next. Experimenters also assessed the percentage of subjects in each group that interrupted during a 10-minute period.

From what you have learned, you should be able to guess the results.

Subjects primed with words associated with *rudeness* interrupted more quickly than subjects primed with neutral or *politeness* related words. Specifically, subjects primed with neutral words or words associated with *politeness* waited for a significantly longer time before interrupting the conversation than subjects primed with words associated with *rudeness* ($p < .04$). In addition, approximately 67% of the subjects in the *rudeness* primed group interrupted the conversation, approximately 38% of the subjects in the neutral word group interrupted, and approximately 16% of the subjects in the *politeness* primed group interrupted. This trend was also quite significant ($p < .02$).

It should be pointed out that the priming effect was easier to achieve in this instance because the experimenter's non-attentive behavior would naturally trigger an interrupting response from the subjects. Yet, the quickness and frequency of subjects' interrupting resulted from the priming and not the circumstances alone. We know this because all subjects experienced the same difficulty in obtaining the experimenter's attention. This was confirmed in a follow-up debriefing assessment that determined that there was no difference by the three groups of subjects in the perceived level of politeness and courteousness of the experimenter. That is, the perceived level of politeness and courteousness of the experimenter was so similar between the three groups of subjects that the interrupting behavior could not be deemed a result of one group perceiving the experimenter to be more impolite than another group. This further confirmed that the priming words were the factor that influenced the quickness and frequency of interrupting. Yes, manners can be and are primed.

What a phenomenal study with captivating results! Under strictly controlled circumstances, human behavior was manipulated significantly without any conscious awareness by the participants. Once primed, the automatic pilot took control and behavior was influenced. What a powerful force in our lives. This book is about harnessing this power.

Let's further explore the incredible power of priming as revealed through research.

How Many Ways Can People Be Primed? Lots.

This book will focus almost exclusively on priming with words which, in research, is referred to as semantic priming. Webster's dictionary defines "semantic" as "of or relating to the meanings of words and phrases," or, "of or relating to meaning in language." Although the focus of this book is on the influence of priming with words, to fully understand the concept, it is beneficial to understand the many ways that we are primed.

Just about anything that triggers a thought or image can prime. You can be primed and moved to automatic behavior with words, images, scents, objects, environmental cues, people, and your own thoughts. I am particularly interested in this last one. However, before examining how we can prime ourselves, let's explore priming by sensory means.

Researchers in the Netherlands investigated whether behavior could be triggered with scents and odors.[8] They investigated the impact of olfactory stimulation in several ways.

In the first experiment one group of subjects was placed in a cubical in which the citrus scent of cleaning fluid was present and a second group was placed in a cubical with no scent present. Each group was given the task to as quickly as possible identify groups of letters as either real words or simply a string of letters that spell nothing. Of the 40 letter groupings presented, 20 were real words and 20 were non-words. Of the 20 real words, six were related to cleaning and included words such as "cleaning" or "hygiene." Reaction times to identifying words were recorded.

As you may already expect, cleaning related words were identified more quickly when the citrus scent was present (p = .04). As with all such experiments, in the debriefing process that occurred afterwards, researchers confirmed subjects were unaware that the scent in the room was being studied and that it influenced their responses. This confirmed that the influence of the scent on response time occurred at an unconscious level. In this instance, how quickly one could mentally access cleaning-related words was enhanced by the citrus scent commonly associated with cleaning products. As demonstrated here, priming enhances the mind's access to related concepts. Later we will see how this priming attribute is very helpful when priming to create self-change and self-improvement.

In a similar study, subjects were again placed in rooms with or without an orange scent and then asked to write down what activities they planned for the rest of the day.[8] Of those subjects placed in the room with the citrus scent, 36% listed cleaning-related activities as opposed to only 11% placed in a neutral odor room. The difference was scientifically significant (p = .04).

Finally, subjects were placed in rooms with or without citrus scent and instructed to complete a questionnaire.[8] After completing the questionnaire, they were moved to a room where they ate a cookie that was brittle and deliberately designed to produce crumbs. Their eating behavior was videoed and rated as to the degree they kept their eating area clean by picking up the crumbs produced. Those who rated the degree of crumb cleaning behavior did not know which subjects had been exposed to the citrus scent and which had not. In scientific terms, video raters were "blind" as to which subjects were in which group.

As you must expect by now, participants exposed to the citrus scent displayed significantly more crumb removal behavior than the no-scent group (p = .02). Specifically, subjects primed by the citrus scent removed crumbs over three times more often on average than the non-primed group. Post-experiment debriefing revealed that participants were unaware that the orange scent influenced their behavior. Once again, the automatic pilot was triggered and resulted in behavior of which no participant had any idea of the cause. It's a bit spooky.

The Effects of Hot and Cold—Can You Feel It?

Here's another mind-boggling study. Researchers Lawrence Williams and John Bargh tested the impact of temperature on people's perceptions.[9] (By the way, if you are interested in priming, study John Bargh's work; he is one of the foremost experts on the topic.) This time they were investigating whether simply having subjects hold either a hot or cold drink would influence their perceptions and subsequent ratings of a person of whom they had a general description only.

In order to subtly introduce the influence of temperature, the researcher asked subjects to hold his/her drink while the researcher completed paper work. This was done during subjects' elevator ride to the laboratory. For one group of subjects the drink was hot, for the other group the drink was cold. Once in the laboratory, subjects were provided a general description of a person and asked to complete a questionnaire rating the person on ten personality traits. The traits included a measure of how interpersonally "warm" or "cold" the person was perceived to be. As you should suspect, subjects who held a warm drink rated the person as "warmer" and people who held a cold drink rated the person as "colder." Results were significant at the $p = .05$ level. Furthermore, the temperature of the drink did not influence rating differences on other personality traits. Subsequent assessments revealed that subjects had no awareness that the temperature of the drink was being studied and was influencing their perceptions.

In a similar study the above researchers had subjects hold either a hot or cold therapeutic pad and then decide whether or not to accept one of two types of rewards.[9] One reward was framed as a "personal reward" for him/herself and the other was described as a "prosocial reward" or something to give a friend. The experimenters wanted to determine if hot or cold influenced self-centered reward choices or not. In this study 75% of the subjects primed with a cold pad chose a gift for themselves, whereas only 46% of the subjects primed with a hot pad chose a gift for themselves. Again, this difference was scientifically significant ($p < .05$). Unquestionably, hot or cold temperature influenced whether subjects rewarded themselves or others.

Other studies have confirmed these results and shown that temperature influences the ratings of friends, oneself, and the experimenter, as well as the level of abstraction used in language descriptors.[10] In all instances subjects had no inkling that their behavior was being influenced by temperature. Of greater interest to scientists is that varying sensory input in one area (e.g. temperature) influenced behavior in a completely different area—the perception of others. Would you have ever expected that the temperature of a room or that a hot/cold pad could change your perception of others or change whether you took a gift for yourself as opposed to a gift for another? Perhaps you should keep your house warm and serve hot drinks in order to have others think better of you and give you things.

Can You See the Implications of This?

By now I am sure you get the picture. People can be influenced through priming with words, scents, temperature, as well as other sensory input and their behavior can be changed without their awareness. There is an enormous amount of research investigating the power of priming. However, it is beyond the scope of this book to address even a moderate portion of the findings. Frankly, I agonized over which studies to discuss and constantly have the feeling that I have not included some of the most interesting. Below are some additional studies that illuminate the impact of priming. For brevity, I provide brief summaries that only skim the details and provide results. Those desiring additional study can begin with the references provided that will guide you to the formal research.

A fair number of studies have examined the influence of priming on conformity, fairness, competitiveness, cooperation, hostility, and aggression. Summaries of a few of these particular studies follow.

As noted, priming can occur in many ways and through many means. Researchers as early as 1983 primed subjects through watching videos where either hostile behavior or calm, pleasant behavior was observed.[11] Subjects later were asked to rate the actions of a person in an ambiguous script in which it was very unclear how the behavior of the person could be interpreted. As hypothesized, those subjects primed with hostile models rated the person in the ambiguous situation as more hostile ($p < .03$).

Researchers Kay and Ross[12] demonstrated that priming influenced the title participants chose to label a game of which it was unclear as to the ultimate purpose or outcome. Specifically, those primed with words associated with competitiveness more frequently chose the titles "The Wall Street Game" or "The Battle of Wits"; whereas, those primed with words associated with cooperation more frequently chose the titles "The Community Game" or "The Team Game." These results were quite strong across all measures ($p < .001$). The priming words also significantly influenced the approach that subjects perceived others would have toward playing the game. That is, those primed with words associated with competition thought that others would have a more self-centered approach to playing the game than those primed with words associated with cooperation ($p < .001$).

In a study investigating conformity,[13] two groups of subjects were primed with either words associated with conformity (adhere, agree, comply, conform, copy, customary, emulate, etc.) or nonconformity (challenge, confront, counter, defy, deviate, differ, disagree, etc.). Subjects were subsequently placed in a group in which they were asked to express their views regarding the Scrambled Sentence Test just completed. Unknown to all subjects, all other group members were confederates working for the experimenter who always gave their opinions first. As expected, those primed with words associated with conformity agreed with the confederate group members significantly more than subjects primed with nonconformity words ($p < .05$). This research also noted that priming with nonconformity does not result in rebellious response to group norms, just perhaps less agreement.

In another study regarding competitiveness versus cooperation, mere pictures of items associated with the business world (board room tables, ink pens, men's suits, etc.) resulted in subjects being able to better recall words related to competitiveness in subsequent tasks ($p < .01$).[14]

In a similar study to the one above, the presence of business related items also resulted in subjects being less likely to view vague, ambiguous behavior as being related to ideas of cooperation ($p < .001$).[14] That is, once primed with business related items, the mind tended to move away from ideas of cooperation and toward ideas of competitiveness and adversarial relations when assessing situations that were neutral and not clearly one way or the other.

Finally, those primed with objects related to the business world were less likely to divide money evenly between themselves and another.[14] As might be suspected, those primed with business-related items favored keeping more money for themselves ($p < .01$). Specifically, of those primed with neutral items unrelated to the business world, 10 out of 11 (91%) proposed to split money evenly between themselves and another. Of those primed with business related items, 8 out of 12 (66%) proposed to keep more money for themselves! Wow! Studies such as this point out how powerful environmental cues can be in priming what people choose to do. How often have you found yourself unconsciously, automatically adjusting what you do relative to your surroundings?

Similar findings are pervasive throughout the priming research. That is, once primed with words or images around a theme, other words related to that theme are recognized more quickly and brought to mind more quickly than words unrelated to the theme.[4,15] Such studies demonstrate how words that are input into the mind influence future decisions and actions. These findings are of utmost importance in self-priming and programming your own mind. This research teaches us that it is vitally important to be very precise in choosing the words we place in our mind. Likewise, words linked to ideas opposite of what is desired should be avoided.

How do young children learn cooperation and helpfulness? In a most interesting study[16] researchers showed a group of 18-month-olds photographs of household objects, such as a teapot, book, or shoe..In the background of the pictures were images of two wooden dolls, one wooden doll, or a block of wood. In the pictures that included two wooden dolls, the dolls were either facing and almost touching each other or facing away from each other. It should be noted that the background objects were never mentioned to the children in the conversations that ensued; yet, they were clearly visible. Could the presence and position of the dolls subconsciously influence the children's behavior?

After showing and discussing the pictures, the researcher "accidently" dropped a bundle of small sticks and observed how the children reacted. If the toddlers did not help immediately on their own, the researcher made comments such as, "My sticks, they've fallen on the floor." The results: Infants who saw background images of the two dolls together, whether facing or not, were three times as likely to help with picking up the sticks as infants who saw the other background images ($p = .003$). The results demonstrated how subtle visual cues can prime helpfulness. Indeed, children are primed by subtle cues from adult behavior much more than one might think!

As you can see, researchers really like to determine if they can get people to do things without knowing it. This is the foundational premise that runs through the priming research. In another experiment[17] subjects were assigned a task with a partner who, again, was actually a confederate working for the experimenter. The two sat at right angles to each other and the interaction was designed such that they stayed focused on the task at hand. Now here's the underlying setup. In one group, the confederate rubbed his/her face repeatedly during the task while in the other group the confederate shook his/her foot repeatedly.

The sessions were videoed and coded as to what the subject themselves did and how many times. As you might suspect by now, subjects mimicked what their work partner did.

Specifically, those subjects in the presence of face-rubbing rubbed their faces more ($p < .025$) and those in the presence of foot tapping tapped their feet more ($p < .06$). No subject had awareness that their behavior was being influenced. Moreover, in one group the confederate smiled more than in the other group. Accordingly, it was also assessed if the subject mimicked the smiling behavior of the confederate working for the experimenter. And yes they did, and quite significantly. Subjects mimicked the smiling behavior more when the confederate smiled than when the confederate did not smile ($p < .0001$).

Finally, can you be primed to pursue a goal and not even be aware of it? The short answer is, "Yes." In a series of experiments[18] assessing whether goal pursuit could be primed, researchers obtained significant results when searching for the answers to a number of questions related to nonconscious goal acquisition. In the first study, subjects were primed with either neutral words or words associated with achievement (win, strive, succeed, etc.). Later, subjects were given a word-search puzzle and given 10 minutes to find as many words from a list as they could. Subjects primed with achievement oriented words found significantly more words in the allotted time ($p = .003$).

In the same study a number of other complex experimental designs were used to investigate the impact of priming on goal pursuit. The results were, again, quite astounding. Ultimately these experiments confirmed earlier assertions that goals can be activated without conscious awareness and that nonconscious goals appear to function just like conscious goals.[3] Additionally, these experiments demonstrated that *nonconscious goals* can produce *higher performance rates* than conscious goals. Further, subjects favored resuming nonconscious goals after they were interrupted. The message is the same and is even more profound than originally thought: Goals primed without awareness have a profound effect on behavior, sometimes more effect than consciously known goals.

What studies such as these have shown in the laboratory, we have all experienced in our everyday lives. Have you ever been sitting in one room in your house and gotten up to go into another room to do something only to find yourself unexpectedly doing something else that grabbed your attention? When you left the first room you had no intention of doing what you found yourself doing. You may have then moved to another task that inadvertently took control. After all of this, you then returned to your original task only to wonder what you got up for in the first place! If you have ever had this happen you have experienced how an unconscious goal can be triggered and hijack your behavior. When you experience and understand what has occurred, it's easy to grasp how unconscious goals influence an enormous amount of what we do.

That's Some Pretty Amazing Research

I hope you are now thinking that the priming research is absolutely fascinating and extremely compelling. The results of the priming studies are so phenomenal that people often do not believe them. Indeed, the leading researcher in the area, John Bargh, says that people do not believe him when he tells them the results of the research he does for a living![3] They do not think that people can be influenced in such ways. The powerful results just don't seem possible. Further, they argue that they have never been influenced in such a manner themselves! The average person is unaware that they are being influenced constantly by stimuli around them.

Yet, the fact that our behavior can be influenced and controlled by factors outside of our conscious awareness is now a firmly established scientific reality. It is also a primary area of study for social psychologists. Once stimulated by priming, our mind triggers actions of which we are not aware. We are undoubtedly frequently controlled by an automatic guidance system, and much of the time do not know when it has been turned on and put into action. As will be discussed in detail later, this automatic guidance system is generally referred to as coming from the subconscious and unconscious parts of our mind.

It makes you stop and wonder about just how much we are controlling our own lives. Who and what is controlling me? When you stop and think about it, it's a bit creepy. But I suggest that the better question is: How can I use this knowledge to beneficially control myself? How can I use this knowledge to break my bad habits and mold myself into the person I want to be? How can I use this knowledge to accomplish my goals? Specifically, how can I use this knowledge to stimulate my brain with preparatory thoughts that compel me to do the habits needed to accomplish my goals? The purpose of this book is to answer these questions.

As you will see, priming, habits, and automatic behavior are tightly connected. Repeated priming creates habits and habits are controlled by priming. The connections are so strongly interwoven in our psyche that, across time, they become one and the same. There are no habits without the primes that trigger them, and repeated priming results in habits.

The Ultimate Goal: Automaticity

The ultimate goal of this book is to teach you how to use priming to create automaticity. When I say automaticity I am referring to automatic behaviors or habits that we do without much effort. These are the behaviors that we just seem to do without thinking. We just do them, automatically. Your life is largely determined by your habits. There is no better way to take control of your life than to take control of your habits. The more you control your habits, the more you control your life.

More importantly, I am going to show how to break and create habits in the most direct, effective way I know possible. It is actually much easier than most have thought and experienced. Yet, you have to do it with great precision and consistency for it to work. This book provides the scientific basis for the formula for habit creation.

First, we have to investigate and understand a bit more about priming, ironic processes, and how the mind works. Let's explore the incredible possibilities.

Chapter 1 Key Points

- Priming occurs when something that is presented to you – such as a word, image, fragrance, or object—influences something you do later. Scientifically speaking, priming occurs when an earlier stimulus influences later behavior.

- Priming works by activating preparatory thoughts that always precede actions and behavior.

- Priming is occurring almost constantly in your everyday life and activates any habit, belief, or mental process you have stored in your brain. Priming occurs across a multitude of behaviors, mental processes, and situations.

- Priming can occur with or without our awareness. A multitude of studies have confirmed that we process and act on information without knowing it. We are controlled by an unconscious guidance system much more than we are aware.

- Ultimately, priming can be used to create automatic, habitual behaviors in ourselves that guide us in breaking our bad habits and creating desired ones.

Chapter 1 Footnotes

Footnote 1. Upon attempting to duplicate the findings of this particular study, other researchers did not get the same significant results.[19] This sparked a lively and somewhat fierce debate between researchers regarding the validity of the original research and the influence of unintentional experimenter bias. However, it is important to note that those questioning the results of this specific study did not denounce the overall validity of the priming paradigm and its suppositions.

Dr. Bargh responded[20] to the criticisms by pointing out that strict scientific procedures were used in his study and that two other research studies demonstrated priming effects of words associated with the elderly when moderating intervening variables were assessed.[21,22] He also pointed out that two TV science shows openly demonstrated the priming effects of words associated with the elderly. He went on to cite two comprehensive articles that examined hundreds of priming studies and concluded that the results are statistically reliable and valid.[23,24] Such comprehensive reviews are referred to as meta-analyses in research.

Interestingly, researchers who failed to duplicate Bargh's and his colleagues' original research regarding walking speed suggested that slower walking speed may have resulted from a combination of three factors: word priming, experimenter bias in timing, and unintentional, subtle, experimenter cues that influenced the subjects. The third possibility is most interesting. If inadvertent experimenter cues biased the results, this also indicates how easily people are influenced by the most subtle environmental cues unbeknownst to those giving or receiving them. Consequently, this particular explanation for inconsistent findings gives credence to the premise that people are unconsciously influenced by subtle cues without their awareness and, ironically, supports our understanding of priming in general. Interesting twist.

There are a number of reasons I do not find the criticisms of this particular research of concern and neither should readers of this book. The first is that there is an abundance of research supporting the impact of priming across a multitude of domains.[23,24] Second, as will be explained later, there are numerous variables that may account for different results obtained by different researchers. Third, all studies were conducted by serious researchers under strict scientific practices. Differences in research results are common and do not bring into question the integrity of those conducting the studies. Finally, because of the nature of scientific research and the multitude of unknown variables that may influence results, replicated research often does not obtain the exact results of original studies. This is extraordinarily common in drug approval research. Such is the nature of science as we move toward understanding our world.

Chapter 2

Priming: Explanations and Necessary Details

"Words are the best medium of exchange of thoughts and ideas between people."
William Ross

"Syllables govern the world."
John Selden

This chapter explains what happens in your mind when you are primed with words, the factors that influence how well priming works, and other important scientific details about this most interesting phenomenon.

For those yearning to delve into the priming research in detail, I suggest you start with the references frequently cited in this chapter. Most are summary articles and chapters and provide a comprehensive overview of current knowledge. As previously explained, be prepared for challenging reading.

As an introduction to these details, I am going to briefly talk about words and the influence words have on our everyday lives. This will be followed by the scientific nuances of priming.

A Few Words About Words

The brain makes sense of the world through associations. That is, we understand things in terms of other things. This is most often accomplished with words. The meaning of every word you use is defined by other words you use. That is, all words are understood by linking them to other words.[1] Every single one. Your understanding of the world in which you live is immensely dependent on the links between the words you have in your mind.

For example, if you look up "car" in the dictionary, it will state "automobile." If you look up "automobile," it will state "vehicle." If you look up "vehicle," it will state "car." There is a continuous loop of words defining other words in the dictionary *and in your mind.* As convoluted as this sounds, this continuous loop of linked word definitions works rather well as a system to help us make sense of the world and to communicate.

When we learn the meaning of a new concept, it is always understood by connecting the new concept to already known concepts. Accordingly, the process of learning is the process of connecting new concepts with old concepts. For example, the automobile was initially referred to as a "horseless carriage." People of the time labeled the new invention relative to what they already knew, the carriage. In addition, the salesmen of the day had to convey how powerful the gasoline engine was to buyers who were primarily farmers. They needed to create a concept that farmers could understand relative to what they already knew. The term created to describe the power of the internal combustion engine was "horse power." Clearly, this was something to which the farmer could relate. The world is full of similar examples.

The power of words is also used to manipulate people and ideas. When politicians want to raise taxes they do not talk about needing to raise taxes; they refer to it as "revenue enhancement." Obviously, the word "enhancement" brings to mind more positive, beneficial associations than the words "raise taxes." The creation of wars is framed as "defending freedom" and fighting and dying in them is framed as a "patriotic duty." Such terms carry a much more acceptable tenor to the public. Rarely are the economic windfalls of the defense industry and the related political payoffs mentioned by those in charge. Consequently, the populous is influenced and, in some sense, manipulated by framing decisions and actions with associations that are more pleasing.

Those with a command of language can undoubtedly use the linking of words and concepts to their advantage.

As previously mentioned, in the 1970's McDonald's asked its cashiers to merely ask customers if they wanted fries with their order. The purpose was not to hard sell, but to soft sell by merely suggesting the possible additional purchase. The "tool" for priming the minds of customers was words. And this is an excellent example of linking things together with words in order to influence sales. You are already ordering food and thinking about eating so why not link this to even more food. The six words spoken, "Would you like fries with that?" resulted in millions of dollars in increased sales. Since then this tactic has been used extensively throughout the sales world. Words have great power and salespeople know it.

We think with words, we communicate with words, and we understand the world with words. We create new things by putting words together in new ways and writing words in new ways. Words form the link between the physical, psychological, and spiritual worlds.

Words are a force of nature. Well-chosen words make or break legal cases, decide presidents, and shape the course of nations, as well as individual lives. Words create war and peace. Words are critical to all of life's adjustments.

Bergen Evans, the noted author, lexicographer, educator, and master of ceremonies for the $64,000 Question—a TV game show from the fifties—reminded us that, "Words are one of our chief means of adjusting to all the situations of life. The better control we have over words, the more successful our adjustment is likely to be." The clarity with which you describe problems directly leads to the clarity needed to solve problems.

Millions of people go to therapists to talk about and work through problems. The primary tool used to move through those problems is words. Research regarding the use of words in journaling found that those who wrote once a week about what they were grateful for were better off mentally when compared to those who wrote their complaints. Words form your psychological health.

Words are the primary, fundamental tool for managing living. Your knowledge and use of words is essential for thriving in this world.

Words shape reality. This is why it is important to choose your words carefully in describing everything and, in particular, creating future goals. You want the words you choose to bring to mind all associations that are of benefit, not undesired associations.

Finally, as you have just learned, **words prime actions and control behavior**.

"Language is a living, breathing thing."
Bill Maher

This Book Is About Words

I realize that we also can prime using images and other sensory input such as scents, tastes, sounds, and touch. However, when you closely examine the mental processing we do with these other sensory inputs in everyday life, we often convert them to words in our thinking and in our conversations in order to make sense of and communicate about them. I am aware this is not the case with the musician who thinks with sounds and melodies, or the artist who thinks with colors and shapes. Such thinking is specialized relative to the work at hand. Yet, for the vast majority of everyday thinking we use words.

In this book, the focus on words is for clarity and convenience. There are a number of reasons and benefits to this.

Words are the most common communication medium. It is easier to give everyone specific, detailed instructions with words. You can fine tune your communications by honing in on just the right word and its particular shade of meaning. Imagine I was writing about what to picture in your mind. How would I do that? With words. While the same word may conjure a variety of images depending on the listener's experience, pictures are likely to conjure up even more variety and variability in the minds of individuals. Yet, because better specificity is possible, the impact of words more readily fits what is necessary for scientific measures and rigor. Another reason I will focus on words is because, in my view, it is just too overwhelming and arduous to address all the ways we can be primed.

Most importantly, priming with words is the easiest to explain, understand, and accomplish for ourselves. Those wanting to broaden their study can easily research other priming methods. For the most part, a conceptual understanding of what occurs in the brain when primed with words also applies to other stimuli. For our purposes there is no need to be redundant and add confusion.

But what about the influence of images and pictures? Are they not just as important? Good point. Pictures and images are powerful priming tools and can easily be used to prime ourselves and others. I am well aware of this and suggest that you should take advantage of this power. Yet, for the most part and practically speaking, it is very difficult for the mind to separate words and images. Try it now.

Read this word: Bicycle.

Did you see a fleeting image of a bicycle in your mind? Most likely you did. Try it another way, turn the page and look at the picture on the next page.

Did you *hear* the word that describes that animal in your mind also? Chances are you did. This is known as a "subvocalization." Words and images are tightly linked in mental processing, almost inseparable. When you see an image and think about it, it is extremely likely that you automatically subvocalize the word to yourself.[2,3] That is, you say the word to yourself in your mind. In fact, research consistently confirms that the harder you try not to subvocalize the word associated with a picture and vice versa, the more likely you are to do it.[2,3] As we all have personally experienced, the harder we try not to think of something the more we do. This phenomenon will be addressed extensively in Chapter 3.

So, even though we will focus on words, in most cases those words will automatically trigger images. Separating words and images is virtually impossible. For practical reasons, the distinction between priming with words versus images will not receive attention going forward. If you would rather see an image than repeat words to yourself, then do. It's your brain and, with practice, to a large degree you can control what you prefer to display in your mind's eye. (I state that you can control your thoughts to "a large degree" because Chapter 3 reveals situations where we cannot control what is brought to mind.) The key is to learn to display the right words and images in the correct manner to achieve your desires.

If you discover that your words are quickly converted to images and that you can better impact your life's direction by consistently conjuring up certain images, then do it. I by no means desire to discount the impact of other influences on your mind.

Priming Nuances and Details

Priming is a powerful influence in everyone's life. So let's examine some of the details and nuances of priming. Specifically, the following questions will be addressed in this section.

What happens in the brain when you are primed?
How long do priming effects last?
What factors influence the effects of priming?
Can we manipulate others with priming?
Can priming effects be consciously overridden?
Does it always work?
Can I prime myself and use it for self-improvement?
Is the source of the prime important?
What is the ultimate goal of priming?
Which behaviors can become automated?

(For those wanting immediate answers to the above questions, here they are: Thoughts and actions are stimulated; briefly, unless; many; it depends; yes; no; yes; no; automaticity; all.)

What Happens in the Brain When You are Primed?

Before almost any action is done there is a momentary thought that occurs in the brain that triggers that action. Such thoughts are referred to as "preparatory thoughts." If the action desired has a degree of complexity, then the preparatory thought likely includes a brief, momentary imaging of what is about to occur. The more basic and repeated the action, such as the typing I do to write this book, the more the preparatory thought is deeply ingrained and triggers the action so rapidly that you have no awareness of it. Regardless, except for a few reflexes that are triggered in the spine, the vast majority of action *is preceded by thought* in the brain. Such pre-action thoughts are also referred to as "preattentive" or "preconscious" processing in formal research.[4]

Therefore, although we may not be fully aware of it, we are not haphazardly going from one action to another. No one is randomly going from one behavior to the next without some sort of controlling unit giving the orders of what to do next. That controlling unit is your brain. Because what we are thinking at this moment influences what will happen next, we are, to a large degree, in control of our lives. However, when we are primed by factors of which we have little awareness, we have less control.

Priming triggers preparatory thoughts that activate behavior. We can make ourselves do something by stimulating our own thoughts, or we can be primed from the outside and be stimulated to do something and never realize what triggered the behavior in the first place. This is one of the most fascinating aspects of priming. It's a bit spooky. Yet, preparatory thoughts are occurring constantly, one after another at this moment in your brain.

Semantic priming stimulates preparatory thoughts because all words are linked to other words. As noted, this occurs because all words are defined by other words. Words linked together in structured, recognizable patterns form sentences. Sentences form thoughts. Thoughts program your mind and, thereby, activate movement and control your life.

Priming triggers and brings forward preparatory thoughts that create movement in a particular direction.

More precisely, when you hear or say a word, the neural links to associated words fire off and are momentarily strengthened. I like to think of this as a sort of word chain reaction in the mind with each word activating related words. That is, each word heard, read, or thought creates a momentary explosion of related words in the mind. Because the neural links are momentarily strengthened, the associated words can be "brought to mind" more readily. This has been repeatedly confirmed by research.[1,5] Further, the more you think or say a word the stronger the links to related words become.[1,5]

Thus, when you hear or read or say a word, that word and any word associated with that word, becomes more accessible to the conscious mind. Figuratively speaking, when you say a word, that word and the words associated with that word move from "deep" in the mind to just beneath the surface of consciousness. At this point, all words associated with the initial trigger word are more quickly retrieved by consciousness. That is, it is easier to "bring to mind" words associated with the priming word than words not associated with the priming word. To understand semantic priming, it is critical that you understand this concept.

For example, right now, think of an elephant. When you bring the word "elephant" into thought or consciousness you are also increasing your conscious mind's access to related words such as, "gray," "large," "tusk," "Tarzan," "jungle," "trunk," etc. This has been consistently confirmed by numerous priming studies that investigated subjects' reactions to related words and compared them with reactions to unrelated words. In the brain the links between the words we speak are, literally, neural connections.

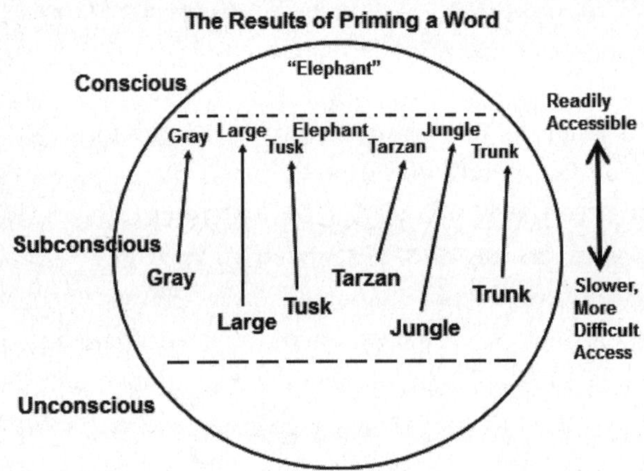

Once triggered, each of the new related words also link to other related words and so on. The same is true for images, sounds, scents, and objects which are also linked together by associations.

This is the basic, unsophisticated explanation of what occurs in the brain with priming. More complex, detailed explanations are available in the scientific literature; yet, this explanation is all that is needed for practical understanding and application.

The implications of this are profound and far-reaching.

For our purposes, the practical significance that emerges from these findings is that, if you want to trigger a certain behavior in yourself or others, you need to bring to mind the exact words necessary to trigger the preparatory thoughts needed to stimulate the behavior desired. Simply put, **the more you trigger words that are likely to trigger the necessary preparatory thoughts, the more likely you will do a desired behavior.**

While this may appear obvious and seem easy to do, I am convinced that most people do not fully understand the implications of this and do not know how to apply this knowledge for self-control. Most people talk to themselves and others in ways that often promote the very behavior they *do not* desire. That is, they say words that trigger the wrong mental links (neural connections) relative to what they want to happen.

Likewise, **those who learn to bring to mind powerful priming thoughts find themselves accomplishing what they desire more frequently and with much less effort. They accomplish more with greater ease because they are not fighting the detrimental influence of poorly chosen words that trigger undesired behaviors.**

For example, think of the parent in Walmart saying to their child, "Now don't you pick that up!" Or, "Don't you hit your little sister!" The triggering words "...pick that up," or "...hit your little sister" will likely have little effect or possibly prime a reverse effect of that desired. Similarly, if I need to get myself up and to work on time and I say to myself, "I don't need to lie here longer," the priming phrase "lie here longer" is likely of little impact and may prime and bring to mind all of the comforts that accompany staying in bed.

Can you see where we are going with this? Can you quickly come up with better words to say and think for the above situations? Much more on this later.

Another way to grasp the importance of words and priming is to realize that each word you think is really a cluster of words. That is, it is an error to think of words as individual, singular concepts. No word stands alone in your mind. A word not linked to other words would be a meaningless mental sound. **You should think of each word as a cluster of related words and concepts that are all triggering each other *and***

future action. This understanding is fundamental to effectively controlling your thoughts and life.

With an understanding of what priming does in the mind, the importance of understanding thought processes grows significantly. What you are thinking at this moment, whether consciously or unconsciously, influences what will happen in the next moment. **Each moment of your life is controlled by the mental processing that occurs in the moment that precedes it. The challenge for all humans is to learn how to control the thoughts that control our actions.** Your mind controls your life and words are the primary mechanism for programming your mind. An understanding of priming gives us the tools for effective mental programming.

How Long Do Priming Effects Last?

Overall, the effects of priming are short-lived.[1,5] Sometimes extremely short-lived, just seconds, depending on accompanying factors. The reason for this is self-evident. Your mind is processing millions of bits of information per second. If a prime does not trigger a behavior that is acted upon, then another thought or prime will enter the mind and override the effects of the current thought. Generally, we should assume singular priming influences fade quickly. Yet, this is not always the case. Some studies have found priming effects remain for up to a week.[6]

The good news is that the deterioration of a prime can be mitigated. As will be discussed in the next section, the singular most important factor that determines the length of time a priming thought will have impact is repetition. Other factors that extend the length of time a prime has impact will also be discussed.

What Factors Influence the Effects of Priming?

There are many factors that influence the impact of priming. These factors have been researched to such a degree that reading through this research is a formidable task. Yet fortunately, the primary factors influencing priming are rather commonsensical and can be summarized with a certain degree of brevity. Also, most of the factors influencing priming overlap a bit in their characteristics and, therefore, reinforce the impact of each other. These factors also provide much information about how to increase the impact of priming and avoid mistakes that decrease its impact. Again, the emphasis here will be on semantic priming, even though the factors have effect across all priming domains.

Priming cannot work unless there is something to link it to in the brain.[5,6] As simple as this may sound, it is a critical component to effective priming. If you hear a word and you know what the word means, by definition your familiarity with the word indicates you have connections to related words in your brain. The more you use the word and have an understanding of its meanings, the more connections. Also, the more connections the more likely the word will have impact and trigger action. Try it now.

Close your eyes, pause, and think "eating." Really do it right now. Chances are this triggered a plethora of ideas, images, and possibly even a momentary inkling of flavors. It may trigger thoughts about your last meal or your next meal. You may have felt a momentary urge to eat or quickly scanned the foods immediately available. Put "eating" in your mind again and observe. Interesting, isn't it?

Now think the word, "absquatulate" (ab-skwoch-uh-leyt). Chances are you did not get much mental reaction because you have never heard the word and do not know the meaning. I can hardly pronounce it myself. To know the meaning of a word literally means you have connections between this word and other words. A prime cannot work unless there is something to link it to in your brain. No connections, no priming. By the way, "absquatulate" means to "flee or run away, usually with something or someone." Now you can build some new neural connections around this word and impress your friends with your vocabulary.

Simply put, the more words you have to accurately describe the specific action you want, the more connections you will have in your mind to trigger that action. The opposite is also true. If you do not

have specific words in your mind to describe and trigger the behavior you desire, it will be difficult to stimulate that behavior.

This idea is directly related to the scientific concept of mental accessibility. Words with high levels of mental accessibility are words that are easier to think, use, and understand. The words you use frequently have high levels of mental accessibility and are more likely to be applied when needed to influence your life.[6] Mental accessibility is a direct result of neural connections between words and repeatedly using those words to strengthen the connections. The more easily you can access useful words and concepts, the more beneficial they become. More on this later.

During my doctoral training I did an internship placement in an inpatient facility that housed preadolescent sex offenders. Yes, pre-teenage sex offenders. It did not take long to realize that they were some of the most confused children one could ever encounter. In my interactions with them I soon realized that most of these children had been given what-not-to-do instructions their entire lives—"Don't hit your little sister," "Don't run," "Don't touch that!" "Don't take that." They literally did not have words in their minds that described *how to act*. They only had words describing what they should not do and, unfortunately, these words triggered the very behaviors that were undesired. These children did not have connections to beneficial concepts in their brain. It was no wonder they ended up in this facility and were so confused about life.

Priming impact increases with repetition and practice.[1,4,5,6] Repetition and practice advance the impact of priming. You may repeat something because it is important to you, because it is important to the task at hand, or a host of other reasons; regardless, repetition is the common element that makes the difference.

Priming without repetition is just a fleeting, transitory event that will likely not have much influence on your overall life. Although it is possible and does happen on occasion, it is rare that a singular priming event changes someone's life. **Priming with repetition becomes mental programming and determines your life.** Repetition is the paramount factor that makes the difference. This means you have to practice. As noted in the introduction, I offer no quick fixes. If you are not willing to consistently apply the techniques across time, don't expect much.

Perhaps this is a good time to briefly delve into the modern scientific findings of the neuroplasticity and neurogenesis research. Neuroplasticity refers to the brain's ability to restructure itself. For example, when certain parts of the brain die, other parts can take over. Neurogenesis refers to the brain's ability to create new neurons and nerve pathways. Both concepts are very closely related.

For years scientists believed that the brain could not generate new cells, repair, and restructure itself. Today nothing could be farther from the truth. New breakthroughs in the ability to measure brain activity and density have definitively confirmed that numerous activities, life events, and stressors change brain structure at the neurological level.[7] The study of neuroplasticity is fascinating, yet, very complex.

There are a host of variables that determine whether or not something results in structural change to the brain. These include brain chemistry, nutrition, amount and duration of practice, exercise, personal motivation, and whether the change is a result of positive or negative events, just to name a few. However, from the studies of neuroplasticity and neurogenesis one all-encompassing, predominant point has emerged: *Repetition* is the singular, necessary, underlying ingredient for change to occur at the neurological level.[8] It takes time for neural growth to occur. If you want to create new neural pathways, you have got to repeat something across time.

This phenomenon has been summarized by the phrase "neurons that fire together wire together" which is a foundational concept in modern research investigating neuroplasticity. The more complete expression is: "Neurons that fire together, wire together and neurons that fire out of sync, fail to link," and is credited to psychologist Donald

Hebb who stated this in 1949. The second portion of this expression is just as important as the first.

(Later in Chapter 6 I will return to the neuroplasticity research when the issue of how long it takes for structural change to occur is discussed.)

Hence, repetition is of the utmost importance and will be driven home throughout this book. I am going to be writing a lot about repetition from here forward. You may get tired of hearing it. Yet, it cannot be emphasized enough. Simply put, you get better at what you practice and the more you practice the more you change neural structures. Not only is this true with physical activities such as sports, playing the piano, typing, cooking, etc., it is also true for thought processes.[7] The more you are exposed to a prime and the subsequent thoughts, the better you get at processing these thoughts. And, the better you get at accessing the preparatory, action-triggering thoughts when needed. Simply put, more frequent priming has a greater influence than less frequent priming.[5,6] This should be self-evident. **You get better at what you practice *and* you get better at what you practice the most.**

Stated another way, the influence of priming is circular. **The more you prime, the more you trigger thoughts that promote action. Likewise, the more you do the action, the more you increase the influence of the original priming stimuli that promoted the action.** Because the influence of priming is circular and cumulative, the fundamental premise of this book is that priming is the ultimate tool for self-improvement.

Directly related to this concept is the fact that, the more a prime is repeated, the shorter the time it takes for the influence to occur.[5] Your brain literally triggers the desired behavior faster the more it is practiced. Ultimately, the desired behavior is triggered so instantaneously and so automatically that you do not have any awareness of it occurring. You find yourself being steered to do things robotically, without effort. Habit!

Also of paramount importance is the fact that, the more a prime is repeated and practiced, the more influence the prime will have in overcoming the influence of distractions and impediments that may obstruct or override the ultimate behavior desired.[5] Thus, repeated priming enhances focus on the task at hand by blocking unwanted reactions and distractions. Repeated priming creates a greater concentration of thought on the ultimate objective.

Repetition of the correct priming stimuli is the cornerstone of good habits. Unfortunately, it is also the cornerstone of bad habits. The secret is to combine the principles presented here to more effectively and more easily create the habits desired.

By the way, do you think that advertisers and politicians are aware of the importance of repetition in influencing consumers and constituents? You bet they are. This is why ads run over and over in an effort to create a link between their products and your mind. Advertisers run ads incessantly on TV to the point you know the entire script the moment the ad begins. This is why those running for office create apparently meaningful, catchy slogans and drive them into the minds of people regardless of their truth or reality. Do you think they are influencing you? You bet.

"If your attention is not your intention, you are being used."

Myke Myers

The more relevant to the immediate task at hand, the more impact priming has.[1,5] This is true whether you are aware of the prime or not. On the surface, this is another rather commonsensical point. If you are standing in front of a smorgasbord, a prime regarding health and long life will be more pertinent than a prime regarding practicing the piano. In this instance, priming yourself with, "I eat healthy every day," will have much greater influence on your dieting plans than, "I practice piano daily." It is easy to understand how the more closely tied to the immediate task a prime is, the more impact it is likely to have.

Remember the experiment where subjects were primed with words such as "impolite," "rude," "obnoxious," and were later placed in a situation where interrupting others was necessitated because they were hindered from getting the additional instructions needed?[9] Interrupting was applicable to the task at hand and, thus, words associated with interrupting had a greater impact on behavior than neutral words.

The most recent prime typically has the most influence in the moment; yet, the most frequent prime has the most influence over the long run.[1,6] If not repeated and "burned" into the mental circuits, the influence of a prime deteriorates rapidly. A comment made in the moment will likely fade quickly unless it triggers a more deeply ingrained, repeated prime that links to thoughts that linger longer. In the long run, frequency overrides recency.

The more specific the prime, the greater the impact.[1] The more specific the prime, the greater the influence of the prime on subsequent behavior. For example, suppose I have a goal to improve my health through exercise. If I say to myself, "I am healthy," this may trigger a multitude of ideas and behaviors, possibly exercise. There is nothing wrong with this priming statement; yet, it is vague and limited in its relation to exercise. If I were to say to myself, "I exercise daily," or, "I exercise every morning," I am much more likely to stimulate preparatory thoughts that promote exercise. The latter statements are very specific to exercise while the first statement is vague and it is not necessarily directly related to exercise.

However, "I am healthy" is not necessarily a poor priming statement. It brings to mind anything associated with health and states it in present tense. Both of these factors are advantageous. Depending on the individual, this statement may be valid as a trigger of a host of behaviors such as eating well, exercising, thinking rationally, getting enough sleep, etc. Yet, while I do not think it is always necessary, priming statements that refer to a specific behavior or action to be done appear to be the most impactful and practical. In the end, the relevance of a prime is dependent on the individual and what thoughts he/she wants to trigger. More on this later.

The more personally relevant and meaningful, the longer lasting the priming influence.[6] Priming a matter that is of greater personal concern will deliver influence longer. We have all had someone make a comment that triggers something of deep personal concern that resulted in a multitude of thoughts that followed and lingered. Such primes may trigger obsessive thoughts that continue even if not wanted. Those who are aware that certain comments trigger a rant or emotional outburst in one of their friends become acutely aware of what to avoid in conversations.

The reason for this is almost self-evident and directly tied to the idea of accessibility. Things that are important and meaningful to you are thought about more often and, therefore, have greater accessibility by the mind. Things that are not important to you are not thought about often and have less accessibility by the mind. Thus, mental accessibility and personal importance become inseparable concepts and, when present, result in priming influences that last longer once triggered.

This reality directly applies when seeking to create self-priming statements that have impact. The more the priming statement can tap into something that is personally meaningful, the greater the impact and the longer the impact will generally last. For impact, you need to fine tune what you say relative to what is important in you. For one person, "I am a good model for my children," may be meaningful programming for smoking cessation. Yet, for another, "I save money," may be more meaningful. Depending on the underlying personal values, mental programming that works for one person may not be beneficial for another.

Priming works best for those with a strong need for closure.[5] It appears those who do not have a strong need for closure or who have a need to avoid closure are less likely to be influenced by a prime. This makes perfect sense in that priming triggers action toward accomplishing goals. Goal achievement by definition necessitates closure. Thus, any underlying mental programming for delaying or avoiding can override the influence of a prime necessitating or requiring closure. (Perhaps those who avoid closure need to program their mind to seek closure?)

Priming effects can be influenced by competing goals.[5] If you are primed to do a behavior that competes with another behavior you are currently doing and you deem the newly primed behavior as more important, the influence of the new prime can override the initial behavior. In other words, if you are primed to drink water while doing something, the prime to drink water may override the desire to stay on task. Here your desire for water overrides the desire to complete the task. Of course, the opposite could also occur. It could be that the priming to stay on task overrides the priming to drink water. This all depends on the relevance of the competing primes.

As will be discussed later, if you consciously prime the brain with a known objective that is of importance to you, the brain will automatically filter out conflicting goals. The prime perceived as more important relative to the situation at hand tends to dominate.

People cannot be primed to do things against their morals.[5] This is directly related to the previous points. If you have a deeply ingrained moral conviction, you cannot be primed to go against it in the moment. Here again you are presented with competing goals and the one that is the most deeply ingrained and personally relevant will dominate.

Please note that I am referring to momentary primary here. Brainwashing, which exploits repeated priming as well as other manipulations across time, can result in people doing many curious things, including suicide. It is beyond the scope of this book to delve into the complexities and implications of brainwashing. Suffice it to say that the mind grows from that which it is fed. The focus here is on the advancement of personally desired, beneficial behaviors.

In summary, these are some of the factors that influence the impact of priming. There are many others of course. Yet, this book is not intended to be a full scientific analysis. It is self-help. The above factors are more than adequate in understanding how to create powerful self-priming statements.

Can We Manipulate Others with Priming?
Can Priming Effects Be Consciously Overridden?
Does it Always Work?

For those of you worrying about people controlling your behavior, I have good news and interesting news. The good news is, if you are aware of a prime and do not want to act on it, you can override the prime and do otherwise.[6,10] Returning once more to McDonald's french fry sales we see an example where priming can be overridden. As previously stated, when ordering your burger and asked, "Would you like fries with that?" you are clearly aware of the prime and can answer, "No." In this instance, you can easily override the influence of the priming suggestion. You are not compelled or forced to do anything. As noted, about half of the people do not allow the priming suggestion to influence them; yet again, about half of the people end up eating fries. Interesting. **Having mental power does not always result in using mental power.** Then again, it is likely some really wanted fries!

As explained previously, the reason this particular prime works is because the prime is strongly tied to the task at hand which is eating. If you were buying aspirin in a drug store the same question would appear absurd. Yet, when purchasing a burger the question appears highly relevant. I know this is commonsensical; however, how often do we actually study and analyze the significance of words relative to various situations?

Also as mentioned above, research has shown that priming someone to do something deemed "...morally wrong, culturally objectionable, or socially undesirable" is ineffective.[5] If currently implanted mental programming is strongly against the behavior triggered by the prime, people will not do it. If this were not so, we could prime people to do all sorts of illegal or immoral acts. Obviously, priming works best with acceptable behaviors that are related to the task at hand. If it is important to the person, it works even better. (By the way, the reason priming objectionable behavior does not work is because previous repeated priming has deemed the behavior as objectionable. You were not born with such thoughts or mental programming.)

On the other hand, as we have repeatedly observed from the research mentioned in Chapter 1, if you are not aware of an automatic behavior being triggered and the prime is relevant to the current situation, you are more likely to be influenced.[10]

I do not believe we should necessarily consider this reality as negative.

This fact can work for you as well as against you depending on the situation at hand. We are all being primed and preparatory thoughts are being triggered throughout our day. This is how we get most of our daily routine tasks accomplished. We are also being primed by stimuli that may not be so common in our life; yet, we do not see results that are always negative. For example, it is obvious that much creativity is likely a result of new priming stimulating new ideas.

To always deem priming of which we have no awareness as harmful or negative is unjustified. Yet, understanding that we may be influenced by things beyond our awareness can help us avoid undue, negative influence. Remember, it is extremely unlikely that we can be primed into doing anything we do not believe is morally right. Unfortunately, we are sometimes primed to buy things in the spur of the moment that we later realize we did not need. Similarly, we are primed into ordering food that we know is not good for us and so on. The degree of negativity from a prime is dependent on the situation.

Understanding and being aware of what is influencing us gives us power over priming influences in some circumstances. While research has shown that people's behavior can be influenced, research has also shown that, if subjects become aware that someone is trying to manipulate them, they can choose to do the opposite[6,9] The issue of harm from priming is a philosophical discussion beyond the scope of this book. The focus here is on using this phenomenon for our benefit.

The short answer to the question of whether or not priming always works is "no." As noted above, priming influences can be mitigated by degree of repetition, specificity, immediate and personal relevance, need for closure, competing goals, morals, and other factors as well. Consequently, when attempting to prime others there are a host of factors that influence the outcome. With regards to priming yourself, if the priming statement is suited to your needs and mental processing, and you genuinely desire the outcome and vigilantly follow the method, it will work. These issues will be addressed in detail later.

Can I Prime Myself and Use It for Self-improvement? Is the Source of the Prime Important?

Yes, you can prime yourself for self-improvement and the source of the prime does not matter. You can and do prime yourself regularly. Priming researchers have confirmed that it does not matter from where the prime originates.[10] The prime can come from the outside, from a word read or spoken to you, or from the inside from your own thoughts. Research has shown that you can be fully aware of the prime and its influence and still have the effect it produces on your behavior[4,5,11] Vital to the purpose of this book, the source of the prime does not have to be covert or secret for the influence to be effective. You can deliberately trigger preparatory thoughts that put into motion behaviors you want. How do you think you get things done now? This book will teach you how to do this more effectively to rid yourself of bad habits and create better ones. Let's learn how to do this well. Your life is shaped by it.

What is the Ultimate Goal of Priming? Which Behaviors Can Become Automated?

The ultimate goal of priming is to create and instill desired habits or automatic behaviors that improve your quality of life and success at viable goals. Habits or automatic behaviors are created and triggered by priming preparatory thoughts. All behavior becomes automatic behavior through repetition and practice of precise preparatory thoughts. Inevitably, all habit formation or automation of behavior is accomplished through priming. This book teaches the most direct method to accomplish this.

Any behavior can be automated[5,10] and, therefore, become more efficient. This level of efficiency can become such that any behavior can occur without conscious awareness. Ultimately, this can happen to such a degree that the mental process will occur and exert its influence on behavior even if consciously unintended. As researchers Forster & Liberman state, "Any process...may be automated and become more efficient, unaware, and unintended"[5] (p. 203).

All of these points will be discussed and referred to throughout this book as we learn to utilize priming.

Circling Back to Words

The influence of words is immensely underestimated by most people. Writers, philosophers, psychologists, motivational speakers, and spiritual leaders have been saying this for years. Unfortunately, much of what has been said in the popular literature regarding affirmations and positive thinking has been too loosely presented and poorly formulated to be effective. Some of this stuff is so farfetched in proclaiming what can be accomplished that it readily falls into the category of new age mumbo jumbo. Yet, research has now confirmed that precisely delivered words have a decisive impact on behavior.

The sad reality is that much of what has been previously stated as intuitive conjecture does not provide the details necessary to make it truly effective. Just because you say you are rich, does not mean you are or will be rich. The nuances of proper mental programming are significant and must be addressed for it to work. I suggest that to effectively program the mind with words, a precise formula must be followed that is based on what we have learned about how words influence behavior.

The key is choosing the precise triggering words to say to yourself. If you choose the wrong words to describe yourself and describe life, you will unconsciously guide yourself in directions you do not desire. This will happen even if you consciously desire the opposite results. At a minimum your efforts to change and reach your objectives will be filled with excessive internal conflict and struggle.

The bottom line of all of this discussion is that words are powerful forces in shaping how you think and what you do. Each time you say a word, you are triggering a multitude of mental connections and associations that are triggering behaviors. **Words program the mind, the mind controls actions, and actions create results. Your life is a series of actions that are programmed into your mind largely through words.**

Unfortunately, this mental programming process is further complicated by the way words are processed in our mind relative to the behaviors they trigger. The next chapter will discuss *ironic process* theory, the major stumbling block we must face and overcome in order to execute impactful mental programming.

Chapter 2 Key Points

- All words are linked and connected to other related words. When you read, hear, or say a word a chain reaction of links to associated words occurs in your mind and those associated words become more accessible and influential.

- All behaviors and actions are stimulated and triggered by preparatory thoughts in your mind. Priming stimulates and triggers preparatory thoughts.

- Priming cannot work without something to connect to in the mind.

- Unless there is repetition, the influences of priming fade rapidly. The most recent prime usually has the most influence in the moment. The most frequent prime has the most influence over the long run.

- The effects of priming are dependent on a number of variables including relevance to the situation, personal meaningfulness, biological drives, specificity, need for closure, competing goals, and moral beliefs to name a few.

- Priming does not always work. If you are aware of a prime you can override the influence by sheer willpower. If you are not consciously aware of a prime, it may or may not work depending on the factors listed above as well as others.

- You can and do prime yourself. It does not matter what the priming source is.

- The ultimate goal for self-improvement is to reach a point of automaticity and to make desired, important behaviors habitual. Any behavior can be automated. Repetition is the most important factor in creating automation or habits. Repeated priming is the most direct approach to this end.

Chapter 3

Ironic Process: The Mind Cannot Avoid, The Mind Can Only Attend*

*It works even when you don't want it to; you cannot, not prime.

"It is hard, if not impossible, to suppress thoughts."[1]
Forster & Liberman (p. 224)

Let's Play Mind Games

Read this brief paragraph doing this exercise and observe what happens. Close your eyes and think about a rose. Create a vivid image of a rose in your mind along with the word "rose." Think only about a rose for as long as you can. Keep the word and a vivid image of a rose in your mind continuously. Think this one thing. Stop everything else you are doing and do this now.

If you observed your thoughts carefully, you noticed that there were moments when you did not think about a rose even though you wanted to focus exclusively on the rose. During these off moments when a rose left your mind a mental monitoring system kicked in and noted that you were not thinking about a rose; and, when you became aware that another thought was in your mind, you returned your focus to the rose. When you try to consistently think of a rose this happens repeatedly, no matter what.

This is what happens to everybody every time. You can do the exercise again and again, and it will always be the same. You may also notice that it takes a moment of time to obtain an image of a rose when you first begin. Thought takes time. Self-directed thought focused on something specific also requires that you become aware when you are not focused on it. **That is, conscious, focused thought necessarily requires awareness of moments when you are not focused on the thought.**

How interesting! And what a bind!

No matter what you consciously, intentionally concentrate on, you will always have intruding thoughts that are unwelcome and, most of the time, the opposite of what you desire to be thinking. Note that we are referring only to self-directed, intentional thought at this point in the discussion. The importance of willful intentionality (or not) will become evident shortly.

The monitoring system that checks to see if you are thinking about what you intend to think about is built-in. It appears to have been "hardwired" into your brain's circuits from birth. It does not have an on-off switch. That is, you cannot shut it off at will. You cannot shut it down by directly trying. In fact, it works harder to stay on when you try to turn it off. Interestingly, you can shut it down by not trying. This will be explained shortly.

What you have just experienced is called "ironic process theory" in the scientific literature.[2] Dr. Daniel M. Wegner is credited with developing the theory and is the name to search first for further investigation. In precise scientific lingo, Wegner states that, "…attempts to influence mental states require monitoring processes that are sensitive to the failure of the attempts and that these processes act subtly yet consistently in a direction precisely opposite the intended control.…when efforts to implement the intended mental control are undermined in any way, the monitoring process itself will surface and ironically overwhelm the intended control to yield the opposite of the mental state that is desired"[2] (p. 34). Did you get that? Sometimes it's a bit hard to decipher the technical language.

What Wegner is saying is that, when the mental monitoring system recognizes that you are not on track with the thoughts you desire, it will bring to mind the undesired thoughts to a *greater degree* than the desired thoughts. It is as if the mind "shows" you the undesired thoughts to let you know you are not on track. And it shows the undesired thoughts so intensely that they take over and dominate your thoughts momentarily. Once you become aware you have drifted off course toward the unwanted thoughts you can then move back to the wanted thoughts. However, unwanted thoughts will return and the process will be repeated.

The automatic system that checks your thoughts is exceptionally vigilant. So vigilant that the theory also states that the harder you try to control your thoughts under conditions of stress and pressure when it is really important, the more the unwanted thoughts creep into your mind. We have all experienced the harder-you-try-the-worse-it-gets phenomenon. As has been confirmed, when subjects in experiments were given tasks that overloaded their mind or that put them under pressure to perform, they did worse.[2] We have all had this happen to us, likely on numerous occasions. We tend to choke when the pressure is on. When we try to not think something, we think it more.

This is not a new idea by any means. Freud called it *Counterwill*. Baudouin called it the *Law of Reversed Effect*. It is the basis for therapeutic approach known as *paradoxical intention* which suggests deliberately practicing a neurotic habit or thought in order to remove it. The theory being, if you cannot get rid of a neurotic thought or worry by trying to get rid of it, then the way to get rid of it is to try to think about it. The historical predecessors of the scientific study of this phenomenon are nicely presented in Wegner's article.[2] Those desiring an in-depth study of this phenomenon would do well to start with this article and branch out from there.

Understanding ironic process theory is vital when you are attempting to trigger preparatory thoughts that produce desired actions. This is because, when you are trying to trigger certain preparatory thoughts, unwanted thoughts of an opposite nature are inevitably going to sneak into your mind! Dang! It looked like it would be so easy, now this! What a pain. How are you ever to control your preparatory thoughts to create the behaviors you want when built-in mental systems work so hard against you?

The good news is this mental monitoring system can be managed. Ironic processes can be maneuvered. In order to maneuver them, you must first understand how they work. So let's take a detailed look at how ironic process works.

Research supporting ironic process theory has been conducted in a number of ways. Some of the most interesting experiments at demonstrating the effect have involved putting golf balls and trying to hit target areas in the midst of varying instructions and pressures that bring to mind negative thoughts contrary to the putting goal. Before I provide a basic review of the studies, I want to point out that I am not going to delve into the specifics of all of the variables studied. Most of these studies investigated multiple influences on missing golf putts. Only the essential findings relative to ironic process theory will be addressed here. In scientific terminology these findings are referred to as the "main effects." Those desiring additional study can easily proceed from the references provided.

Researchers Wegner, Ansfield, and Pilloff[3] had subjects hit a golf ball at a glowing spot on the floor and recorded their accuracy. During practice shots subjects were instructed to "...land the ball on the glow spot." However, during the final test putt the instructions were to, "...land the ball on the glow spot, but be particularly careful not to *hit the ball past the glow spot: don't overshoot the glow spot.*"

To measure the influence of additional mental overload and pressure, one group of subjects was asked to keep a six-digit number in their mind while the other group was given no such distracting thought.

Trying to remember a six-digit number while simultaneously hitting the final test putt was more taxing to the mind and created an additional degree of stress and pressure. Based on ironic process theory, it was hypothesized that this additional degree of stress and pressure would make it more difficult to counter unwanted thoughts and their influence. Therefore, Wegner predicted that subjects trying to hit the spot in the final test condition when given instructions "…not to hit the ball past the glow spot," and when also told to keep a six-digit number in mind, would be *more likely to overshoot* the putt than those not required to remember the number.

Sure enough, just as predicted, subjects overshot the glow spot significantly farther when trying to remember a six-digit number than when given no such additional task ($p < .05$). On average, the golf balls stopped just a bit over a foot farther for the group trying to remember the number and under the most pressure.

In a similar study,[4] researchers allowed subjects 15 practice putts before one final putt. Before the final putt they were told that if they landed the ball entirely or partly on the target they would receive 50 British pounds or approximately $100.00. Obviously, this "money-shot" was intended to add significant pressure and stress and stimulate ironic process influences. The theory asserts that, under stress, the unwanted thoughts of ironic processes get worse and, thus, should impair putting performance. As in the previous experiment, before the money-putt the researcher commented, "Try to land the ball on the target, but be particularly careful not to *hit the ball past the target. Do not overshoot the target.*" This study investigated a number of variables related to ironic process but again, we will only address the most pertinent.

The study was particularly interested in subjects' degree of nervousness or anxiety and its effect on putting performance on the "money-shot." Just before the last putt, anxiety was measured in two ways. The first was by asking subjects to indicate their degree of worry and tension on a brief test. The other was by measuring subjects' heart rate. Obviously, the first measure assessed how the subject knowingly presented themselves—how they wanted to appear outwardly. The second measure was derived directly from physiological measures outside of subjects' conscious control. You might say the second measure came from the heart. (Pun intended!)

The general finding was as expected: Those subjects who displayed high anxiety did worse on the final money-putt. Of particular interest here was one specific group of subjects. Subjects who outwardly indicated that they were not worried or tense over the last putt (the money-putt), but whose heart rate increased significantly were labeled as "repressors." Repressors try to repress their anxiety. They are either in denial of their nervousness or are trying to put on a "good face" and present themselves as more confident than they really are. Generally, repressors are defensive regarding their anxiety. The theory is that they are so preoccupied with avoiding anxiety, that it will decrease performance even more. It was hypothesized that this group would be particularly vulnerable to ironic process effects because they outwardly tried to avoid the ironic process influence; yet, under pressure their heart rate indicated increased anxiety. The hypothesis was supported. Repressors overshot the target significantly more on the money-putt than all other groups ($p < .05$)!

Once again ironic process theory was demonstrated! The more we attempt to minimize the influence of negative intruding thoughts, the worse they get. The more people try to avoid ironic process effects, the more effects they have. **Negative intruding thoughts get worse under pressure and stress.**

The findings of one more putting experiment are worth noting. In a similar putting study[5] researchers were particularly interested in thought and image control in relation to putting performance. In this experiment, subjects were given various images to think before some of the putts. What was most fascinating were the findings regarding the impact of positive or negative images on putting performance. I will summarize some of the most pertinent results.

First, even though positive images generally improved putting performance, some subjects thinking positive images *still reported having negative thoughts creep into their mind.* Second was the finding that intentional attempts by subjects to suppress negative putting images appeared to have actually *increased* the occurrence of negative images. Finally, attempts to suppress negative images resulted in overcompensation in performance. Here, overcompensation means that, in attempting to avoid the influence of the statement to "*...not hit the ball beyond the spot,*" subjects did the extreme opposite of the negative thought. That is, when trying to avoid thinking about hitting the ball beyond the spot, subjects often hit the ball *short of the spot* and vice versa.

This experiment indeed substantiated just how dominating the ironic processes can be. And perhaps of most importance was the finding that **intentional, active attempts to control or override negative images only makes them worse.** Keep this in mind as it becomes crucial in learning to manage the negative images produced by ironic processes of the mind.

Researchers have studied a number of behaviors with regards to ironic process, some of which we are all familiar. Perhaps one of the most familiar experiences of ironic process influences is with insomnia. We have all had nights when it was difficult to fall asleep—an event that requires a passive "letting-go" and that can never be intentionally controlled. The more we become aware that we need to sleep, the harder it is to fall asleep. Then we try not to think about our need for sleep. Yet, regardless of our thoughts, we become acutely aware that we are awake! No matter which way our thoughts lead us, we lose the battle. The opposite can also occur when trying to stay awake. Who cannot remember trying to stay awake during a boring speech or sermon only to find ourselves nodding off in the midst of our attempts to stay awake? Research has confirmed such effects (As if we need research to confirm this!) and also confirmed that a mild distraction is one of the methods to actually aid sleep.[6] This is why so many find it helpful to fall asleep with the TV on.

The other area in which we have all experienced the torment of ironic processes is with thought suppression. Who has not become obsessed and worried over some troubling situation and fought the futile battle of attempting to stop thinking about our concerns. If there ever was a losing proposition with the mind, this is it. An active, conscious mental directive to not think about something is virtually worthless.

Indeed, it was research into attempts to suppress thoughts that prompted the formulation of ironic process theory.[7] You may have heard of the somewhat legendary "white bear" experiments where subjects were instructed not to think about a white bear only to discover that their mind kept returning to that very image. Included in the findings was that attempts to avoid thinking about a white bear actually increased sensitivity to the image rather than decreasing sensitivity. Other related experiments confirmed that the more people were taxed with time pressures and other tasks that overloaded their mind, the more words to be avoided burst forth.

Remember the research mentioned in Chapter 2 that indicated that it is very difficult for people to see a picture of something and not subvocalize the word naming the object in the picture?[8] This research also validated ironic process theory. In this study subjects were shown a picture and instructed 1) to not subvocalize the name of the object in the picture and 2) to not count the number of letters in the word naming the object. Notice that the instructions brought to mind the very thing subjects were told *not to do*. Thus, in order for subjects to check to see if they were following the instructions, they had to bring to mind the very thing they were instructed not to think. How would you know that you did not subvocalize the name of an object without bringing the word to mind to check whether or not you thought it? The task is virtually impossible. This is why ironic process theory states that, the harder you try not to think of something, the more you will think it. As you should have guessed by now, the primary finding of the study was that, when instructed not to, subjects both subvocalized the name of the object ($p <$

.001) and counted the letters in the name of the object at significant levels ($p < .001$).

These findings are directly related to the problems encountered by those experiencing depression, anxiety and other psychological problems. Attempts at countering such mood states often fail as a result of ironic process influences coupled with increasing pressures to move away from the undesired state. Psychotherapists have long been aware that attempts at avoiding emotions that accompany depression, anxiety, grief, trauma, etc. only make things worse. With this knowledge, they seek supportive ways to move clients into and through difficult emotions in order to get past them.

Other studies examined ironic processes related to the efforts to control the direction that a pendulum held in the hand swings, to avoid prejudice, to relax, to present ourselves well in social situations, and to avoid pain.[2] How easy is it to stop your tongue from constantly checking that mouth sore to see if it is still there? In all of these studies the primary findings consistently emerged. **With intentional thoughts, the greater the effort to avoid unwanted thoughts the more likely they were to occur.**

Stated another way, ironic process comes down to this: **The mind cannot consciously avoid, it can only intentionally focus and attend.** If you try to avoid thinking about something, you always have to define what to avoid and then constantly check to see that you are not thinking it. This process, by default, results in you thinking the undesired thoughts. Even when you try replacing undesired thoughts with new thoughts, you still have to check that you are on track with the new thoughts and, once again, encounter negative thoughts. This is a fundamental characteristic of the conscious mind presented later in Chapter 4.

While we must contend with the perils of ironic processes, this does not mean that it is futile to try to reprogram your mind and behavior. Ironic process is introduced here only to point out what you must deal with in order to change. Mental reprogramming is possible and occurs constantly. It's just that you have to learn the proper way to do it in spite of ironic processes. Hence, any serious discussion of mental programming must include an excursion into ironic process theory. Failing to understand ironic process theory frequently results in a great deal of the failure when attempting habit change.

Those who do not realize what they must face, often lose the battle. When attempting to break habits, they let the negative thoughts that emerge dominate. They do not understand that the negative thoughts are an absolutely natural part of mental systems that control behavior and that understanding them and managing them *is change*. Let me repeat that. **The process of change is all about managing the negative thoughts that emerge as a result of the thought monitoring systems built into the mind. All successful mental programming is contingent upon the successful management of unwanted thoughts.**

An understanding of all of this becomes vitally important to programming your mind and successfully managing the negative voices that are inevitably aroused. I will return to these concepts in Chapter 4 and Chapter 8 when I present characteristics of the mind and the repercussions that occur with new mental programming.

How Do We Overcome the Perils of Ironic Process?

At first glance, it is as if the mind has a built-in system that works against us. Yet, this is not the case. The monitoring system that brings forth negative thoughts has a vital purpose: This monitoring process alerts you if you are not on course for any task including new mental programming. If you desire change, you must have some kind of system to monitor if you are moving in the desired direction. Understanding this, it is easy to see that the monitoring system is essential for new programming and staying on track with any task. The problem is the process of keeping you on track feels as if it is sending you off track. Yet, in the long run, it is your friend.

Controlling the ever-vigilant thought monitoring system is a bit tricky. Remember, it is a harder-you-try-the-more-you-fail system.

Though the system that focuses attention is conscious and can be voluntarily controlled, the system that monitors whether or not we are on track is unconscious and, therefore, it responds automatically regardless of our wanting it to or not. Consequently, the monitoring system cannot be turned off consciously. It cannot be "willed" or ordered to stop functioning. While I can gather my thoughts and consciously decide to focus my attention on something, I cannot "decide" to not have uninvited intruding thoughts thrust their way into my mind. Direct use of willpower is futile in controlling it. Approaches to managing ironic processes must elegantly negotiate these dynamics.

The first step toward managing the ironic processes is to understand them. Be knowledgeable regarding how they work. Be aware of pressures and distractions that intensify their effects. The experiments described above provide excellent examples of the primary dynamics at work. Hopefully this discussion has provided a clear understanding of how ironic mental processes function.

There is one primary thing you have to understand in order to move toward controlling the ironic process monitoring system: **Ironic processes only happen when you are trying to control them; they do not happen when you are not trying to control them.** As Wegner states, "The occurrence of both intentional and counterintentional effects of mental control are dependent on an important precondition: The person must be attempting control"[2] (p. 39). In other words, ironic processes only kick in when you are trying to avoid them. When you are wholly focused on a task and not bothered or trying to avoid unwanted thoughts, the system turns off.

Thus, the second step toward managing ironic mental processes is to intensely focus on the desired outcome and to use your understanding of negative thoughts to move to a position of accepting them when they occur. Accept that ironic processes will always be present when conscious effort is exerted. Let it happen and simply watch it happen with a neutral attitude toward its occurrence. Flow with it. If not totally focused, accept that negative voices are a part of any new endeavor.

Hence, if fighting ironic processes works against you and makes it worse, then accepting that they will happen moves you through them. Develop an attitude of complete passivity towards them. Don't fight them. Don't love them. Don't watch them; don't try to not watch them. Just let them be. Because that's the way to get beyond them. (I realize this is not as easy as it sounds when reading these words because even moving to these attitudinal states requires a management of ironic processes!) Recognize that intentionality is your enemy in the management of ironic processes. Effort is what triggers them. Direct effort against them is your nemesis. You cannot directly avoid them; all direct attempts to avoid them will backfire.

Remain calm and focused in the midst of the negative thoughts and simply use them as a signal to move your thoughts back to what you desire. Recognize that the intruding thoughts of ironic processes are your friend. Without the monitoring system letting you know when you are off track, you would not know to get back on track. The monitoring system is a necessary ingredient to mental focus. It is your ally in the quest for concentrated thought. You want to develop a detached appreciation of them.

This approach to accepting intruding thoughts is used in all meditation practices and hypnosis procedures. Allowing the intruding thoughts to gently guide you back to what you desire is a healthy way to utilize this built-in system.

Once you learn to do this you can then move to one of two highly related states.

The first is to practice doing something to the point it becomes automatic and you do not have to consciously think about it. Practice the thought and action to the point that you do not have to actively monitor if you are on track or not—it just happens. You have, in essence, moved to a place where you do not try, you simply do. You reach a state where you avoid effort. Effort requires monitoring; effortlessness requires no conscious monitoring.

This is what is happening as I am typing these words. I have typed so many hundreds of thousands of letters that I do not have to monitor if my fingers are moving in the right direction or not. I do not have to counter the difficulties of ironic process. Automaticity occurs at such an ingrained level that counterproductive, intruding thoughts do not enter into the picture. The preparatory thought is fired off and the behavior is triggered before I even consciously know I am doing it. Thus, the complications that accompany ironic process are circumvented. Remember, ironic processes only occur with *intentional* preparatory thoughts. I had to contend with them when I first learned to type, but not now. Currently, automatic preparatory thoughts bypass the unwanted intrusions of negative thoughts.

More importantly, once new patterns of thinking and behaving are deeply ingrained to the point of automaticity, ironic processes begin working for you! What initially appears to be your enemy in changing behavior becomes your strongest ally in maintaining newly established behavior. Your apparent enemy becomes your known friend.

In fact, once a behavior is mentally programmed to the point of automaticity, the reverse phenomenon occurs—*it becomes hard not to do the behavior*. Behaviors that have reached this level of consistency are deemed "habits" and, as we all have experienced, they become very difficult to alter. Habits are behaviors that are so strongly programmed into your mind that it takes great concentration and intentional efforts *not* to have them occur. The neural pathways are so burned into your mind that they fire off effortlessly. The preparatory thoughts of habits appear to have their way, no matter what we want. At this point, ironic process thoughts usually consist of statements and images proclaiming that the habitual behavior can *never be stopped*! The forces of ironic process are working in the opposite direction from when the habit was first formed. If we want to break a habit, we now have to work to create a new set of thoughts that trigger the opposite response to the habit.

Another interesting fact about this level of automaticity is that, once accomplished, it is often hard to do the task consciously. Most of us have "dialed" a phone number (literally speaking, pushed buttons) to the point that our fingers move to the correct numbers automatically. Later, when someone asks for the number, we have to imagine a key pad and "see" where our fingers go to in order to recall the number! This level of automaticity has left our conscious mind almost helpless at doing the task itself.

Those who have learned songs on musical instruments have also experienced the phenomenon of our fingers moving to the correct notes effortlessly. Attempts to play consciously when trying to think about where to place our fingers, fail. I have seen musicians who, when asked to show what they played—to show where their fingers were placed on the instrument—could not do it consciously. They often struggle and laugh at themselves when trying to demonstrate slowly with awareness of what they are doing.

This is true of everyone who has practiced any task repeatedly to a high level of skill. All successful athletes, surgeons, musicians, dancers, therapists, brick layers, carpenters, drivers, stenographers, gamblers, seamstresses, chefs, etc. have reached this state with their essential skills. In many ways, the skills we pay others for are largely the skills that have reached high levels of automaticity. **The key to life is automatic thought.**

The second approach to managing ironic process thoughts is highly related to reaching a state of automaticity. In this instance, in order to overcome unwanted, intruding thoughts you must become engrossed in a task to the point where we shut down the inner ironic processes as well as the outside world. This is referred to as a state of "flow." The term "flow" was coined by Mihály Csíkszentmihályi who wrote a popular book entitled *Flow: The Psychology of Optimal Experience.*[9]

When you are in a state of flow, you are fully immersed in the task at hand. Your being becomes completely absorbed in what you are doing and effortlessly focused all of your attention on it. You often find that you lose track of time. Yet, when you come out of flow you appreciate what you have done. States of flow are intrinsically rewarding. Of particular interest is that, while you experience a sense of control over what you are doing, you also "lose" yourself. Specifically, you are not self-conscious. You forget that you exist as you become intensely focused on what you are doing. Another essential aspect of flow is that your emotions are aligned with what you are doing and not fighting against you. Negative emotions do not emerge in states of flow. Although there must be some effort to what you are doing, it feels effortless.

This state is almost the complete opposite of the state that brings forth the negative voices of ironic processes. In the golf experiments described above, subjects were very self-conscious as pressure was put on them to do a task of which they were not familiar. Emotions ran high when they were offered real money for their putting performance. There was great awareness of the task at hand and emotional pressure to do well. As noted, ironic processes occur when intentionality is present. Intentionality calls forth effort and, with effort, we become acutely aware of what we are trying to do. This, in turn, arouses the negative voices of ironic processes. In the state of flow, these characteristics are absent. **The state of flow is activity absent of negative voices.**

To some degree, you can enter a state of flow with activities of which you have little practice. Here you get lost in the task that you are trying to accomplish and, in doing so, the critical voice of the monitoring system is not present. You may be trying to learn a new task or solve a problem or repair something of which you have little knowledge; yet, you accept that you do not know exactly what you are doing without inner disapproval. You allow your mind to cut you slack regarding your lack of skill in doing the task at hand. With this high level of inner self-endorsement you proceed focused on the examining, learning, and adjusting necessary to move toward your ultimate goal. Obviously, some abilities to accomplish the task in which you are engrossed are automatic; nonetheless, you can fumble forward in the areas of little skill without ironic process voices rearing their head.

If you become absorbed in the task and are doing it reasonably well, eventually the monitoring system will limit the intrusions or shut down altogether. The state of flow is a pleasant, enjoyable blending of conscious effort with unconscious mental operations. Csíkszentmihályi argues that this is the true state of happiness and that we should be seeking it rather than the shallow pursuits of happiness we so often see.

The key to accomplishing all of this is, of course, repetition and practice of the precisely correct thoughts. Remember, I told you that repetition was going to be emphasized over and over. (No pun intended.) I am going to repeatedly point out the critical role repetition and practice play in successful mental programming and, ultimately, in success at any endeavor. All of this requires that you understand and manage ironic process systems.

I will return to the points of this discussion later when addressing the natural backlash that occurs when new mental programming is introduced. The approaches for managing the intruding thoughts of ironic processes are similar to the techniques used to manage the inevitable backlash from the negative voice that emerges with new mental programming.

The next chapter will summarize and clarify the most common model used to understand the mind and levels of thought. The material addressed should provide a bit more understanding of mental processes and further elucidate these concepts.

Chapter 3 Key Points

- When there is conscious, intentional effort at thinking a thought, ironic processes will automatically be activated and bring into awareness opposing thoughts. This is because conscious, effortful thought necessitates knowing when you are not thinking what you want to be thinking. Thus, when the mental monitoring system that checks to see if you are thinking what you want to think recognizes that you are not, it will bring to mind the undesired thoughts to a *greater degree* than the desired thoughts in order to make you aware you are not on track.

- While the system that focuses attention is conscious and can be voluntarily controlled with intentional thought, the system that monitors whether or not you are on track is unconscious and, therefore, it responds automatically regardless of our wanting it to or not. The monitoring system cannot be directly controlled or "willed" to stop functioning.

- The more pressure put on people and the more taxed the mind, the greater the impact of ironic process effects. With intentional thought, the ever-vigilant monitoring system is a harder-you-try-the-more-you-fail system.

- The first step to managing ironic processes is to understand them and accept them. Recognize intruding thoughts as your friend that informs you when you are off track so that you can get back on track. Embrace and develop a detached appreciation of this built-in system. Cultivate an attitude of complete passivity towards it. Just let it be.

- Ironic process systems dissolve if you practice doing something to the point it becomes automatic and you do not have to consciously think about it. Moving into states of flow also disengages the thought monitoring system.

- The mind cannot avoid thought; it can only focus and attend.

Chapter 4

The Mind Has Minds of Its Own: Understanding the Conscious, Subconscious, and Unconscious Minds

"We must give up the insane illusion that a conscious self, however virtuous and however intelligent, can do its work singlehanded and without assistance."[1]
Aldous Huxley

In this chapter I will address and clarify the differences between conscious thought, subconscious thought, and unconscious thought. These subdivisions of thought are commonly referred to as the conscious, subconscious, and unconscious minds. In addition, unique, distinctive, one-of-a-kind characteristics of each will be explained and discussed.

Read and study this chapter carefully. It is from an understanding of these concepts that the key principle that guides us in programming our own mind and controlling our behavior is constructed. Through understanding and applying these characteristics we mold our being and control our life.

I believe these characteristics should be taught to everyone—even elementary school students. To me, it is painfully evident that the vast majority of people have no idea how their mind functions and goes about doing its job. A lack of understanding of these characteristics is apparent in a considerable amount of the communications I experience. I cannot say enough about the significance of understanding the implications of the material in this chapter.

The conscious, subconscious, and unconscious minds have been explained and written about extensively. Because explanations abound, I will endeavor to be as brief and concise as possible in explaining the characteristics of each. For those familiar with this material, this will be a review of what has been said many times before and you can skim much of the chapter. Discussions of the distinctive characteristics of each mind are not as common. Hence, please tune in to the unique features of each mind, particularly the conscious and subconscious minds.

Much of what is addressed here has been alluded to previously and is supported by the priming and ironic process research. You can view this chapter as the summation of what the priming and ironic process research is revealing about how the mind works. Additional points are also presented. However, here it will be explained in everyday, lay language. Hopefully, these explanations will provide clarification and specificity to key points regarding mental processing.

For those seeking to read about these concepts from a more scientific perspective, I highly recommend you start your study by reading *The Unbearable Automaticity of Being*[2] by John Bargh and Tanya Chartrand. This article offers a wonderful review of the priming research that provides substantiation for the ideas summarized here regarding levels of mental processing.

Interestingly, the conceptualization of the conscious, subconscious, and unconscious minds has been written about from an intuitive perspective by numerous authors over the years. Philosophers have long observed that mental processing appears to occur at different levels within the mind. Yet, these ideas have only been corroborated scientifically in recent years and primarily from the priming research. Therefore, not only do we owe the understanding of how we can be influenced through priming to this research, but we also can credit the priming research with illuminating a much deeper understanding of how the mind works as a whole.

That being said, it is important to realize that what we are talking about are concepts, nonetheless. The terms conscious, subconscious, and unconscious are used to provide a conceptual map by which we explain thinking and behavior. They are a metaphoric map; they are not definitive things you can hold or carve out in a map of the brain. So, don't look for them on a chart of the brain, even though some have argued this possibility. In spite of their elusiveness, these conceptualizations are quite useful for explaining the thinking that manifests behavior.

Historically, Freud is generally credited with bringing these concepts into the awareness of the populous. It was Freud who pointed out that there is an abundance of mental processing occurring of which we are unaware as we live our lives. This was one of Freud's greatest contributions. Freud noted that some of this mental processing can be brought into awareness and that there is some of which we may never become aware. It might be noted that Freud regarded the term subconscious as confusing and he did not use it. The concept that he used that most parallels "subconscious" was "preconscious." He did, however, refer to the unconscious frequently.

Today, the most common lay usages are conscious, subconscious, and unconscious. In science, these terms are typically conscious, preconscious, and unconscious. For simplicity and to avoid confusion, I will use the term subconscious exclusively. For those more accustomed to the term "preconscious" please substitute in your mind when you read "subconscious." Your mind is very capable of doing this. Because of my early readings on the subject, I am more comfortable with "subconscious" and I believe it is a better descriptor. Yet, I am certain there are others with the opposite experience. There are times I just wish everyone could settle on a term.

The term, "mental processing" will be used as a catch-all term regarding all types of thinking at all levels.

Basically, conscious mental processing is simply the thinking you are doing of which you are aware. Subconscious mental processing is the thinking your mind is doing of which you are unaware, but that you can readily bring into awareness if desired. Unconscious mental processing is the thinking your mind is doing of which you are unaware and cannot bring into awareness or that takes great effort to bring into awareness.

Before we examine these differences in detail, I feel it is fitting to briefly review recent findings regarding the enormous capacity and processing power of our brain. The current estimates of mental processing power provide a window into understanding just how powerful the human mind is. These estimates also validate that there is an enormous amount of mental processing occurring outside of conscious awareness and substantiate the occurrence of subconscious and unconscious mental processing. Upon reviewing the numbers related to this we should live in awe of our mind's computing power and potential. This is the one computer you should learn to program.

Just How Much Capacity Does Our Brain Have?

Lots. Beyond comprehension.

Our knowledge of the brain at the neurological level has grown exponentially in recent years. As I write this book, mathematical estimations of the brain's mental processing capacity at the neurological level are becoming a workable possibility. While it is not the purpose of this book to address extensively mental change at the neurological level, I will delve into relevant neurological findings on occasion. To begin this undertaking, let's take a moment to examine recent estimates of the brain's processing capacity. You might categorize this as "mental fun facts." They are quite impressive.

Estimations of the brain's processing capacity vary considerably depending on who you are reading. Search the internet and estimations abound. The problem is that most estimations are extrapolated from limited information. What scientists are trying to measure is so microscopic (neurons are less than a thousandth of a millimeter in diameter) and the numbers are so large that error is inevitable. New estimates using the latest technology appear every few years. So, please allow for error rates in the trillions, and that the numbers presented here will undoubtedly change.

For years it was generally estimated that there were approximately 100 billion neurons in the brain. That is, until Dr. Suzana Herculano-Houzel took actual brains and turned them into a sort of "brain soup" and then took a precisely measured sample of the soup and counted the neurons in it.[3] From here she extrapolated the total of neurons in the average human brain to be around 86 billion (86,000,000,000). Great work. Others have estimated up to 200 billion nerve cells.[4] So, at the time of this writing, it appears that we can loosely state there are somewhere between 86 and 200 billion neurons in the brain. For our purposes, the conservative numbers will suffice and are still amazing.

Each neuron has somewhere between 1000 to 20,000 connections (technically, synapses) to other neurons depending on the type of neuron and whose estimates you are using. Stanford researchers have recently developed a method of taking pictures of neurons by using fluorescent molecules that attach to them and glow in different colors. These same researchers estimate approximately 125 trillion—that's 125,000,000,000,000—synapses in the brain.[4] Even with the enormity of this number, this is one of the more conservative estimates. To give you an idea of this number, these researchers estimated it to be equal to the number of stars in 1,500 Milky Way Galaxies. These researchers concluded that the brain has more synaptic switches than all the computers on earth have electronic switches or gates. Wow! Yet, others have estimated as high as a quadrillion (1,000,000,000,000,000) neural connections.[5] Again, we will stick with the conservative numbers.

So, with all of these connections, just how much computing is going on in your brain?

Researchers at the Okinawa Institute of Technology Graduate University in Japan and Forschungszentrum Jülich in Germany recently set out to answer this question.[6] To approach the problem they used the fourth most powerful computer in the world, the K computer in Kobe, Japan. Based roughly on the numbers presented above they created an artificial neural network simulating 1.73 billion nerve cells with 10.4 trillion synapses. The result was that it took 40 minutes using 82,944 processors in the K computer to equal just 1 second of human biological brain processing time. Yes, that's right; the computer you bought at the store is no match for the one you were born with.

Stated another way, with the typical neuron firing between 5 to 50 times a second, your brain is processing over one trillion (1,000,000,000,000) bits of information per second. (Some estimates are as high as 100 trillion bits a second.) Conservatively, that's a trillion bit-per-second processor. Yet, you are only aware of an extremely small amount of this processing. Even if you take the most conservative estimates, the processing power of your brain is staggering.

Here are a couple of other interesting fun numbers from the internet. The average 20 year old has about 100,000 miles of nerve fibers in his/her brain. Also, the brain uses between 20 to 30% of the calories we take in. For those wanting to burn calories, think more!

Simply put, the brain is the most complex organ in the universe. Period.

The processing power of your brain is astronomical. We were each born with a computer that has processing power far beyond any computer manufactured to date. As of this writing, not even the most powerful computers on the planet can compete with the processing power of your brain. Yet, we generally know very little about how to systematically program this computer—this gift from nature.

Naturally, this startling information only provokes more questions. For example, what is all of that unknown mental processing about? Why was the mind structured such that we are not allowed awareness of so much that is being processed? And most importantly, how do we access and program all of that neural processing that is determining our behavior?

Let's look at this information relative to the conscious, subconscious, and unconscious minds. There is much continuity between what we can now estimate about neural processing and how mental processing has been conceptualized.

Just how much processing occurs in the consciousness versus the subconscious and unconscious? In introductory psychology classes it has often been taught that the average person can only hold between five to nine objects in working memory at one time. (Scientifically stated as 7 plus or minus 2 objects.) This is known as Miller's Law. This capacity could be increased with chunking or placing objects into meaningful groups and remembering the groups. According to current estimates, this comes out to a maximum processing ability of up to 2000 bits of information per second for the conscious mind. Compared to the overall processing that is going on in the brain—over one trillion bits of information per second—the amount of processing in the conscious mind is beyond miniscule.

Yet, as will be explained, the small amount of processing that occurs in consciousness is our link to the subconscious where the vast majority of behavior is controlled. This conscious-subconscious link is so critical to our lives it is important to understand the qualities and features of the conscious and subconscious minds. In the next section we delve into some more important characteristics of the conscious mind.

Fun Facts: Current Conservative Estimates of Your Brain's Computing Power

- The brain is the most complex organ in the universe.
- The brain contains approximately 86 billion (86,000,000,000) nerve cells.
- Each cell has between 1000 to 20,000 connections to other cells.
- There are an estimated 125 trillion (125,000,000,000,000) neural connections in the brain.

- Your brain is processing over 1 trillion (1,000,000,000,000) bits of information per second.
- You are only aware of about 2000 bits of info being processed per second.
- The typical neuron fires 5-50 times per second.
- In a recent simulation experiment it took the 4th fastest computer in the world with 82,944 processors 40 minutes to do what the human brain can do in 1 second.
- The average 20 yr. old has about 100,000 miles of nerve fibers in his/her brain.
- The brain uses 20-30% of the calories we consume.

The Conscious Mind

Conscious processing is the thinking of which you are most aware. It is the mental processing you are doing that you know you are doing. Thus, it is thinking you are doing that you "think" you are doing. Likewise, it is the thinking you are doing that you can think about immediately after you do it. It is the voice and images in your head that you can immediately tell to someone. It has been reasoned that conscious mental processing *is awareness*.

The conscious mind also controls deliberate body movements—movements that you think about doing as you do them. These physical movements require that you concentrate on them in order to do them. When you first learned to type you had to concentrate on where to place and move your fingers. When you first learned to drive a car you had to think quite deliberately about pushing the gas pedal and turning the steering wheel and shifting the gears. When you first learned to play a musical instrument or swing a golf club or knit or any new physical task, you had to concentrate very deliberately on what to do with your fingers, arms, or body, and your conscious mind was in command. All of these movements were initially done intentionally and were controlled by the conscious mind. Once trained by the conscious mind, the vast majority of these bodily movements are turned over to the subconscious mind, thereby, freeing the conscious mind to learn more new things.

The conscious mind also has the capacity to make decisions and set into motion actions in order to accomplish something. In such instances, it is the decision making center of the brain. Hence, behaviors that emerge after considerable weighing of options and consequences are conscious mind activated. In this capacity, the conscious mind is your free will or self-control center.

Thus, when you have to stop and think about what course of action to take and assess which course will be the best, all of this mental processing flows through the conscious mind. Again, this is the thinking you are doing that you are aware you are doing. Philosophically speaking, it is the mental processing done in the conscious mind that lets us decide the direction our life will take as much as is possible. Hence, it is this mental processing that gives us free will or self-control. It is the mental creation of willpower and self-determination. In a moment I will expand on the philosophical implications of this.

Interestingly, research has indicated that this self-control capacity can get overloaded and depleted.[2] It appears that the more you have to use your self-control or willpower in one area, the less self-control is left for use in another area, at least for the moment. This is referred to as "decision fatigue" or "ego depletion."

Basically, the more decisions you have to make and/or the more willpower you have to use in following through with decisions, the less mental energy is left for other decisions and tasks. In this sense people often state that their mind is "tired." Those desiring to study this phenomenon can search the internet for discussions or read *Willpower: Rediscovering the Greatest Human Strength* by Baumeister and Tierney.[7] Research regarding the topic is included within. The implications of decision fatigue and the practical applications for habit change that follow are also addressed in *Habit Stacking: 127 Small Changes to Improve Your Health, Wealth, and Happiness*[8] by S. J. Scott.

Decision fatigue is perhaps why it is important to slow your mental activity through techniques such as meditation. Here you take a mental break, so to speak, in order to rejuvenate the conscious mind's self-control abilities. Fortunately, we have the subconscious to lessen the load and take control once a conscious decision has been made. As we will see, the subconscious unburdens the conscious mind by automatically following through with the minutia needed to accomplish something.

As noted, relatively speaking, the capacity of the conscious mind is quite small.[2] While it has the ability to control intentional things we do, it does not control most of the things we do. When you analyze all of the minute things that must be managed even to do the most mundane behavior such as walking, you quickly realize that the conscious mind is not doing most of the processing. It needs considerable help in completing the behaviors it sets into motion.

Fortunately, although the conscious mind can only hold a small amount of information in it at one time, it can quickly switch between the information it is processing. Because the conscious mind can rapidly jump from one idea to the next, it often appears to be a large component of mental processing. In reality, the conscious mind is an extremely small part of mental processing. That the mental processing in the conscious mind appears to be so immense is an illusion of thinking. Without an understanding of how the mind works, we fall prey to this illusion and inadvertently give up control of our lives to other influences. The amount of mental processing that is occurring of which we are unaware is astronomically larger.[2] Recognizing that the greater part of thinking and mental processing is going on elsewhere is vitally important in understanding how to approach mental programming.

Yet most importantly, the conscious mind is the tool by which we access and control other mental programming. The conscious mind is the biological window into the subconscious we have been given. It is the control panel nature gave us to operate the rest of our mind. It gives initial instructions to other parts of the mind that then take over. Too many people think that conscious thought is all thought; this is patently wrong. We would be much better off thinking of the conscious mind as a control panel that contains the instrumentation to manage subconscious processes (and, ultimately, some unconscious processes).

More specifically, the conscious mind has two highly related functions. When you have any outside sensory input that you "think" about, this "thinking" is done with the conscious mind as it continues on into the subconscious mind.(see footnote 1) For example, if you smell a rose and note the fragrance consciously, this input continues on to the subconscious by way of conscious thought. As you read and become aware of the words on this page they continue on to the subconscious by way of recognition in the conscious mind.

The second function of the conscious mind is to conjure up a thought from within. This, by the way, often requires the retrieval of stored subconscious information. Here, the source of the thought is the mind itself. Isn't it useful and pleasing that we can bring a thought into consciousness without outside sensory input? This self-generated, internal thought will, in turn, stimulate the other subconscious links associated with it. This entire process is referred to as thinking.

Drawing an analogy to your computer, conscious mind is the screen, keyboard, and mouse or touch pad. When you move your mouse to a certain point on the screen and click, there are millions of internal electronic switches (technically, microprocessor gates) that are switching in various combinations to ultimately produce what you see on the screen. While I might move and click one time to reach a website on my screen, thousands upon thousands of electronic switches are activated that result in the internal programming possible to produce the outcome you see on the screen. Many apps and programs are launched when a website is reached, loaded, and made functional. Together, all of the programs launched require thousands of minute electronic functions. Yet, we do not see any of this. We only see the results on the screen.

Such is the case with the conscious mind. In the conscious mind, we set into motion and immediately observe the results of the millions of neural pathways that must properly connect with other neural pathways. In this sense the conscious mind is both the keyboard and the computer screen. Yet, while the conscious mind directs and observes the outcome, there is much more neural processing going on below the surface that it only sets into motion.

Clearly, the reason for developing an understanding of the characteristics of the conscious mind is that **your conscious mind is the control panel you have been provided to initiate and manage all mental processing that is controllable. It is the gateway to the subconscious, the part that ultimately controls your life.** With this understanding it follows that learning how to program the conscious mind to properly trigger the appropriate responses from the subconscious is *the key* to controlling our habits and our being. Acquiring this skill is the ultimate goal of this book.

There are two unique characteristics of the conscious mind that I want to point out and expand upon. These two characteristics structure and shape conscious mental processing and guide us in formulating effective mental programming.

"I used to think I was smart, then I realized
where the thought was coming from."
Unknown Comedian

The Conscious Mind Can Think About What it is Thinking About

Your conscious mind has one of the most unique characteristics of any machine or organism on the planet: It can think about what it is thinking about. Not only can it think about what it is thinking about, but it can think about what it is thinking about what it is thinking about...and on and on. Thinking about thinking is called metacognition. Philosophically speaking, it is "knowing about knowing." Stated another way, the conscious mind is capable of self-observation. It can "watch" itself as it is thinking. Is that not amazing?

As a case in point, as I sit here writing this material I am thinking about what I am thinking about and then writing it. I am aware of how mind boggling, unique, and functional this concept is! When you think about it (pun, get it?), the entire process of writing a book requires that you are constantly involved in the circular process of thinking about what you are thinking (metacognition) and then communicating your thoughts in writing.

A meta-thought can also be the thought that lies "behind" a thought. Many times we appear to quickly reach a conclusion without immediate awareness of the logic upon which the conclusion is based. When this happens, we can slow down our thoughts and go back and explore how we reached the conclusion. This re-examining or sorting out of thoughts is quite common. Now this is going to sound a bit weird. When you re-examine and sort out the logic behind a conclusion, this is an example of a meta-thought about a meta-thought, or a thought about a thought.

The implications which arise from the ability to think about thinking are enormous and, while it is not the purpose of this book to explore these implications in-depth, I will very briefly note a few.

That you can think about what you are thinking about is really self-evident when you think about it. (I am chuckling as I write this.) We can do this consciously, at will, if desired; therefore, it is definitely one of the characteristics of the conscious mind. (I suspect that the subconscious and unconscious are capable of some form of self-observation also. But, for now, let's stick to discussing this ability as a conscious mind skill.)

As odd and redundant as it may sound, thinking about thinking is thinking. Most conscious mental processing consists of doing this over and over. And, it is this ability that gives humans great power to analyze, assess, and decide in our minds before taking action or creating something new. What a powerful, self-insight we are given with this ability. This gift is a powerful, time-saving feature of our conscious mind.

It is this singular, unique ability that puts the human mind in a category of one. No other organism or machine has to the ability to control and guide itself to the degree of the human mind. Nothing. While we are rapidly approaching a car that can drive itself, it cannot tell itself where to go. Somewhere in the equation, a human will always have to give some sort of direction. While we are rapidly approaching self-programming computers, they still have to be programmed by a human who has a true self-observing mind-computer.

With the conscious mind, there is no separate operator and machine; the operator and the machine are one and the same. Within the conscious mind, there is no separation between the controls and controller; this is the natural way the conscious mind works.

Those philosophically inclined are likely having thoughts regarding willpower and free will at this moment. I would argue the circular ability of the mind to control and guide itself is the foundational component of free will. That is, free agency is a result of the mental dynamic of metacognition. This is because metacognition is the fundamental, key prerequisite to self-awareness.

The logic goes something like this: Because we can think about what we are thinking, we know we exist. We know that we are. Perhaps the most well-known metacognition statement came from Descartes who is famous for stating, "I think, therefore I am," which is a metacognition and a statement of self-awareness all rolled into one! That's why this statement is so famous and fundamentally profound. *Metacognition is self-awareness*. We think about our thinking and we are aware that we think about our thinking; therefore, we are aware of our self. Metacognition is self-awareness in action. This is what makes us human and unique.(see footnote 2)

Self-awareness leads to a multitude of implications not the least of which is that we can take information and lessons from the past and project outcomes that might occur into the future. This could not happen if we did not have self-awareness. The reasoning is simple: I know I exist; therefore, I know I existed in the past and will exist in the future. I can think about what occurred in the past and think about what may occur if I do various behaviors in the future. Therefore, I can think about and plan future courses of action *before I get there* and change that course of action based on perceived outcomes--that is, meta-thoughts.

The profound upshot of all of this is that I am not controlled by the factors of the present moment only. The stimuli of the moment may have influence, but I have the ability to override their influence and change my life direction through my ability to meta-think. Thus, my life is not solely the result of the urge of the moment like my cat. I can override the urge of the moment through meta-thinking.

"In between stimulus and response there is a gap,
and in that gap lies our freedom to choose"
Victor Frankl

I would argue that most other animals do not have this ability.(see footnote 2) That is, other animals go through their day being motivated solely by biological urges and whatever stimuli happen to be around them at the moment. They do not have the ability to think situations through and make alternative choices. Consequently, they do not have free agency or free will. Humans do have free will because we can think about a situation before it occurs and decide on a course of action regardless of the biological urges and associations from the stimuli around us. We do not have to repeat what we did in the past. We can change of our own accord. Therefore, metacognition is the foundational prerequisite to self-awareness which leads to freewill. Ultimately, metacognition, self-awareness, and free will are all one and the same. The only difference is the perspective from which they are explained and viewed.

Metacognition is a unique skill that forms the foundation for the premises put forth in this book. That is, that you can program your mind-computer to better control your life. We can think about what we are thinking and change that thinking to subsequently control our being. I suggest that the most amazing, fundamental characteristic of the conscious mind is that it can self-observe. Think about it.

Related to the self-awareness implications that stem from metacognition abilities are other implications regarding self-regulation, the development of ethical and moral principles, and intelligence in general. All of these human characteristics and philosophical struggles are possible because of the unique ability to meta-think. It is not the purpose of this book to delve into all of the philosophical implications rooted in metacognition. Suffice it to say that metacognition abilities are unique and powerful and central to being human. I am going to leave this point for the moment. If you desire to read more about metacognition and the enormous philosophical implications that stem from this ability, simply search it on the web. You can read for days.

The Conscious Mind Cannot Intentionally Delete a Thought: The Conscious Mind Can Only Attend

These two characteristics are really one concept presented from two different perspectives and were initially mentioned in Chapter 3 on ironic processes. They are two sides of the same coin, so to speak. They are discussed and summarized here because they are foundational to understanding why many people fail when pursuing intentional habit formation. The primary reason most people do not effectively program their mind and mold their behavior for successful outcomes is rooted in these fundamental conscious mind characteristics. Their understanding is of such importance that I make no apologies for reiterating them.

The first point is that you cannot delete a thought—consciously that is. You cannot make yourself forget anything. Forgetting is a sub- or unconscious process outside of conscious mind control. There are many times when it would be convenient to just forget an uncomfortable memory or to be able to block out an event that has you preoccupied and obsessing, but you can't. Forgetting is uncontrollable. Forgetting is the process whereby a thought is removed from conscious mind access and you did not deliberately control it happening.

Forgetting is to your mind as deleting is to your computer. The difference is you can press a button to delete on your computer; however, you do not have any conscious control over the mental process of forgetting. There is no mentally accessible delete button. You cannot deliberately forget.

Also, when you delete a word or picture on your computer, most of the time you can immediately retrieve it. You can go into that part of your computer that is still holding it, and bring it back to the screen. Still further, if desired, you can also go into that part of the computer that stores deleted material and permanently delete that material by wiping your hard drive clean so you can never get it back. Not so with the mind!

We cannot consciously decide not to think something and then not think it. The reason for this is simple and was explained in Chapter 3: You must think what the thought is in order to be aware of what you do not want to remember and, in the process, you constantly remember what you want to forget. Wow! What a paradox! A computer, on the other hand, can have its programming wiped out, literally. In the brain, the only comparison to completely removing something from your computer is memory loss due to injury, dementia, or amnesia. Brain injury literally breaks the neurological connections—the mental wiring, so to speak—so the thought is no longer accessible.

Now, we often momentarily forget things during our day only to later remember them. You might call this every day, unintentional forgetting. In such instances, you likely get so busy with what you have to do that all of the thinking about the current activities overrides remembering the other things you intended to do. What you wanted to remember never gets a chance to enter your mind because your mind is too busy concentrating on current activities. Remember, conscious mind has limited capacity and can get over taxed. Generally speaking, forgetting occurs because there are no cues to stimulate the conscious mind about the desired thought. Most often this type of forgetting is only a temporary loss of the mental connection to a thought.

Another reason we forget is that we have deeply ingrained, unconscious programming that instructs our subconscious mind to not allow the "forgotten" thought to enter consciousness. If the forgotten material is virtually inaccessible to the conscious mind, the process is referred to as repression. This unconscious programming has occurred without our awareness. Repressed thoughts can be very difficult to recover. Research suggests that this is one way that the unconscious protects us from traumatic thoughts.

It is easy to see that, for humans, forgetting is quite paradoxical. When we do not want to forget, we often do; when we want to forget, we remember. We cannot consciously force the process. Remember the tale of Rumpelstiltskin!

Of course, the processes for forgetting and for trying to forget tie directly into the ironic process research discussed in Chapter 3. In that chapter we reviewed research that revealed that unwanted, usually negative, thoughts enter our conscious mind at the very times we least desire them. Subjects were not able to delete or forget unwanted thoughts at will. The ironic process research illuminates the fact that there is no immediate, straightforward conscious control that allows us to instantly forget or delete a thought.

Additionally, the ironic process research demonstrated that, the more you intentionally desire to forget a thought, the more that thought will intrude into consciousness. Things you want to forget emerge at the most unwelcome times. Deliberate attempts at forgetting or deleting a thought create the *opposite effect.*

The flipside of the fact that we cannot directly remove a thought was also summarized in Chapter 3 with the point that the conscious mind can only focus. It can only attend. The conscious mind cannot, not attend. This would, of course, be forgetting. Effort to not, not attend invariably stimulates unwanted thoughts. This is the second, flipside characteristic of the fact we cannot consciously delete a thought.

Returning to the analogy with your computer, not attending would be equal to completely switching your computer off. When your computer has been fully switched off there is no electricity running through it. Nothing is happening. There is only one human parallel to switching off the brain: You are dead. The brain switches on the moment you are born and switches off when you die. There is no switching off the brain as long as you are alive. It is always on and doing something.

Even if you are in a coma, parts of your unconscious are still working to control bodily functions.

You might say that being asleep is equal to your computer temporarily shutting down but not being completely switched off. The analogy is so accurate we often refer to our computer as "asleep." At such times, the keyboard controls are not functioning and the screen is not producing new material. Parallel to mental functioning, the conscious mind or mental controls are not functioning when you are asleep. Yet, underlying mental processes are still working. Therefore, unless in a coma or some similar state, the mind is always focusing and attending to something.

This is easily tested. Try to not attend to anything. It almost sounds ridiculous to suggest this. There are times when we go into a trance like state and the conscious mind is not focused on the immediate surroundings. However, it is still focusing on the internal fantasy or whatever internal mental flow you are creating from within.

The bottom line regarding these points is this: **The conscious mind can only attend. Conscious, deliberate, immediate forgetting is impossible. Awareness, attention, and focus are the only processes that the conscious mind is capable of doing.**

Stated from yet another perspective, in the conscious mind there is no "nothing." Your mind is always on and processing something. It is always thinking even when you are tranced out. It is impossible to think about the absence of something without thinking about the something being absent. When your mind thinks "nothing" it always jumps to something. Even thinking the word "nothing" is something in your mind.

There is no mental nothing.

Other than the words themselves, there is no picture in your mind of "no" and "not." "No" and "not" only function with regards to something. Close your eyes and think "no" or "not" only for a moment. Notice what happens. You likely got an image of the word and immediately jumped back to an awareness of your mental chatter or an association of something you have with one of the words. Attempting to get to nothing or no or not in your mind always results in something—a mental trap so to speak.

Philosophically speaking, it has often been said that nature abhors a vacuum or that nature fills all voids. There is no place where this is truer than in your conscious mind. This is a sort of strange, funny aspect of life and thinking. But, it is a very important point to understand and to learn to use. **Because you always have to think something and that something is guiding your behavior, why not think something that guides you to where you want or need to be?** All attempts at no thought fail. Consequently, you must constantly choose what to put in your thoughts.

That the conscious mind can only attend also leads back to previous discussions on methods of overriding thoughts stimulated by ironic processes.

The only way to remove a thought from your conscious mind is to focus and attend exclusively on another thought by one means or another. In computer terms, this would be equal to overwriting something. The only way to intentionally get rid of a thought is to (effortlessly) replace it with another thought. There is no other way short of drugs, brain injury, or repression. The first two are not good options and the third is not always beneficial.

Exclusive, focused attention for the purposes of overwriting a thought is not as easy as it sounds and certainly not as easy as overwriting on your computer. To overwrite a thought you have to actively engage in an activity that occupies your mind to the point that you automatically, subconsciously replace the unwanted thought. And you have to let it happen involuntarily without conscious effort. Hence, the replacing of thoughts occurs at a subconscious level but can be assisted and fostered by repeated conscious activity. Typically you do conscious activity to the point it becomes subconscious activity and *then* forgetting automatically occurs. While we do have a mechanism for eliminating unwanted thoughts and mental programming, it is not nearly as convenient as the overwrite key on your computer. How much easier life would be if we had this capability!

As a common example of this, imagine you have troubling thoughts and then go to the movies. Once in the movie we get absorbed in the story and plot and forget our own troubles momentarily. Here we have overridden the troubling thought with thoughts of the movie plot. Note that this occurs as we passively become absorbed in the plot. Similarly, if we can continuously create new thoughts to override troubling thoughts, then old, unproductive thoughts will eventually diminish or perhaps go away completely. Yet, we have to do this to the point of automaticity; that is, by way of subconscious control. This is what happens with most unintended forgetting.

Fortunately as noted, there are things we can do to promote thought deletion. If you think a thought *without effort,* without trying to think that thought only, you can rid yourself of other, undesired thoughts. That is, when you are simply concentrating on something without concerns of intruding thoughts, you eliminate intruding, negative thoughts. When you reach this state of thinking, your thinking is actually being controlled largely by the subconscious mind. The conscious mind is not working very hard at all at attending; it just attends. Your thinking is on automatic pilot. This again is a state of flow or effortless concentration explained in Chapter 3. It is a wonderful place to be.

As stated, the absence of intruding thoughts occurs in states of flow where outside distractions disappear. In flow we are totally focused on the task at hand to such a degree that distracting, unwanted thoughts do not emerge. We say things like you "lose yourself," which really means the conscious mind is relaxed and not working to stay focused on the task at hand. You are "lost" in the task which really means self-consciousness is absent. The subconscious mind is front and center and you do not know it at the time! Stated another way, the conscious mind has temporarily stopped thinking about itself and, as a result, ironic processes switch off.

Similarly, if you practice a behavior or action to the point of automaticity where conscious effort is not necessary, you eliminate unwanted thoughts and actions. Again, the behavior is subconsciously controlled and conscious effort is not necessary. Therefore, unwanted aspects of the behavior or action do not occur. This is the state professional athletes enter when they are in the "zone." Mental programming suggestions for athletes offered in the last chapter of this book are all in an effort to move into the zone.

This entire reality is quite paradoxical. We can only remove a thought from conscious mind by replacing the thought with a new thought and doing it without effort. As you read the last sentence it almost does not sound like it makes sense. To remove a thought from conscious mind, you must replace the thought with another thought, but, you must do this in a state of effortlessness relative to the thought removed. You have to "just do it" regarding the new activity and be completely passive regarding the thought deleting/forgetting process.

So again, we have a unique operating characteristic of our mind. This one does not initially appear to be as useful as meta-thinking. Yet, it is important to understand that we must live with it and learn to think in ways that work in harmony with it. Ultimately, we want to learn how to take advantage and utilize the fact that we can only attend and focus.

The takeaway is this: **If the mind can only attend and focus, then give it something to focus on, not something not to focus on. Conversely, if the mind can only attend, then attend; but pay very close attention to what you are attending!** If the mind can only attend and focus, we must be very finicky, meticulous, and specific about what we provide it to attend to and focus on. The question for mental programming becomes, What am I providing my mind to focus on? What *is* my mental focus?

The primary principle of mental processing offered later is formulated with full understanding of this characteristic. Without an understanding of this point most attempts at mental programming are useless, or worse, detrimental. If we mentally program in a manner that brings to mind the very thing we desire to eliminate, our mental programming will fail. The same is true for communication. If we communicate in a way that brings thoughts into the minds of others that are disadvantageous, our communications are more likely to fail or have a negative impact. We will return to these ideas later.

The Subconscious Mind

"Civilization advances by extending the number of operations which we can perform without thinking about them."[9]

A. N. Whitehead

Basically speaking, the primary characteristics of the subconscious mind can be explained through its two major, overlapping functions.

First, the subconscious contains all of those pieces of information in memory that can be accessed readily if needed. From this perspective, the subconscious mind is memory. At least, it is the memories that you can remember at will. Any information that you are not currently thinking but that you can recall and bring into thought and awareness—into the conscious mind—is stored in the subconscious mind. And that's a lot of stuff!

In addition to memory storage and retrieval, the subconscious mind is controlling all the things you are doing that you are unaware that you are doing unless you stop and think about it. Stated differently, the subconscious controls all the things you are doing and unaware of doing unless the conscious mind commands that you bring the knowledge that you are doing them into awareness. Or, stated a bit differently again, subconscious mental processing is all the thinking you are doing that controls behaviors of which you are not immediately aware but, of which you can become aware if you desire.

Most importantly and inherent in these points is the fact that the subconscious creates and controls all habits. All automated behavior is created and controlled by the subconscious.[2] That's an overwhelming amount of behavior. Remember those trillions of bits of information being processed every second of your life? Most of that processing is occurring at the subconscious level. You might say the subconscious is where the real mental action is occurring; that is, the real mental action of which you can gain access and control.

Because of the phenomenal multitude of things we do that are controlled by the subconscious, it is going to get a lot of attention. This translates into saying that I am going to write a lot about it from here on in this book.

The subconscious tells your eyes when to blink and your lungs when to breathe. It controls all the muscles that allow you to walk and keep your balance without conscious effort. It does all of those little behaviors like scratching an itch, adjusting in your seat, turning your head to listen or to look a particular direction, chewing your food, or even talking. When you get up in the morning or go to bed at night and you do all of those redundant, automatic bathroom behaviors, you are likely on automatic pilot while your conscious mind is thinking about your day. Your subconscious is controlling all of the thousands of movements for brushing your teeth, doing your hair, shaving, or putting on make-up. You never have to stop and think about doing any of this. Most people brush their teeth with such automaticity that they sometimes leave the bathroom and can't remember doing it!

As I am currently typing these words my fingers automatically go to the proper letters and press while my conscious mind thinks about what I want to write. I no longer have to stop and think where to press my fingers; they seem to just know where to go. If I had to stop and think where to put my fingers, I would never get this book written. How convenient that my subconscious works so well for me.

As a guitar player of many years, my fingers instinctively know where to go to play certain licks or riffs—those repeated patterns that appear to flow from my hands. If you had to stop and think how to play every note, music would never flow. It would also not sound very good.

When you first learn to drive a car the conscious mind is working hard to push the pedal, turn the wheel correctly, look where you are going, put on the signal, watch for other cars, read street signs, etc. After months of practice driving a car becomes quite automatic as the subconscious takes over. It becomes so automatic that many times we drive to work and can't remember doing it. We often drive on the highway for ten or fifteen minutes at sixty-five or seventy-five miles per hour without conscious awareness of where we are or where we have been or what we have been doing! The subconscious mind has been driving your car while your conscious mind has been off in la-la-land thinking about who knows what!

To make matters more complicated for our subconscious, we switch on the radio, engage in a conversation, chew gum, smoke cigarettes, eat and drink, put on makeup, yell at kids, and/or talk on the cell phone while driving! We bombard the mind with a mass of sensory input to sort out and process. Yet still, the subconscious manages to process thousands of pieces of information and keeps us on the road.(see footnote 3) When all of this is considered it makes sense that we are processing trillions of bits of information per second.

More specifically, during all such complex behaviors, there is a continuous communication occurring between the conscious and subconscious minds. It is from this constant dialogue that most of your behaviors originate. **When you think about it, the vast majority of your actions are a result of the constantly occurring "conversation" between the subconscious and conscious minds. Consequently, the words stimulated and used in this mental conversation determine your life's course.**

What is so interesting is how, at times, the conversation appears to quiet down and the conscious and subconscious minds appear to go their own way and do their own thing, as if there were no connection between them. Yet, the connection is never broken. The lines of communication are always open; they just become less active because the subconscious is so good at managing automatic, habitual behavior on its own. The communication is only amped up when either mind recognizes a need to call on the other to sort things out. These mental operations are occurring constantly in your life.

While the driving example is fitting in demonstrating the power of the subconscious, the same is true for a multitude of other behaviors. For example, imagine the amount of information that is being processed by an air traffic controller or a short-order cook at Waffle House. I once had a secretary who could type 70 words a minute while having a conversation. How's that for a well-programmed subconscious! Have you ever tried to sing and play a musical instrument simultaneously? People do it all the time. And you can bet it would be impossible without the subconscious taking over and managing for us. The list of complex multi-action behaviors we do is enormous.

You are experiencing the power of the subconscious right now as you read these words. The subconscious quickly interprets the shapes of letters, then the groupings of letters that form words, then the combinations of words that form sentences and, almost instantaneously, provides your conscious mind with the meaning conveyed in the writing. This is occurring at a phenomenal speed. It is occurring so fast that you can continue to read at an amazing pace while "understanding" the abstract concepts being conveyed.

As noted, during this complex task of reading, an internal communication between conscious and subconscious processes is continually occurring. If the meaning of something read is not readily apparent, there is a lightning-fast dialogue and exchange of information between the conscious and subconscious minds that uses logic and reasoning to sort out the meaning. How fascinating!

Just how do we determine how much the subconscious is controlling a particular behavior? This is easy. **The degree to which a task can be done while doing another or competing task, determines the degree to which the task is automatic or controlled by subconscious processes.** In other words, if you can do something while thinking about something else, the subconscious is at work controlling the behavior. For example, brushing your teeth while planning your day mentally. Driving a car while having a conversation. Preparing a meal while directing children or having a conversation or listening to the TV. This ability has enormous implications.

It goes without saying that the subconscious is the "master mind" controlling the vast majority of the mental processing needed to accomplish everyday tasks—every single one of them from the most basic to the most complex. The conscious mind simply cannot handle all of the mental processing necessary to do all of what you must do to get through your day.[2,10]

All of this leads us to a crucial point: **Everything you do well is controlled by your subconscious.** This is so central and vital to understanding the subconscious, it deserves repeating. Everything you do well is controlled by your subconscious. Everything! This is an undeniable reality. The degree to which you are successful in your endeavors is directly related to the degree to which that behavior is automatized and controlled by the subconscious. This is one of the greatest fundamental facts that we know about the operations of the mind. Whether it be playing a musical instrument, typing, writing, throwing a football, knitting, painting, talking, sewing, parenting, swinging a golf club, carpentering, machining, filing, fixing, lecturing, teaching, surgically operating, and on and on, if you do it well, it is subconsciously controlled. This is so commonly accepted and written about in the literature on mental processing, that it deserves little more discussion.

Please note that "doing well" in this context does not mean doing perfectly or precisely. If you practice doing something poorly or imprecisely, your subconscious will automate your poorly executed, imprecise behavior. Practice makes perfect, only when practiced perfectly.

When we sum it up, the subconscious is that part of the brain that "contains" or holds all habits and skills programming. Everything you do repeatedly is stored in the subconscious. **Everything you do well, you do well because you have programmed the subconscious to do it**

automatically. The subconscious is the automation center of the brain. It is hard to comprehend the amount of habitual and skilled behaviors contained in the subconscious without serious, deliberate examination.

I could rant about this for hours. The point being that you were born with the most powerful computer on the planet in your head—much more powerful than the one you bought at the store. Yet, most people have little or no appreciation of what this computer is doing and is capable of doing. They too often are haphazardly programming their mind-computer or are depending on outside forces to program their mind-computer for them. Perhaps the first step to success is acquiring an understanding and appreciation of the power of your mind and a comprehension and appreciation of the power that has been put at your command.

Of course, the automatized behavior of the subconscious ties directly to the limited capacity of the conscious mind. The more things that can be controlled by the subconscious, the fewer things the conscious mind has to do and attend. Consequently, the more work the subconscious does, the less strained the conscious mind becomes and the more conscious mind power we have in reserve.[2] As noted above, it appears that the conscious mind can get overloaded and "depleted" if there are too many decisions or too much processing in a short period of time. When this happens we experience "decision fatigue" or "ego depletion" and the conscious mind needs a bit of time to rest and rejuvenate. Here is where subconscious control becomes even more essential.

This automating and creating of habits has other benefits, still, that we sometimes do not appreciate. **The more an action can be done automatically by the subconscious, the easier it is to get it done.** When you stop and think about it, for many activities, conscious effort is actually detrimental!

This may initially appear to be contradictory and counterintuitive; however, it is self-evident by what we observe all around us. The most obvious examples come from professional athletes who perform amazing physical feats while making them appear effortless. Who has not been amazed by the contortions and body twisting of professional basketball players making shots these days? Such movements are happening so fast that it would be impossible to consciously think through them in the moment. They are clearly a result of daily practice that has resulted in subconscious control at an exceptional level. Of course, conscious mind control of such complex movements was necessary when they were first learned; but, by the time you see them perform such shots on the court, the conscious mind is only very minimally assisting the subconscious in execution. **Generally speaking, once a complex behavior is thoroughly learned, conscious mind effort becomes a hindrance to its performance.** That is, if you have to stop and think about what to do, you can't get it done as easily.

Because the subconscious mind is controlling most of what we do and is accessible and controllable through the efforts of the conscious mind, it is of great interest here. To this end there are three highly interrelated characteristics of the subconscious that require attention. They are intertwined to such a degree that I hesitate to discuss them separately. However, for clarity, I am going to separate them into three characteristics. Keep in mind that, in all practicality, they are inseparable.

The Primary Drive of the Subconscious is to Automate

Take a moment and think about everything your subconscious does for you. All of those talking, walking, driving, eating, sitting, typing, writing, thinking, dishwashing, cleaning, musical instrument playing, sewing, athletic endeavoring, internet searching, cell phone pecking automatic behaviors that you do without conscious effort. All of those repeated behaviors that you can do while thinking about something else. Every one of these subconsciously controlled behaviors has common origins and underpinnings. Each is a repeated behavior that, once learned, does not require that you learn it again. *Each has been automated by the subconscious.*

When you think about what the subconscious does, it becomes self-evident that the primary purpose of the subconscious is to automate behaviors. More precisely, the subconscious is driven to automate and create habits. **The subconscious exists in order to automate every repeated behavior you have ever acquired that was not biologically hardwired into your genetic neurological programming.** The greatest parts of what constitutes your life are the automated behaviors that are subconsciously controlled. What an incredible realization.

This drive is phenomenally powerful. Think of the subconscious as addicted to automating anything it gets the slightest hint will be repeated. The subconscious is constantly observing the instructions and orders you deliver to the conscious mind and assessing if what you are doing needs automating. If it gets the slightest hint that you will be repeating a behavior, it initiates internal automating processes.

Understanding this extremely powerful drive and purpose leads us directly to the processes of mental programming. It is this drive that actually lets us mentally program ourselves. The fact that the subconscious is driven to automate paves the way to self-programming. The takeaway is self-evident: **If you want something to become ingrained and occur at an automatic level, repeat it. The subconscious is driven to automate. Consistency is the road to subconscious automation. Subconscious automation is the road to success at any endeavor.**

Unfortunately, this is also true for unproductive, negative behaviors. Whatever you are consistently repeating will be automated whether it is procrastinating or getting things done. Whether it is overeating or eating in a healthy manner. Whether it is exercising or sitting. Whether it is smoking or breathing clear air. Whether it is dreaming or working. Whether it is piddling or engaging. Whether it is saving or spending, and on and on. The subconscious does not really care if what you are doing is beneficial or not. In this sense it does not judge behavior. It only assesses if the behavior is being repeated and instinctively acts from there.

The Subconscious Mind is a Pattern-Seeking Organism

The subconscious mind is a pattern-seeking machine/ organism. While the conscious mind is busy tending to the immediate thoughts and tasks, the subconscious is ever alert seeking patterns *everywhere*. This pattern-seeking instinct is the first step toward automation. The pattern-seeking instinct of the subconscious is extremely prevalent and dominant.

Your mind seeks patterns, looks for patterns, and appears to have an inner drive to find repeating configurations in everything it does. At the same time, your mind quickly recognizes when patterns are broken. Both characteristics result from the pattern-dominated nature of mental processing. The pattern-seeking nature of your mind is far-reaching and ever present in our lives. I will briefly describe some examples of our pattern-seeking and how it relates to our lives. There are many more implications beyond this brief discussion.

Your daily routines are patterns. Much of your day is the chaining together of patterns of behavior. Daily routines are the primary behavioral patterns that make up our lives. Your pattern of getting out of bed, your bathroom preparation patterns, your food preparation patterns, your morning conversations, the way you drive to work (which is so patterned you likely cannot remember doing it), your patterns of work, returning home, etc. How often do you really do something completely new? Most of your day is a repeat of habits and routines.

Conversations are so patterned that husbands, wives, partners, and close friends can predict what others will say with great accuracy and humor. Acceptance of others' patterns could be considered a component of love. If you are in a long-term relationship, you had better get used to it.

People looking at clouds eventually see familiar patterns and start pointing out animals and mountains and silhouettes of various objects. We connect the dots whether we want to or not. The classical conditioning and operant learning approaches taught in introductory psychology courses are both a result of pattern seeking.

In order for information to be stored and retrieved from memory a pattern must be recognized or created. It is through this pattern creation that memories are created, stored, and retrieved.

We quickly see patterns in bricks and wallpaper and building construction. And, when the pattern is broken, we are equally quick to notice something is not consistent with the pattern our mind has recognized. We notice the book that is not perfectly aligned with other books on the shelf.

We are so pattern seeking that we find patterns and create patterns where there are none. We recognize and create patterns whether they are meaningful or not. We find patterns in both meaningful and meaningless noise. We believe that people are going to do things based on their previous behaviors and are surprised when they don't. Researchers have confirmed that stock traders see patterns in random data where there are none.

To demonstrate how powerful the pattern-seeking drive is, read the sentences below.

Aoccdrnig to rscheearch at an Elingsh uinervtisy, it deosn't mttaer in waht oredr the ltteers in a wrod are, the olny iprmoetnt tingh is taht teh frsit and lsat ltteer are at the rghit pclae. The rset can be a toatl mese and you can sitll raed it wouthit porbelm.

Notice how quickly the mind makes a known pattern—a known word—out of a bunch of scrambled letters. There are actually two pattern making drives at work here. The first is the need to unscramble the letters to create a recognizable word. This drive is aided by the typical patterns found in sentence structure. Whether aware of it or not, because certain types of words typically follow other words, we mentally anticipate which words we will read next in sentences. Understanding what to expect helps us to make sense and a pattern out of the above scrambled words. Sentence structure itself is a type of pattern stored in our mind.

Animals and humans will seek patterns in experiments that result in the creation of superstitious behavior in a laboratory. This is because two unrelated occurrences that transpire within close proximity to each other will be assumed to be related and a pattern is supposed.

Imagine that, years ago, a farmer had some good fortune. Perhaps he survived an accident or had a good crop or found a bride or won the lottery. Regardless, through a series of random events something good happened. However, when he recognized his good fortune, he happened to have a rabbit's foot with him. He paired the two events and assumed that the rabbit's foot brought him good luck and, unfortunately, told everyone about it. From this false pattern presumption, a ridiculous social pattern of assuming a rabbit's foot will bring good luck was created. There is no telling how many rabbits have suffered from our pattern creating need.

In the world of science this is referred to as an illusory correlation and they abound in our lives. Illusory correlations occur when we create false, unsubstantiated patterns. They typically occur because unrelated events are erroneously associated with each other. How many people have you known that have a lucky this or that they carry with them? Usually it is a lucky piece of clothing or jewelry. Athletes are notorious for establishing patterned rituals that are performed before games based on illusory, senseless associations. They think these rituals will bring them good luck.

As I was writing this book a story came on the news of a person wanting to get rid of an Ouija board. She was convinced that, since the time of the Ouija board purchase, a series of negative events had occurred in her life. How ridiculous! Yet, her subconscious observed an illusory pattern and she was acting on it.

At the extreme, paranoid individuals see an excessive amount of patterns in others' behavior that really do not exist. They believe that everyone around them who is talking is talking about them. When viewed this way, paranoia is a result of excessive pattern recognition and an error in interpreting the meaning of the patterns.

As Dr. Michael Shermer states in his lecture on TED talks regarding the problems with pattern seeking, we seek patterns because they help us make sense of our world and make good decisions.[11] Also, the cost of not recognizing a pattern and responding can be significant; for example, the pattern of stopping for a red light. The pattern and association that you stop for red lights is taught and deeply ingrained. Failure to respond to this pattern could be deadly. Thus, many recognized patterns are essential for cautious living and survival. Stopping at stop signs, locking the doors, brushing our teeth, exercising, and wearing seat belts are all admirable, healthy patterns.

The lack of a pattern is confusion. When an assumed pattern does not pan out, does not complete, or make sense, we are confused. The task of making sense of the world is largely one of pattern recognition and completion. Confusion results when there is no discernible pattern or a broken pattern. Similarly, not only does our mind seek patterns, it is also very bad at recognizing unfamiliar patterns. This is why chaotic families without stability and regular patterns of behavior raise troubled, confused children.

When a person you know well does not respond as you expect, an assumed pattern is broken. When you can't find your purse or wallet before you leave the house and you thought that you left them in the usual place, a pattern is broken. When your dog or cat does not return home when you call, a pattern is broken. When husbands and wives have affairs, the conventional social pattern of monogamy and trust is broken. Clearly, we do not generally like broken patterns of behavior. We seek stability in patterns and do not like the confusion that results when they are not present.

I typically park my car in the same parking lot at work. On some days the lot is full and I am forced to park in some out-of-the-way place. This is not too much of a problem until I return to my car—usually walking in a trance on automatic pilot--and not paying any attention to where I am going. When I arrive at the parking lot, to my dismay my car is nowhere to be found. I then have to actually think about where I parked. I have had momentary thoughts that my car was stolen. To my amusement and a bit of embarrassment, I have walked great lengths in search of my car. When my parking routine is disrupted, so is my life for a few moments.

Our pattern-seeking need is so great that we create patterns in just about everything we do. Once we set up our smart phone and computer screen layouts we remember the icon pattern instinctively. Can you remember the last time your computer for some unknown reason just changed the organization of your screen? Was that not a freak out for a moment until you got it rearranged back to the familiar layout you covet? The pattern-seeking and creating drive is insatiable in humans.

> *"If one cannot think without mental patterns – and, in my belief, one cannot – it is better to know what they are; for a pattern of which one is unconscious is a pattern that holds one at its mercy."*
>
> Arnold Toynbee

Relating these ideas to the purpose of this book, imagine that you begin to say new words to yourself in ways that do not initially appear to make sense or to be fully truthful. I am not talking about learning a foreign language which is also pattern construction. I am talking about using the words of your native language in a new and different manner, that is, the creation of a new word pattern. This too would be quite awkward and you would likely have an uncomfortable reaction to it initially. Yet, this is what one has to face when introducing new mental programming into his/her mind. In order to change, you have to be prepared to accept the awkwardness of new patterns. Get ready, because this is what this book is about doing.

What it all comes down to is that humans crave patterns in everything we do and all mental programming is based on creating and maintaining patterns of neural connections in our brain. That is, the mind is programmed through the recognition, creation, and repetition of patterns which are directly translated into a pattern of neural connections in the brain. If you had the tools capable of doing it, you could dissect your brain and see that all the patterns in your life have a corresponding pattern of neural connections in your brain. All patterns on the outside have a neural pattern on the inside.

Very obviously, pattern recognition is prerequisite to the automation discussed in the previous section. These two characteristics are inseparably intertwined. Automation cannot exist without pattern recognition. There have been numerous books written about the brain's pattern recognition drive. Those desiring to learn more about this phenomenon might begin by reading Leslie A. Hart's *Human Brain and Human Learning*[12] in which six major patterns are identified. You can also search this topic on the internet.

Again, it is not the purpose of this book to go into detail about this predominant, far-reaching characteristic that dominates our subconscious mind and our lives. This characteristic is noted because we want to learn to use it to our advantage. The takeaway is this: **Because the brain is a pattern-seeking machine, let's consciously, deliberately provide our brain with some beneficial patterns from which it can automate.**

What patterns are you providing your brain each day?

The Subconscious is Constantly Seeking Guidance from the Conscious Mind

Again, this next characteristic is inseparable from automation and pattern seeking. You might say that these topics are "attached at the hip." There is no having one without the other. Yet, as I noted, for clarity, I am discussing it separately.

Directly related to the pattern recognition drive is the fact that the subconscious is constantly seeking guidance from your conscious mind with regards to establishing new patterns of behavior. The subconscious is constantly "watching" what you do and "listening" to how you consciously think in an effort to discover the next behavior that it perceives you want to make automatic or habitual.

The subconscious also receives information from the unconscious mind and outside sensory input and cues of which we might not be consciously aware. As noted, even when some input goes through the conscious mind we may not be aware of the influences it is conveying to the subconscious. Remember the priming and ironic process research discussed in the first three chapters? The information was going directly into consciousness; however, the conscious mind was unaware of the underlying influence on the subconscious. Quite interesting. Because we have very little control over the unconscious mind, we are not going to discuss it here.

The point is that the pattern-seeking subconscious is always looking to the conscious mind for cues and guidance regarding what to automate. If the subconscious recognizes a pattern in the words you are consciously thinking, it will begin transforming those word patterns into habitual behavior. And *we can control conscious thought.* Therefore, we should constantly be aware that the subconscious is vigilantly seeking guidance from our conscious thoughts.

We too often fail to understand that the subconscious that controls our lives is seeking guidance. It wants feedback. It craves feedback and direction in the form of patterns. We too often approach life as if it happens to us and not from a perspective of personal control. **When you recognize and approach life from a perspective that the subconscious is seeking guidance and that everything we do repeatedly becomes that guidance, everything changes.**

Remember, the conscious mind is not merely the vessel for the thoughts you currently think, it is also the *control panel* you have been provided for managing the subconscious. It is the *only* control panel you have been given. Much of the time, people go through life flipping from one thought to another without realizing those thoughts are controlling the subconscious. The subconscious is constantly "watching" and observing conscious thought. You might think of the conscious mind as the parent and the subconscious mind as the child seeking guidance. However, be careful how you raise your child! As many parents will tell you, their behavior may come back to haunt you.

With this awareness, the question of what information you are feeding the subconscious through conscious thought becomes paramount.

What we are consistently thinking is providing guidance to and programming the subconscious. This is unavoidable. When we think of thinking (meta-thought) as the roots of mental programming, thoughts take on a whole new meaning. **Consciously think a thought once and not much happens; consciously think a thought thousands of times and the subconscious will certainly take note and respond.** Interestingly, the priming research discussed in Chapter 1 substantiates that even brief periods of thought stimulation can result in subconscious activation of behavior. As will be discussed, the effects were short-lived because they were not repeated across time. **What we think consistently is the origin and cause of subconscious programming.**

The takeaway: **Because the subconscious is always seeking guidance from the conscious mind, we should use the conscious mind to actively provide guidance regarding what we want to occur, what we want to automate. Don't fight the system; feed the system to your benefit.**

The Subconscious is Programmable and Can Be Consciously Programmed

At this point in the book, I know this goes without saying; yet, I am going to say it anyway just to make it inescapably clear. Because we can learn to do a host of basic and complex behaviors to the point of automaticity and because we can choose which behaviors we want to learn, it is self-evident that the subconscious is programmable.

As self-evident as this point is, I submit that this is one of the most heavy-duty, philosophically profound ideas in this book. When you think about life as a whole, that your being is extensively determined by what was programmed into your brain from birth turns life on its head. Many people live as if who they are and what they do is determined by mystical forces from outer space and beyond their control. Nothing could be farther from the truth. **An extremely significant degree of who**

you are and what you do has been programmed into your brain and, as such, can be reprogrammed.

Just as computers can be programmed to do the same task over and over with consistency, the subconscious mind can be programmed to do the same behaviors over and over automatically without conscious effort. By far the vast majority of what we do each day is automatic, habitual behavior.

Thus, the subconscious is moldable. It is pliable. You were not born with any of the habits or skills you currently possess. You were only born with the mental wiring for basic survival. All of the habits you have, all of the daily patterns you repeat without conscious thought, and all of your skills were acquired. Every pattern of behavior that you did not have hardwired into your brain from birth was acquired through practice. Once learned, you repeat these patterns without conscious effort. It is absolutely amazing the millions of mental processes your brain computes and directs each hour of your day. All of these acquired skills are stored in the subconscious.

Of great importance here is the fact that the subconscious mind can be programmed consciously with full deliberateness and awareness. **Just as the conscious mind can observe itself, the mind as a whole can program itself.** This programming takes place as a result of the interaction between the conscious and subconscious minds.

The fact that we program our own mind is not something that most people fully understand. It is not something that we readily keep in immediate conscious awareness. It is not something that you hear people talking about directly.

How often have you had someone discuss with you what he/she is currently programming his/her mind to do? Almost never. However, we do discuss these matters; we just frame them in a manner that does not appear as if we are talking about mental programming. We make comments such as, "I am trying to learn to…," or "I am trying to break myself of the habit of...," or "I am trying to get the hang of…."

Sometimes the discussion regarding mental programming is framed as desires or wishful thinking. Here the comments may sound something like, "I wish I could get myself to...," or "I wish I had your discipline to...." What is really being said is, "I want to program my mind to have me do _______." Or, as a more complete statement, "I want to program my mind to have me do _______, but I do not know how or I have not taken the time to practice or I have not used a mental programming technique to move me in that direction." While I suggest that the last statement is the real meaning behind what is being said, it is extremely rare that it is acknowledged in such precise terms. Rarely do we talk to ourselves or others with such complete and thorough thoughts.

That we do not think in terms of mental programming appears to be particularly true of those seeking to change themselves—the very people who need to understand this most. When it comes to breaking bad habits it appears as if people attribute the bad habit to some outside mystical force that controls their life, as if they were powerless against it. For some reason, when it comes to habit control, we tend to frame the situation as if we are victims of voodoo.

My sense of why this happens is that it has something to do with the perception that changing habits requires suffering and, as we do not want to do the necessary suffering, we frame the situation as one in which we have little control. The logic is something like this: Because I have little control over the situation, there is little I can do to change, and, therefore, it is useless to go through the perceived suffering. As will be explained later, change need not require such suffering when activated and prompted through mental programming.

The idea that our behavior is a result of some unseen force may also be related to another sequence of logic. That logic goes something like this: If I have control over changing the habit, I also must have had control over starting the habit; therefore, I must accept responsibility for my current situation. Unfortunately, accepting this responsibility does not always feel good. It arouses feelings of ineptness, guilt, disappointment, blame, culpability, incompetence, defeat, or disenchantment. So, rather than face uncomfortable feelings, we distance ourselves from the possibility that we have control over the habit. The logic goes something like this: If I am not in control, then I do not have to feel the negative feelings that accompany taking responsibility for my habits. As a result of these two rationalizations in combination, we tend to distance ourselves from the possibility of control when it comes to bad habits. Sometimes the fact that a habit is a "bad" habit results in even greater distancing because of the psychological discomfort that is aroused.

Yet, we do have control over our habits. The subconscious that contains the habit is pliable, moldable, and reprogrammable. Each of us played a role in creating our current habitual behaviors and each of us can "undo" the habit and reprogram our subconscious. This is true for even the most difficult behavior patterns such as alcoholism or smoking. Listen closely to the story of the former alcoholic who has been sober for ten or fifteen years and you will hear the story of a person who worked hard to reprogram his/her subconscious mind. Yet, this ability seems to be little understood and discussed. **It is amazing how many people live their lives as if their habits are out of their control—as if their life was a result of mystical forces. Yet, it is most evident that we program our subconscious.**

Perhaps this is a good time to point out again that the subconscious can be programmed consciously or by outside influences without our conscious awareness. As has been demonstrated by the priming research discussed in Chapter 1, people can be influenced without knowing it—without conscious awareness. This influence is often temporary, yet, it can be made to last longer through repetition. How people reacted, how fast they walked, how often they interrupted, the name chosen for a game, whether or not they tidied up after eating a cookie, whether they judged someone as cold or warm natured, and where they putted a golf ball were all a result of programming the subconscious and occurred without any conscious awareness.

The primary take away is that the programming in the subconscious is so deeply ingrained that there are likely thousands of things that can trigger the program into action. Words, images, scents, and objects have all been shown to trigger subconscious behaviors. We are doing it to ourselves and it is happening to us.

The programming in your subconscious is the summation of all the influences acting on your life—your parents, your childhood, the media, religion, politics, socioeconomic factors, friends, your country of origin, and most importantly, your own conscious thoughts. All of the factors that have influenced, currently influence, and will influence your life culminate in the subconscious. **Yet, in spite of all of the outside factors that have programmed your subconscious, you can reprogram it if desired.**

Perhaps this is also a good time to remind ourselves that the subconscious is primarily programmed with words and images which most often occur together. Although the mind can also be programmed by other senses, words and pictures are the most accessible and frequently used method of programming. In a modern world dominated by media, by far the greatest influences come from words and images. Most self-priming is through words and images. While possible, rarely do we think in terms of the programming power of scents, tastes, and touch when compared to the power of words and images.

The bottom line is this: **You were born with a computer in your head that you have the power to program to have you do virtually any behavior automatically without you having to consciously think about it.**

Once Programmed, the Subconscious Is Resistant to Change

Of equal importance to the fact that you can program your subconscious is the fact that, once programmed, the subconscious is remarkably resistant to change. This almost goes without saying. Once programmed, the programming in the subconscious is exceptionally stable. To many it may appear as if it is immoveable. Because it functions this way consistently, it is apparent that the subconscious is genetically wired to seek and establish stability and constancy. **Thus, the subconscious is genetically wired for consistency, stability, and resistance to change.**

This is both a convenient, beneficial aspect of the subconscious as well as a hindrance to quick, easy change.

Resistance to change is an extremely convenient feature of the subconscious, for once you have learned something well, you do not have to learn it again. Once you learn to ride a bike, or write, or type, or wake up at exactly the same time daily, or talk, or play the piano, or drive a car, or thousands of other behaviors, you do not have to relearn them every time you do them. In fact, the stronger the habit or skill, the more automatic it becomes and the more you can do the habitual behavior while thinking about doing something else.

How convenient it is that we do not have to constantly stop and think how to do things. We can go about our repetitive, daily activities almost effortlessly. In fact, for the vast majority of the things we do for most of our day we are on autopilot. It is likely that 99% or more of our daily activities and actions are subconsciously controlled. Conscious mind only has to take control when we do not know what to do and must make a new decision or learn a new behavior. Yet, these moments occur sporadically and, even then, the process for resolving which action to take has a subconscious component.

Simply put, the vast majority of the time, the subconscious is in control. Further, it is very consistent in maintaining control and it resists disruptions to the patterns of which it has been programmed. The subconscious works ferociously at maintaining stability in the behaviors it has been programmed to do. As with many aspects of life, the strength of the subconscious is a pain in the butt when it is working against your desire to change your deeply ingrained habits.

Thus, when we desire change, we must contend with this ferociously stable force that appears reluctant to change. **Reprogramming the subconscious is challenging to those who are not skilled in how to go about doing it.** Without the knowledge of how to change the subconscious, many succumb to its will. They end up stuck in previous programming. However, this does not have to be the case when proper methods of change are employed.

Here is a brief experiment you can do with yourself to test the power of the subconscious mind. The next time you sit down at your computer keyboard open your word processing program and try typing the sentence below at a *normal speed* except *without any spaces between the words.*

I am now typing this sentence at normal speed but leaving out all spaces.

Once typed, the sentence should look like this.

Iamnowtypingthissentenceatnormalspeedbutleavingoutallspaces.

Boy is that awkward! Did you notice how many times you hit the space bar even though you were trying not to hit the space bar? Did you notice how trying to concentrate on avoiding the space bar messed up typing the other words? Even when the conscious mind was trying to override the influence of the subconscious mind it had great difficulty. Once the subconscious is programmed it dominates our actions. The key to all success is to harness this power to work for you and not against you.

Here's another fun experiment you can do to test the power of the subconscious. If you are one of those people who always brushes your teeth each night before you go to bed, you can easily do this. Go to bed without brushing your teeth tonight. Skipping one time will not hurt. As you lay in the bed you will become overwhelmingly aware of the urge to brush your teeth. See if you can fall asleep without first brushing your teeth. Really give it a try, just this one time. Experience the power of the subconscious to maintain this habit as you feel the urges and nudging it produces in your being. The power of the subconscious is almost irritating. Your bedtime patterns are so strong at triggering brushing your teeth that it is almost impossible to shut them down.

To further grasp the qualities of the subconscious and what it takes to promote change, I offer the following analogy. Imagine three statues all with the exact same shape. One is made of whipped cream, one is made of firm clay, and the other is made of very hard stainless steel. Each of these materials represents the ability to form skills and change habits. When whipped cream is formed into a statuesque shape it immediately begins sagging and drooping and losing its shape. We are not like whipped cream and incapable of maintaining a shape (i.e., a habit) for any period of time. If we only had the consistency of whipped cream, all behaviors would have to be learned anew each time we did them. We would never have any stability in our actions. We would have to be reshaped over and over every time we learned something new.

We are also not like hard, cast stainless steel that, once shaped, is extremely difficult to change. A statue cast in stainless steel would require extreme heat and high pressure to be reshaped. While it would be possible to reshape a stainless steel statue, the extreme force necessary to reshape it is not representative of what it takes to reprogram the subconscious.

Our subconscious mind is like firm clay. Once moved into a shape, that shape is maintained. If we need to reshape a statue made of clay it is possible; however, it does take firm, consistent force to move the clay into a new position. It also requires the proper tools. You cannot reshape hard clay by fanning it or blowing on it. You must reshape it with a tool that applies consistent leveraged pressure such as a spatula. Yet, even a child could push the clay into a new shape. Anyone could reshape a firm clay statue into any form desired just as anyone can break old habits and form new ones. It would take consistent pressure with the proper tools, but once you have re-sculpted your statue, it will remain in position until pressure is applied again. The only question is, what shape do you desire your statue and what tools are needed to re-sculpt it? You will have to decide the shape. The tools are forthcoming in the next chapter.

In summary, once thoroughly programmed, the subconscious maintains that programming until that programming is disrupted and changed with the proper tools applied with consistent force.

The Unconscious Mind

Although we can logically conclude we have an unconscious mind, it is a bit of a mystery. I do not know what my unconscious mind is doing; it is out of my awareness. It is, by definition, unconscious because it is out of my awareness. And, I cannot get it into awareness—at least, not as easily as I can subconscious information. Generally speaking, in order to bring unconscious information into awareness I would have to do some probing or meditating or therapeutic exercise and the unconscious itself would have to "decide" to release the information to my conscious mind. Hence, the unconscious is all of that mental processing you are doing that you do not know that you are doing and cannot readily access or perhaps will never be able to access.

Theoretically, what is in the unconscious can stay in the unconscious and remain locked away for your entire life. Nevertheless, we have all, on occasion, had a long forgotten memory pop into our mind out of the blue after some idiosyncratic trigger resulted in our unconscious releasing the information. We most likely could not have remembered the event if we tried; yet, when the unconscious decided to release the information, it became available to the conscious mind. Such is the nature of the unconscious.

You can also logically conclude that the unconscious is controlling certain behaviors. The unconscious is controlling all of the bodily processes that you cannot or would have great difficulty controlling easily. For example, there are numerous chemicals—enzymes, hormones, neurotransmitters, oxygen, nitrogen, calcium, to name a few—that must be constantly balanced in your body. All of these balancing processes are ultimately controlled by the brain through glands and completely out of our awareness and conscious control. The muscles that move food through your stomach are unconsciously controlled as are many other bodily functions such as the release of antibodies.

While looking at a particular object can be consciously or subconsciously controlled, the focusing of the eyes is largely an unconscious process. It is very difficult, if not impossible, to take full control of the focusing process and cause your eyes to go in and out of focus at will.

The other mental process that provides evidence that the unconscious exists is forgetting. Some forgetting appears to be in the exclusive control of the unconscious. This is the forgetting that is extremely hard to recall and appears to only come into consciousness when the unconscious allows it. As noted, the psychological term for this is repression.

Obviously, the unconscious has much work to do and is very busy doing it. While we are largely at the mercy of unconscious processes, this is likely more beneficial than not. With all that must be done to keep our body functioning, it would be overwhelming to have to "think" about everything that must be tended to. How convenient that our unconscious is there taking care of business for us without conscious effort.

As previously alluded to, the question that may arise is: Can and do the subconscious and unconscious think about what they are thinking about. In other words, are the subconscious and unconscious minds doing their own metacognitions of which we are not consciously aware? I believe the inescapable answer is, "Yes." This is what is taking place in all of those billions of bits of mental processing which are occurring of which we unaware. However, that we have metacognitions beyond our awareness is only assumed from conscious mind observations.

That sub- and unconscious meta-thoughts occur is evidenced when we have a thought "pop" into our head. Perhaps you were searching for the name of a person you could not recall and, after you finally gave up your efforts, the name popped into your conscious mind twenty minutes later without any apparent effort. This is commonly known as the tip-of-the-tongue phenomenon. It is as if the name was inserted into the conscious mind automatically. The work in searching for the name was taking place at the sub- and unconscious levels. Outside of conscious awareness, there were metacognitions occurring which were processing through the needed logic to find the name sought. We have all experienced this phenomenon from which we can conclude that thinking must have been occurring outside of conscious mind awareness. It was one of the first things that Sigmund Freud wrote about and from which he partially built a case for the existence of unconscious processing beyond our awareness.

Additional evidence of metacognitions at the sub- and unconscious levels is also found in the world of dreams. While we do not always understand our dreams, they appear to be a window into the metacognition processing of the sub- and unconscious minds. I have conducted many dream analyses in my classes using the methods of the Gestalt therapists. On many occasions students have found that a dream that was never before understood became very understandable and meaningful after the technique was employed. I suggest that this too provides evidence for sub- and unconscious metacognitions. Therefore, it is quite reasonable to assume that metacognitions occur at the subconscious and unconscious levels.

Awareness and the Enigmatic Dividing Lines

Take note of the importance of "awareness" in describing the three levels of mental processing. The degree to which we are or can become aware of internal information is what defines the level at which that information is conceived to be processed. We are either aware (conscious mind), not aware and can quickly become aware (subconscious mind), or unaware and only rarely can become aware (unconscious mind) of various levels of information processing.

Also note that the "dividing lines" between the conscious, subconscious, and unconscious are nebulous. In many instances, the momentary control of behavior is a result of a tightly orchestrated interaction between conscious and subconscious processes.[2] For example, as discussed above, when you are driving your car you are constantly moving between a conscious awareness of what you are seeing and doing and a subconscious processing of all the motions necessary to successfully drive. This interaction is so fluid that we never notice it. It is so fluid that we cannot even bring to mind the ever present continuous interactions between consciousness and the subconscious. The same is true for a host of other behaviors.

Similarly, it is also difficult to discern from which part of the mind a behavior originates. In examining our everyday lives, it is not clear from where exactly in the mind something was put into motion. This is particularly true for deeply ingrained automatic behaviors that we do. Some behaviors are done so automatically and are so deeply ingrained that it could be argued that they are done unconsciously and do not even emerge from the subconscious. How could anyone tell exactly?

Take for example ironic processes. The conscious mind is aware that they are occurring—that negative intruding thoughts pop into awareness and enter into the conscious mind. Yet, just where is this control system "housed?" If ironic processes were programmed into the subconscious then, by definition, they could be reprogrammed because the subconscious is programmable. But, it does not appear that ironic processes, as such, can be directly controlled in the moment. Remember, research subjects reported that unwanted thoughts entered their minds regardless of efforts to the contrary and even when replacement thoughts were provided.[13,14] Thus, the ironic process mechanism appears to be implanted in the unconscious to some degree and has proven to be quite difficult to control in the immediate moment.

Yet again, ironic processes can be overridden by programming the subconscious to the point of automaticity. As noted, the only way to override the unconsciously programmed ironic process system is by programing the subconscious mind until the behavior functions automatically. So, the system that appears to be genetically programmed into the unconscious and that cannot be directly controlled by the conscious mind, can be counteracted and neutralized by programming the subconscious mind through repeated conscious mind efforts. What an interesting, enigmatic system. Obviously, the nature of ironic processes is also evidence that there are unconscious processes outside of conscious control.

Yes, the mind has minds of its own.

Generally speaking, the more deeply ingrained a behavior the more automatically it occurs and the more it is assumed to be coming from a deeper level in the mind. Whether it comes from deep in the subconscious or the surface of the unconscious is inconsequential. We have no definitive method of assessing where some behaviors originate. Fortunately, the vast majority of behaviors of which we are concerned are controlled by the subconscious. This is very easy to discern through the fact that I can take conscious control of them if desired.

For those nebulous behaviors that it is difficult to determine where the mental control originates, I really do not care that I do not know. Such issues make fun philosophical debate, but are irrelevant from a practical perspective. What is important to understand is that most behavior originates beyond consciousness. Of importance is the fact that the behaviors we most often want to change are subconsciously controlled and, therefore, are very changeable.

Summary

The above characteristics are the foundation for developing and maintaining effective mental programming. While I am certain there are other characteristics of the mind, these qualities give us a considerable amount of knowledge from which to build and understand what it takes to properly program our mind. Note them well. I also want to note that there are many nuances related to each of these characteristics that are not mentioned here. When you study the scientific research regarding these concepts, many variables influence how each principle applies. Fortunately, a basic understanding of these concepts is enough to develop an effective approach to mental programming. The above characteristics in combination lead to the key principle presented in the next chapter that guides us in programming our mind.

Those desiring to learn more about the incredible influence the sub- and unconscious minds have on our lives would enjoy reading *Subliminal: How Your Unconscious Mind Rules Your Behavior*[15] by Leonard Mlodinow, or John Bargh's new book, *Before You Know It: The Unconscious Reasons We Do What We Do.*[16]

Chapter 4 Key Points

- Even if you take the most conservative estimates, the processing power of your brain is staggering and beyond comprehension.

- Conscious mind processing is thinking you are doing that you "think" you are doing. It has been reasoned that conscious mental processing is awareness. The conscious mind is the control panel given by nature for all other controllable mental processes.

- The conscious mind can think about what it is thinking about; it is capable of self-observation or metacognition. The capability of self-observance or metacognition gives humans great power to analyze, assess, create, and decide in our minds before taking action or creating something new. Philosophically speaking, metacognition is foundational to having free will, the ability to self-regulate, for the development of moral principles, and the development of intelligence in general.

- The conscious mind cannot deliberately delete a thought or forget; the conscious mind can only focus and attend.

- The subconscious mind is accessible memory. In addition, the subconscious mental processing is all the thinking you are doing that controls behaviors of which you are not immediately aware, but of which you can become aware if desired.

- The subconscious forms and controls all habits, skills, and automated behavior.

- The subconscious is a pattern-seeking machine whose primary drive is to automate.

- The subconscious is constantly seeking guidance from the conscious mind.

- The subconscious is programmable and, once programmed, it is resistant to change. The mind as a whole can be self-programmed as a result of the interaction between the conscious and subconscious minds.

- The unconscious mind controls all of the mental processing you are doing that you do not know that you are doing and cannot readily access, or perhaps will never be able to access.

Chapter 4 Footnotes

Footnote 1: It should be noted here that research into subliminal stimulation has shown that information can get into the subconscious without the conscious mind ever being aware of it or "thinking" about it.[2] However, several points of understanding are crucial here.

First, this is not what was done in most of the priming research discussed in this book. In most of the research discussed in this book subjects were conscious of the words and sensory input presented. This is particularly true in the studies using The Scrambled Sentence Test. Because subjects read the words themselves, they were consciously aware of the words presented. This is known as supraliminal stimulation, not subliminal stimulation.

True subliminal stimulation is possible. That is, under the precise conditions, information can be delivered into the subconscious mind while bypassing conscious mind awareness. Some researchers study the influence of priming using methods that do this and have obtained astounding results. However, true subliminal stimulation requires precise laboratory controls, and is not easily accomplished in everyday life settings.

Second, so-called subliminal recordings that use sound masking and that are touted to magically reprogram your subconscious do not work as promoted.[17] The influences advertised from anecdotal reports are more likely placebo effects resulting from users knowing what is supposed to occur. This is easily understood when you think about sound waves themselves.

Sound masking obliterates the underlying vibrations that created the original, underlying sounds. You might think of the masking vibrations or sounds as "devouring" the original vibrations or sounds. When this occurs, the eardrum cannot vibrate in accordance with the underlying vibrations or sounds. With subliminal tapes the underlying vibrations originally formed words and messages. Literally speaking, these messages would have to be delivered to the brain in the form of a neural firing pattern. Yet, if the eardrum cannot vibrate to register the underlying words because the word vibrations are obliterated, there is no message available to send to the brain. As a result, there is no discernable, underlying "subliminal" message sent to the brain for processing. My own research confirmed this.[18] Try to hear what your friend is saying while standing next to a freight train passing by. If change and influence were this easy we would all just listen our way to being perfect and advertisers would be manipulating us into purchasing even more than we do. Change resulting from so-called subliminal recordings that use masking should best be viewed as an urban myth.

Footnote 2: There are degrees of self-awareness. Research indicates that chimpanzees and other apes, monkeys, elephants, dolphins, magpies, and perhaps other animals have some level of self-awareness. The degree of this self-awareness is not clear. What is clear is that the level of self-awareness of such animals is not equal to that of humans. Other animals do not wake up, read the paper, look at the calendar, plan their day, go to work, talk with their therapists, repair broken appliances, practice the piano, or create something original from an image in their mind. All such complex activities require a level of self-awareness far beyond what is seen in other animals. Relative to this book, other animals do not display self-consciousness to the degree that they go on self-improvement programs and deliberately take control of their habits. Yet, research indicates that some animals do know, at some basic level, that they exist. While the vast majority of animal behavior appears to be hard-wired, problem solving and reasoning abilities have been observed. Interesting.

Footnote 3: While the subconscious does an amazing job processing information with most people most of the time when driving, there are limits when distractions fully occupy the conscious mind. Thus, in glorifying the power of the subconscious with the example of driving I am compelled to point out that, with the use of cell phones when driving, we are clearly overtaxing the conscious mind with its limited processing capacity. This is compounded by the rapidly occurring traffic and environment changes.

While the subconscious does the lion's share of the information processing, it depends on the focus of the conscious mind through which this information passes even when we are largely unaware. Clearly, when the conscious mind gets focused away from the road and on cell phone conversations and buttons, the subconscious is helpless in saving us from information it cannot receive regarding driving decisions. It follows that the tragedies that result are from driver error and not errors in subconscious processing.

The subconscious processes best when there is not information overload at the conscious level. The best example of this is meditative states. When meditating, we quiet the conscious mind and allow the subconscious to work undistracted. In such states, the subconscious often delivers insights that we may not easily receive when the conscious mind is taxed. When you think about it, overloaded, distracted driving is the exact opposite of a meditative state and, when driving, information processing can get strained.

Below are some statistics gathered from various internet sources regarding cell phones and driving as of this writing. This data illuminates two things. First, the conscious mind has its limits and there are consequences for pushing these limits relative to driving or any situation. Second, the subconscious cannot help us if it is not provided the information to process. The conscious mind is the control panel we are given for all mental processes. This control panel provides the information that guides the subconscious in the processing it does. If the conscious mind is focused on the cell phone, it cannot gather data to send to the subconscious. The foot cannot automatically press the brake if the conscious mind does not provide information to trigger the subconscious reaction. The bottom line: **The mind cannot process what it does not receive.** The data below is readily understood when systems of mental processing are fully comprehended.

- The National Safety Council reports that cell phone use while driving leads to 1.6 million crashes each year.
- Every year, about 421,000 people are injured in crashes that involved a driver who was distracted in some way.
- In 2013, 3,154 people were killed in distraction-related crashes.
- When talking on the cell phone, you are four times more likely to have an accident.
- When talking on the cell phone, you lose 31% control of your car.
- When texting, you are 23 times more likely to have an accident. At the moment of texting, you lose 91% control of your car. The accident typically happens 3 seconds after the text.
- 11 teenagers die every day as a result of texting while driving.
- 21% of teen drivers involved in fatal accidents were distracted by their cell phones.
- Texting while driving is 6 times more likely to cause an accident than driving drunk.
- Answering a text takes away your attention for about five seconds. Traveling at 55 mph, that's enough time to travel the length of a football field.
- Texting while driving causes a 400% increase in time spent with eyes off the road.

Chapter 5

The Decisive Factor: The Dominant Thought

"You will never be greater than the thoughts that dominate your mind."
Napoleon Hill

Having presented the research and concepts of the previous chapters, I would like to now turn to the practical application of what has been stated thus far. Combining the implications from the priming and ironic process research with an understanding of the basic characteristics of the mind presented in the last chapter, I believe that mental programming boils down to one overarching, fundamental principle. The mind that governs your life is molded and shaped primarily through an understanding of one idea regarding mental processing. What I offer is a principle or axiom, if you will, that summarizes what has been presented and should guide you in all thinking.

Before providing this fundamental principle, let's briefly review the definition of a principle or an axiom. A principle is defined as a fundamental, primary, or general law or truth from which others are derived. The Oxford American Dictionary defines a principle as "…a basic truth or a general law…that is used as a basis of reasoning or a guide to action or behavior." An axiom is defined as a universally accepted principle or rule.

More specifically, an axiom is a proposition that is assumed without proof for the sake of studying the consequences that follow from it. The concept presented below readily fits the definition of a principle or axiom. It is a self-evident truth that governs all mental processing and subsequent action. If you do not accept this principle, fine; instead, use it as a starting point for the studying of mental processes. Disprove or refine it. Hypothesis test it. This is your choice. Yet, I would argue that it is supported by the research presented earlier. I view it as an overarching conclusion summarizing the findings of the priming and ironic process research and building from the fundamental characteristics of the mind presented in Chapter 4.

At first glance, the principle below may appear to be an oversimplification of a very complex system. Yet, what this principle is conveying is very powerful. Having studied and trained on this topic for years, I have evidenced its application and potential. I have learned to appreciate the uncomplicated clarity it offers. It always rings true, and I cannot come up with a scenario to disprove it. I ask that you give it some thought and actively test it yourself. Allow yourself the chance to observe the principle in action. I am confident you will grasp the significance and practicality of its implications.

For the scientists and philosophers I suggest you should be thinking Occam's razor at this point. Occam's razor is a philosophical principle regarding theories and explanations. It basically states that the simpler explanation is the better. Another way of saying it is that the more complicated an explanation, the more *unlikely* it is correct. Ultimately, the simpler explanation is usually the better approach, and simplicity does not negate the importance or functionality of an explanation.

Before presenting the principle, let's do a simple experiment—a bit of a mind game. Astute readers may likely know where I am going with this. Even if you can guess what is coming and where I am going, do the experiment anyway. It will not make any difference whether you are aware of the purpose of this experiment or not. Just do it. Oppositional types are welcome to try to fight the forces at work.

Right now, at this moment, close your eyes and think of a deer.

Notice what your mind did. Chances are an image of a deer appeared in your mind. Only for an instant of course, but there it was.

For a fleeting moment, you recalled an image of a deer that you had stored in your mind. By the way, it is also likely that many neural connections associated with "deer" were also fired off; yet, these connections may not have reached conscious awareness.

Now, read the next sentence, genuinely concentrate, and do exactly what it says.

Close your eyes and *don't* think of a deer.

What happened this time? As you well know by now, the exact same thing.

It does not matter whether you were directed to think of a deer or not. Once the sentence was read, the results were the same. The moment the phrase "...think of a deer" was read, your brain triggered the mental program to produce the image of a deer *regardless* of whether you were instructed to or not, *regardless* of whether you wanted to or not. Your emotional desire had no impact on the end results. What you logically intended had no impact on the results. The words "think of a deer" dominated the momentary mental processing.

After the image was triggered you may have quickly redirected your thoughts elsewhere in an attempt to avoid the image of a deer; yet, for a brief moment, "deer" ruled. Even if you directed your mind elsewhere, in order to assure you were not thinking of a deer, you had to continually examine your thoughts to determine if you had "deer" in them to assure you weren't thinking of a deer! And again "deer" dominated your thinking. Some may have found that you were switching back and forth between a deer and some alternative image you conjured up in attempts to focus on something other than a deer. Nice try.

Of course, you already knew what would happen because the ironic process research you read about in Chapter 3 has been confirming this for years. Your mind did not respond to the "don't" in the second example. In fact, as we have learned, it can't. As we noted in previous chapters, there is no way not to think of something. The mind cannot consciously delete a thought. It's impossible. The mind can only attend and focus.

In the above example, the dominant thought is "...think of a deer." **And it is always the dominant thought that determines the program triggered in your mind at the current moment.** The dominant thought is where the mind is focused, and thus, where it is directing you. Once the dominant thought of the above sentences entered your mind, for the next instance, you had *no control over what occurred.* Regardless of the wording, the image of a deer came forth. For an instant, you are powerless to the directive of the dominant thought.

With these points in mind, the cardinal rule below explains and governs the mental processing that determines all actions. Learn and consistently apply this principle and you will be the master of your fate as much as is possible. It is the key to breaking old habits and creating new habits that guide you toward your goals. It is fundamental to all success. With consistency, you can forge your life from this principle. The principle is this:

> **The subconscious mind moves you and your listener in the direction of the dominant thought regardless of whether that thought is stated in the positive or the negative.**

While I have never heard it stated exactly this way previously, it has actually been stated in much more general terms before by many writers and philosophers, some of whom I will note in Chapter 10. So what does this principle mean exactly? What is this principle indicating about mental processing? To answer these questions we have to first understand another associated principle regarding the subconscious.

The above principle is built upon a basic assertion or principle regarding the subconscious that is also demonstrated in the priming and ironic process research. This second foundational principle is this:

Most of what we do is controlled by the subconscious mind and the subconscious mind is controlled by the dominant thought.

This is the foundational assertion from which the dominant thought principle is built. You might say it is the assertion supporting the assertion; or, the principle behind the principle. In actuality, it is of greater significance than the dominant thought principle just presented. Even though this second assertion is the underlying assumption which leads directly to the dominant thought principle, it needs to be examined independently in order to build a rationale for dominant thought theory. Dominant thought theory is built upon these two principles in combination.

Take a moment and contemplate this second principle. All automatic behavior is controlled by the subconscious mental processing; but what triggers and stimulates the subconscious to think what it does? Answer: The dominant thought.

Your life is largely a set of repeated behaviors controlled by the subconscious and the subconscious is controlled by the dominant thought. This is why it is termed the "dominant" thought. The dominant thought takes the number one position in your mind *and automatically triggers everything associated with it as it guides and directs your subconscious.* Stopping the momentary influence of the dominant thought is virtually impossible. More specifically, stopping the neurons that fire off momentarily as a result of the dominant thought is next to impossible.

That the subconscious mind is controlled by the dominant thought is not well understood by most and, consequently, it is often overlooked. This is the mental quality that is frequently *not used* to people's advantage when habit change is attempted. Unfortunately, it becomes the stumbling block to which so many fall prey when attempting personal change. Consequently, habit change becomes more difficult.

Take a moment and think back to the priming research presented in Chapter 1, particularly the research involving semantics or simply the "placing" or stimulating certain words in subjects' minds. In the semantic priming research, subjects interrupted more frequently and quickly, walked slower, chose certain names for a game, as well as a host of other behaviors all because certain words were read by them. Simply put, the dominant thought words controlled the subconscious reaction and response. As we know, this occurred without subject awareness. This is because the words triggered behaviors that were done automatically. The dominant thought ruled.

The exact same thing happened in the ironic process experiments. Remember the putting experiments and how the experimenter's comments, "...to be careful not to *hit the ball past the target*. Do not *overshoot the target*," resulted in missing the shot more, especially under pressure.[1,2] Efforts to bypass the dominant thought failed. Because the instructions to subjects were "do not" instructions, we saw the impact of the dominant thought on the subconscious even more clearly. This is why the principle includes the statement, "...regardless of whether that thought is stated in the positive or the negative." The dominant thought words influenced; the "not" in the statements was inconsequential.

In both the priming and ironic process experiments, the words placed in the minds of subjects resulted in automatic behaviors of which subjects were unaware and, consequently, were not consciously controlling for the moment. Ultimately, both types of research confirmed that the subconscious was controlled by the dominant thought of the words presented and that increased effort and stress only amplified the impact of the words.

This is so simple; yet, so profound. Please allow this to sink in. If you do not grasp what you just read, please read it again until it makes sense. The implications are ever so compelling.

Words! Can we say enough about the importance of words? I doubt it.

The impact of dominant thoughts is amplified by the fact that, when you think a word, you are triggering a chain reaction to all associated words it stimulates. As noted previously, these additional words, in turn, become more readily accessible to the conscious mind.[3,4]

Always be aware that each word you think should be conceived as a cluster of words all manifesting their influence on the subconscious. Accordingly, one dominant thought can trigger a host of related concepts which can be used for your benefit *or not,* depending on the associations stimulated.

Having explained the basics of dominant thought theory, allow me to explain an adjustment I usually make in stating the fundamental principle. Without a full understanding of the conscious and subconscious minds and for the sake of reaching the most people with the most readily understandable statement, I typically remove the word "subconscious" when presenting the principle in trainings. I find this wording to be too academic relative to most people's knowledge. Thus, I most often state the principle as:

> **The mind moves you and your listener in the direction of the dominant thought regardless of whether that thought is stated in the positive or the negative.**

I have much more desire to teach the greatest number of people than to impress with academic rhetoric and nuance. Also, I have found that omitting "subconscious" does not diminish the message. Readers of this book most certainly understand that the subconscious is being influenced by the dominant thought by way of the conscious mind.

Detecting and Identifying Dominant Thoughts

Finding dominant thoughts is easy. For statements directing you to not do something, the dominant thought is what remains when you remove the "no's," the "not's," the "shouldn'ts," the "wouldn'ts," the "don'ts," and the "won'ts" or similar words directing the ceasing of some action. Perhaps the most common word directing one to cease an action is "stop." In statements such as, "I need to stop procrastinating," or "I need to stop drinking soft drinks," the dominant thought always follows the word "stop." (Incidentally, the word "cease" just used in the sentence above carries the same meaning but is not as often used in everyday language.) All such statements are negatively worded and, ironically, the dominant thought is the opposite of what is intended. Unfortunately, such negatively worded statements or thoughts dominate too much of our conversations and our lives. The pervasive prevalence of negatively worded dominant thoughts will become self-evident as you gain understanding of the concept and observe every-day conversations.

For a positively worded statement, the dominant thought is the primary focus of the statement or simply the content of the statement itself. This is usually a noun or verb used as a directive. Many times it is a verb and noun used in conjunction with each other. If I say, "Close your eyes and think of a deer," there are two directives, "close your eyes…" and "…think of a deer." In positive statements, the dominant thought is triggered directly by the content; no other words are present to trigger other mental processing.

In negatively worded statements the dominant thought is opposite of the grammatically stated directive. With negatively worded statements, the brain is priming one thought while attempting to consciously do the opposite of the prime. At the least, the brain is momentarily thrown into a conflict that it has to sort out to accomplish the directive. That is, the brain has to distinguish between the grammatically desired statement that is opposite of the dominant thought presented. What is desired and what is mentally triggered are opposite and it is much more difficult to obtain the results you want as the mind struggles with the paradox. Why create the struggle in the first place? Yet, because the mind has to resolve such discrepancies frequently, this is fairly easily accomplished most of the time.

Because we often resolve such linguistic discrepancies, the dominant thought may not appear to be of great significance. At least, not at first glance. This is particularly true when the dominant thought is deer or elephants. You could argue that people give instructions in the negative all the time and it works. For those who might argue that do-not-do statements actually produce the desired results, I agree for many circumstances. If you tell a child not to walk in the street, most frequently, he or she will walk on the sidewalk.

Interestingly, much more often than you would ever suspect the prime ends up directing behavior and the intended grammatical directive is not accomplished. The parent who admonishes the child in the toy store by saying, "Don't pick that up," has brought to mind the very behavior not intended. The child has no idea what *to do*. The teacher who has the student write one hundred sentences of "I will not talk in class" is triggering the very behavior not desired. More importantly, the worrywarts who constantly tell themselves "not to worry" are programming nothing into their mind toward reaching the desired state. The people with a fear of public speaking who say to themselves "don't be nervous" are programming absolutely nothing into their brain of benefit. Remember, the mind can only attend or focus. Dominant thoughts are the root triggers of all behavior.

Let's examine this more closely.

Dominant Thoughts in Everyday Conversation

Let's look in detail at one basic example mentioned above. Imagine the teacher who has the student write "I will not talk in class" a hundred times as an attempt to punish and stop inappropriate talking behavior. The dominant thought is obviously "talk in class" because the "not" is inconsequential relative to the internal neural links activated. As this statement is written by the student it is generating mental access to every word and everything associated with talking in class. This might include other words such as "speaking," "saying," "dialogue," "communicating," as well as the associated feelings of fun, friendship, pleasure, deviancy, and the attention that follows. In this instance, all associated words and feelings are triggering the very response not desired by the teacher.

What would be a better sentence to have students write? How about, "I listen with respect when the teacher speaks," "I sit quietly and pay attention to what is said," or "I only speak after raising my hand."

Have you ever heard of a student writing one of these sentences one hundred times? Have you ever thought these thoughts yourself?

From this example we can also see that dominant thought theory comes into play when we are communicating with others or when we are attempting to motivate others to act a certain way. Every time you talk with others you are momentarily triggering priming that arouses that person toward some action. The parent who yells, "Don't hit your little sister," is triggering a completely different set of actions from the parent that says, "Keep your hands to yourself, play fair, and be cooperative." In understanding this difference, the question is not, Are my words influencing? The question becomes, In what direction are my words influencing others and myself at the moment? Remember, even very brief comments have been shown to significantly influence what people do.

Read the list of common everyday expressions below in which the dominant thought has been italicized.

Don't *hit your little sister.*
Don't *forget to…*
You're going to *fall and break your neck.*
Don't *be nervous.*
Don't *hesitate* to call.
Don't *blow this assignment.*
You will not *fail.*
Don't *give me a hard time.*
I don't need to *eat that chocolate cake.*
I have to stop this *procrastinating.*
I need to stop *smoking.*
I need to lose some *weight.*
Don't *speed.*
Stop *arguing.*
Quit *fighting.*
Don't *pick that up.*

Take a moment and imagine the ideas and behaviors being triggered in the mind by the italicized words. Now, think of how many times people fail in getting the results they want. When you consider dominant thought theory and the behaviors triggered by these phrases, it's amazing we get beneficial results to the degree we do.

Now, let's look at the list of common expressions again along with alternative statements with different dominant thoughts.

Don't *hit your little sister.*	Keep your hands to yourself, play fair.
Don't *forget to…*	Remember to…
You're going to *fall and break your neck.*	Maintain your balance. Get a firm footing and grip as you move from branch to branch.
Don't *be nervous.*	Remain calm and relaxed.
Don't *hesitate* to call.	Call me when you need me.
Don't *blow this assignment.*	Maintain your poise and complete the assignment.
You will not *fail.*	You are succeeding.
Don't *give me a hard time.*	Thanks for cooperating.
I don't need to *eat that chocolate cake.*	I eat healthy.

I have to stop this *procrastinating.*	I do now, now I do.
I need to stop *smoking.*	I breathe clear air.
I need to lose some *weight.*	I am healthy, I am fit.
Don't *speed.*	Drive safely.
Stop *arguing.*	Pause, listen, and respect each other.

Notice the different dominant thoughts triggered by the alternative statements. Some are familiar and some are quite different from the commonly spoken. Regardless, the alternative statements trigger and stimulate thoughts and behavior regarding what *is desired* instead of what is not desired. While this idea appears rather simple, the impact can be tremendous.

If you become acutely aware of such language subtleties, you will start to observe the impact everywhere you go. Simply go to Walmart or Toys-R-Us and listen to the parents talking to their kids. You are likely to hear statements such as, "Now don't you *pick that up*!" or "Don't *hit your little sister*," or "Stop *running*." I have observed this with great sadness too many times. My urge to correct the parents is overwhelming and I have to work hard to keep myself in check. I once heard a parent in Walmart telling their young son, "You're worthless; you're so stupid." Imagine the impact of the words "worthless" and "stupid" on the child. The damage done to the self-esteem showed on the child's face. I wanted to call child protective services but I knew it would be of little consequence.

You really don't need hard core scientific research to confirm any of this; it is right before our eyes. Observe.

Dominant Thoughts, Habits, and Self-Control

Perhaps now is a good time to examine what you are saying to yourself regarding your desires and the influences on your subconscious. For those of you dieting are you saying things like, "I shouldn't *eat this chocolate cake,*" or, the ever-popular jest, "I *gain weight* just *looking at food!*" If so, observe the direction the dominant thoughts are leading the subconscious. A detailed analysis of the mental programming errors of these examples is provided in Chapter 11 along with strategic, advantageous alternatives.

Similarly, the procrastinator who constantly focuses on "not *procrastinating*" or the fingernail biter who thinks about "not *biting my fingernails*" are very likely doomed to fail. Parents who say that they "...need to stop *yelling at the children,*" or bosses who consistently tell their sales force to, "not *blow the deal*" are stimulating the very behavior they want to avoid.

The habit of procrastination is one of which many of us have struggled and can identify. So, let's look at it in detail for a moment. Here's a bad habit that appears to be largely defined by one singular concept, "procrastination" or "procrastinator." Other common expressions regarding this habit are to "put things off" or to "delay." Yet, when asked to define this bad habit, most use the words "procrastinate" and "procrastinator."

However, are these words what we want to bring to mind when breaking this habit? Not in the slightest. Is there anything about the word "procrastinate" that creates or stimulates action? Say the word to yourself now. Do you experience a call to action? I don't. It only triggers delaying and waiting and postponing and the accompanying uneasy, negative feelings associated with inaction. So, how can these words be of benefit when wanting to stop procrastinating?

As you have read these two paragraphs, I'll bet some of you have already linked into something you have not gotten done. Isn't it interesting how this works?

Let's change the subject.

What's the positive opposite of the words associated with this bad habit? We have a number of words in our language; some are quite common while others are rarely heard. I suggest the opposite of the word mentioned above (we now avoid) is "focused movement" or "focused action." How often do you say that dominant thought to yourself? Probably never. Other opposites might include:

I start and finish.
I act meaningfully.
Now I do, I do now.
I exploit the moment.
I use time effectively.
I use my minutes.
I am a model of focused action.

How often do you hear such expressions? How often do you use such expressions? How dominant are they in your mind? How foreign do these statements sound and feel to you? As you read the statements, if they feel foreign or even uncomfortable to you, it is likely that you have cultivated this unproductive habit of which we do not want to now refer.

By the way, the more foreign and uncomfortable dominant thoughts feel is not reason to reject them. To the contrary, the more foreign and uncomfortable, the more likely this is the dominant thought you should utilize. That a dominant thought feels foreign and strange can be an indication and clue to its utility.

A detailed list of opposites of procrastination is provided in Chapter 11. For now, I want you to grasp the impact of language on our mental processing and our efforts to change and create new behaviors. Procrastination just happens to be one of the clearest examples available that represents how language puts us in binds and impacts behavior.

Returning to an earlier point, much of the time we correct for negatively worded statements and do the opposite of the prime. Yet, taken in the context of someone trying to move toward focused action, dominant theory becomes incredibly important with regards to priming movement and accomplishment.

The same applies to all other bad habits or desired outcomes including being chronically late, exercise, getting organized, showing understanding, doing your homework, flossing, being better at a sport, being successful at work or in your home life, writing a book, fingernail biting, or any other behavior you want to stop or create. Dominant thought theory provides the fundamental roadmap for effectively programming the mind to break old habits and create new ones.

The implications of the dominant thought are enormous and powerful. All mental programs, all of those trillions of bits of mental processing power discussed in Chapter 4, are triggered by dominant thoughts or other stimuli that trigger behavior.

"Most powerful is he who has himself in his own power."
Lucius Annaeus Seneca

Personal Experience

Allow me to provide a personal example that perfectly exemplifies these points.

A number of years ago I learned this powerful lesson about how the mind works. I had decided to do some self-improvement. To this end I began by listing a number of bad habits I possessed. I had a number of areas that needed work. In order to overcome each bad habit, I wrote out new personality characteristics I wanted to develop.

One area that needed improvement was my conversational skills. I know this because I had been told rather emphatically that I had the bad habit of interrupting people when they spoke. In an attempt to correct this flaw, I wrote out the following personality characteristic: "I will not interrupt people when they speak." I was determined to change this habit. Thus, I then began repeating this statement to myself regularly. I can distinctly remember running over my list of self-improvement characteristics nightly before going to bed. This one included. At the time, I thought I was practicing positive thinking—a term that is overused, poorly defined, rarely fully understood and, subsequently, overvalued.

However, to my surprise, I did not improve. In fact, I got worse, almost effortlessly. I found myself interrupting others more! In addition, I had a greater awareness of my interrupting others when they spoke. It was as if the entire endeavor had backfired. I was going nowhere and I knew it. How could this be? I genuinely wanted to change. I earnestly repeated and drove the sentence I had written into my mind believing it was the characteristic I wanted to acquire. I told myself to "not interrupt people when they speak." I can remember failing so miserably that I went through a period of serious doubt as to whether self-change was possible without considerable suffering. I later learned that this suffering was something I did not have to endure to create change.

Let me tell you now that I am convinced that **self-change can occur without undue suffering.** The secret to changing yourself and reaching your goals lies in understanding how to properly program your mind. Learn this and you learn how to control your own behavior without pain and agony. Fail to properly program your mind and you will struggle with acquiring the characteristics you desire; you will be a victim of your old habits and constantly strain in reaching your goals.

Needless to say, the reason I was still interrupting people when they spoke is that I was not properly programming my mind. I clearly knew what I wanted to stop doing. However, knowing what I wanted to stop doing did not lead to viable mental programming. This point deserves clarification and much attention.

> **Knowing the behavior that you want to stop doing is actually of minimal benefit when it comes to breaking bad habits and creating new behaviors. Knowing the behavior you want *to do* is absolutely vital to breaking bad habits and creating new behaviors.**

Proper mental programming requires that you have a precise, clear statement of what you want to *start* doing. What you want to *do*. Where you want to *get to*. You need a viable, effective dominant thought.

In my struggle with the habit of interrupting people I failed miserably. I should have. I was repeating ineffective, negative programming. In reality, I was programming my mind to do what I did not want to do. The results were in accordance with the laws of mental processing—I moved in the direction of my dominant thought which was "interrupting people." I never delivered a dominant thought to my mind that moved and directed me toward the actual goal I wanted. Unfortunately, my conversation skills suffered for a while longer. (Some would say they still do!)

As I struggled with creating this change, I began to develop my theories on how the mind works. From my readings and study of mental programming, I recognized that I was programming my mind incorrectly. I later changed my programming statement to, "I listen with respect when others speak." This statement contains a very different dominant thought. This statement directed me to "listen with respect"—an idea not mentioned in the previous statement. This new statement moved me in an entirely different direction from my former statement. I got results. I got results because I changed my dominant thought.

Also take note that the new dominant thought was short and sweet—precisely to the point. I have discovered that the most effective dominant thoughts are often brief and to the point. This is evident in the examples provided in Chapter 11. Don't make it complicated. Complicated has nothing to do with effective.

Here's another example I noted recently. I saw a bumper sticker that read: "Don't postpone joy." As is typical, the intended message and the word choice led the mind into two different directions.

The good news here is the inclusion of the word "joy" which the bumper sticker is promoting. The word "joy" will likely link with beneficial concepts. The bad news is that the word "postpone" was triggered along with a "don't." At the least, this message is confusing to the mind because "postponing" is mentioned regarding the desired state of "joy." The "don't" typically is secondary and does not fully block the concept of "postponing." At worst, the idea of postponing joy is actually triggered. At best, one would have to sort through and untangle the message to arrive at what one should do, which is to seek joy. I doubt most people actually take the time to do that.

As bumper stickers go, this is a nice concept. As a tool for actual mental programming and accomplishing the message, it is weak and lacks efficiency. A much better mental programming phrase would be to state, "Be joyous now," "I am joyous now," "I recognize and embrace joy in many things," or anything that directs your mind to focus on and attend to joy. Note how every word in these alternative statements moves the mind toward and promotes joy. The undesired is never brought into consciousness or, more importantly, into the subconscious.

Considering that, by leaps and bounds, most of our everyday behavior is subconsciously controlled, it becomes apparent that the key to controlling your life is to correctly program your subconscious. **The key to your success at whatever you attempt depends on the precision with which you implant the programming into your subconscious.**

The dominant thought principle is crucial to breaking old habits and forming new ones. It also provides guidance to powerful communications with others. Learn to create dominant thoughts that *lead the mind* to what you want and you can program yourself to create any behavior mentally and physically possible.

I refer to this principle as a "secret" because it is amazing how poorly it is understood and how little it is used in our world today. It is really quite simple. Yet, people just don't seem to live their lives with a clear understanding of it. When it is taught, it is often included among a list of goal setting rules and only briefly discussed. There has been little discussion of the concept relative to the scientific research supporting it. While the broad concept of positive thinking is mentioned frequently, the significance of the dominant thought is rarely expounded upon.

Be aware of your dominant thoughts, they govern and control your life. Carefully choose your dominant thoughts; the degree to

which you control your life is determined by the precision of your mental programming.

The next chapter provides the four practical steps necessary to develop dominant thoughts and utilize them for change.

Chapter 5 Key Points

- Most of what we do is controlled by the subconscious mind and the subconscious mind is controlled by the dominant thought.

- The subconscious mind moves you and your listener in the direction of the dominant thought regardless of whether that thought is stated in the positive or the negative. Dominant thoughts govern your life.

- Knowing the behavior that you want to stop doing is actually of minimal benefit when it comes to breaking bad habits and creating new behaviors. Knowing the behavior you want to do is absolutely vital to breaking bad habits and creating new behaviors.

- Many everyday expressions include dominant thoughts that actually sustain habits and behaviors people want to change.

- In order to create effective dominant thoughts we have to carefully analyze language and often we have to create and hone statements that are out of the ordinary.

Chapter 6

Using Dominant Thought Theory to Change Your Life: The Four Steps

"One critical upshot of this work is the notion that just as we as a society are learning to take more responsibility for our physical health by engaging in the regular practice of physical exercise, so too can we take more responsibility for our minds and brains by engaging in the regular practice of certain mental exercises that can induce plastic changes in the brain and that potentially have enduring beneficial consequences for social and emotional behavior"[1]

Davidson and McEwen

Everything that you have ever done, everything that you are doing at this moment, and everything that you will ever do is processed and controlled by your mind. Doesn't it make sense to learn as much as you can about how your mind works and how to program it? Learn to effectively program your mind and you learn to control those aspects of your life that are controllable. Properly program your mind and you tap into a wealth of ability you never dreamed possible. Yet, I assert that most people know more about how to program their cell phone and TIVO than their own mind. Forgive me as I rant more about this for a moment.

As simple and self-evident as this statement is in our modern, educated world, it is amazing how little people understand about how to program their mind for their own benefit. It also amazing how little credit people give their mind for controlling their actions. This is particularly true when it comes to habits. Most people live as if thinking is merely a dialogue within themselves for analyzing various aspects of the world and as if most of what they habitually do is a result of uncontrollable mystical forces. Many people go about their day as if most of what they think and what they habitually do are unrelated events.

One of the reasons that many have such difficulty crediting their thoughts for creating their actions is that the process by which the mind controls our actions is extremely automatic.[2] In fact, it is astonishingly more automatic than deliberate. That is to say, the most important thoughts that control our actions come from the subconscious mind, not the conscious mind. We go about our daily lives without being aware of the millions of commands that our mind is communicating to our bodies at each moment. This point has been explained and amplified in this book.

Without knowledge of how to properly and effectively program the subconscious, most people stay stuck in habits that they wish they could change. They feel as if they are at the mercy of some uncontrollable, mystical force. They smoke and can't seem to get themselves to stop. They overeat and feel as if they can't get themselves to stop. They know they need to exercise and, yet, continue to sit on their butts. They have work to do that does not get done. They have dreams they want to pursue and, yet, they take no action to accomplish them. They want to save money, yet, spend recklessly. They take pills that they hope will change them that, in the end, only numb them and aid at keeping them in the dark relative to their ability to self-control.

Pills don't program your mind, words do.

Hence, there is a severe lack of knowledge about programing the most important thing that controls our lives. What follows are the four fundamental steps necessary for programming your mind-computer. They provide the formula for mental programming.

The Four Steps

So, what are the steps necessary to program your mind? When you break it down, there are four steps to applying dominant thought theory to your life. Each step must be precisely and consistently implemented in order for the process to be effective. The four steps are:

1. Define what you are currently doing.
2. Precisely define the positive opposite of what you are currently doing.
3. Create a present tense statement that states you are doing the new positive opposite behavior.
4. Repeat the statement created in Step 3 to yourself 500 to a 1000 times a day consistently across time. Likely 2-3 months.

That's it. If you are looking for something more complicated, read another book. If you are looking for something that is harder, try using self-discipline alone without any accompanying mental programming. Please note that using self-discipline alone can be a very successful method of creating change. It is just that, for deeply ingrained habits, self-discipline alone often provokes a tremendous internal struggle that is accompanied by feelings of this-is-too-much-for-me and I'll-never-do-it. For habits that have an added physiological component such as overeating or smoking, the internal struggle and the battle with the body's cries for sugar, nicotine, or pain killers can be overwhelming.

If you think this method is too simple and, therefore, it cannot be effective, then give it a serious trial run and test it. You might be pleasantly surprised by what you discover. In order to fully understand the method, I will discuss each step in detail.

Step 1: Define What You Are Currently Doing

Step 1 is likely the easiest step of the four. This is the step that most people can instantly state. The smoker is smoking. The overweight people say they eat too much. They eat too much junk food. They don't know when to quit. They like food too much. They drink too many soft drinks. The person with the difficult task before them states that they procrastinate. They delay. They keep waiting to know exactly what to do before acting. They worry that it will not be good enough and, therefore, do not act. The person with test anxiety or anxiety about anything states that they are nervous and that they doubt. They worry and their worry prevents them from thinking clearly and doing the very things they need to do to move beyond the worry.

These responses are a good place to start and many times plenty adequate at defining what is currently being done. I really do not want you to spend too much time belaboring thoughts of your current ineffective behavior for they are the culprit which needs to be ousted and replaced. Yet, sometimes people do not have a clear picture of what they are currently doing and this can be a hindrance to an effective Step 2.

As should be obvious by now, the reason the first step is the easiest is because it entails simply labeling the behavior using the terms that most people typically use to describe their problem. Ironically, the first step not only defines the problem, it most often is a large part of the problem. That is, the words used to describe the behavior are the same words that are maintaining the behavior. For example, the procrastinator who constantly talks about the need not to procrastinate is triggering procrastination by using the word!

The reason for the first step is that a clear and precise definition of what you are currently doing often leads to a clear and precise definition of the positive opposite. As I will repeatedly point out, precise wording is key to an effective change formula. Thus, if when asked what you are currently doing, you respond, "Nothing," this is not a clear enough statement for developing a well-defined positive opposite statement in Step 2. You are never doing "nothing." "Doing nothing" is a catch-all phrase that can mean a host of things. It may mean you are sitting. It could mean you are not acting for your own benefit. You are passive. You are delaying. You are piddling. You are continuing to do what you have always done. You are ruminating. However, you are never doing nothing, so be careful to not let a feeble analysis of your current behavior hinder your change.

Sometimes it is a bit of a struggle to define what you are currently doing because you have to "get real" with yourself. You have to honestly confront what you currently feel is an inadequacy or a fault. This self-analysis arouses discomfort and you have difficulty forcing yourself to admit that you do certain things. Here, you may require some pure self-discipline to "come clean" with yourself with an honest assessment of your current behavior. A secondary benefit of this analysis may be that the discomfort of recognizing an undesired behavior in yourself may result in an emotionally compelling reason for change.

Step 2: Precisely Define the Positive Opposite of What You are Currently Doing

Step 2 is the vital, foundational component to applying dominant thought theory. It is here that you create a new, specific, precisely worded dominant thought that clearly defines what you will be doing when you have reached your desired goal or state. Step 2 is by far where most people err in their thinking. Step 2 is *the programming stumbling block* that must be overcome. Poorly worded "get to" statements are, in and of themselves, one of the primary reasons people find it so hard to make changes in their life. Step 2 is where you begin the process of programming your subconscious and, if it is done incorrectly, you could inadvertently program your mind to move you in the wrong direction.

"All things and all circumstances must first be created on the mental plane."

U. S. Anderson

You begin Step 2 by asking yourself what the positive opposite of what you are currently doing is. This may require some serious thought and work. If you were not doing what you are currently doing what would you be doing? This new behavior must absolutely be defined as doing a desired behavior. It should not be stated as not doing an undesired behavior. Careful analysis and internal searching are needed. This is not to be taken lightly and don't be surprised if the positive opposite of what you are currently doing is not a commonly stated behavior. Approach this task with great solemnity and seriousness. Be pleased with yourself if you create a statement that is completely new and has never been used to describe your behavior before.

Because it provides some wonderful examples from which to learn, I will use smoking as a detailed example to demonstrate the task at hand in Step 2.

When I was in graduate school seeking my doctorate I earned extra money by conducting smoking cessation groups for a local hospital. From this experience I became very familiar with the complexities of what people say to themselves about smoking. This experience also helped form and solidify my belief in dominant thought theory.

One of the beginning tasks was for group members to list motivators as to why they wanted to quit smoking and to develop appropriate positive dominant thought statements from those motivators that they would repeat to themselves daily. When first asked, "What is the positive opposite of smoking for you?" the most common answers were, "not smoking" or to become a "nonsmoker." As is obvious, smokers who state, "I need to stop *smoking*," or "I want to stop *smoking*," or some similar statement likely elicit a perilous stimulation of the subconscious with the dominant thoughts aroused. With such statements their mind is constantly being primed to smoke. Nothing in the words is priming any action opposite of smoking. Such statements make it very difficult to break the habit and, to make matters worse, are actually triggering the very behavior they intend to stop!

Let's examine this paradox a step further. What do we call people who do not smoke? "Nonsmokers." Again, what's the dominant thought? Smoking! What a linguistic bind! Stating the desire to become a non*smoker* is also mentally linking to everything associated with smoking. Interestingly, there is no formally defined word to describe those who do not smoke without using the word "smoke." You can bet the cigarette manufacturers love this! Remember, when you say the words "smoking" or "smoker" all associated words and emotions are brought forward in the mind. This could include pleasure, relaxing, feeling good, taking a break, friendship, hanging out, relieving the craving of an addiction, etc. Unfortunately, all of these are associated with smoking and create the desire to smoke.

(Interestingly, "nonsmoker" was originally spelled "non-smoker" with a hyphen. Initially, this was the grammatically correct way to write the word. However, the word has been so commonly used that it is now listed in dictionaries as a noun in and of itself and the hyphen is now omitted.)

Back to the point, the initial most commonly stated opposites of smoking all include the concept of smoking—not a very beneficial or effective thought if you want to quit smoking. Thus, the task before the group was to think of opposites of smoking without using the word or concept of smoking. This proved to be quite challenging for group members.

The problem was that the group members had never thought in terms of what they would be doing if they were not smoking without steering their minds to think about smoking. They were talking and thinking like we commonly talk and think without any regard to the implications of the words they were using. Though motivated, they had not been successful at quitting and were now seeking help through the group. *I am absolutely convinced that one of the primary reasons they had not been successful at quitting was because they were constantly leading their minds toward the very behavior they wanted to eliminate.*

Thus, we began the journey of discovering what the opposite of smoking was for each member. As the group leader I did not want to jump in with suggestions too quickly without first allowing members to develop their own insights. As a therapist I have used this technique many times with people wanting changes in their lives and I can tell you that it is amazing what people come up with. I can also point out that, when you rush in too quickly with your insights and suggestions, you preclude the opportunity for clients to discover opposites on their own.

When the insights come from the client, they carry more ownership and have more potential benefit.

So, what are some behaviors and concepts that constitute the opposite of smoking? Below is a partial list of opposites that clients and others have generated over the years.

I am healthy.
I breathe fresh air.
I breathe clean air.
I breathe clear air.
I take care of this body-temple that I exist in at this level of existence.
I am a good model for my children.
My children are healthy.
I live longer.
I save money.
I am a good kisser.
I have fresh breath.
I am in control.
I love my (wife, husband, children, etc.) and I strive to be here for them.

Wow! What interesting opposites. These are actual statements provided by those with whom I have worked over the years. How often have you heard these statements from smokers? Make note of what each statement does not state, what each primes, and how rarely they are heard. There really are a lot of opposites of smoking, we just never take the time to think of them and think them consistently.

As you study this list of opposites of smoking, notice certain things. First and foremost, there is no mention of smoking, cigarettes, quitting, stopping, etc. No thought is brought to mind that is associated with smoking. There is only a statement of conditions which *cannot exist* if one smokes. With each of these statements the mind is directed to move the "smoker" toward a state or behavior that does not permit smoking. Each statement in its own way is a very good representation of the opposite of smoking.

Second, notice that most of the statements listed are not a common part of our everyday language. How often do you hear someone say, "I breathe clear air." This is a unique piece of mental programming of which I am particularly fond. It is a very accurate counter to the act of smoking. An eloquent expression of a place to be which, for me, also conjures up a picture that is unmistakably beneficial and good. The freshness of the language matches the feeling of the underlying desired state. The "get to" place is unambiguous. Clearly there is power in this dominant thought that directs the subconscious mind to act in a new way. Yet, how often do people ever make such a statement to themselves?

Third, notice that there are many different opposites of smoking. Any one of these is an accurate representation of the opposite of smoking and, yet, they are quite different. For the individuals who created the statements, the statements represent the opposite of smoking for them. If the meaning does not appear to apply to you, that is perfectly fine. Your opposite is not their opposite. Each of us has to determine what our opposite is relative to our world and our habits. Each has a particular meaning for the person who created it. What is meaningful to one individual may not be meaningful to another. What triggers a strong motivation in one person may not in another.

In seeking change it is always beneficial to link into emotionally compelling reasons within the individual. The more an opposite triggers a strong, desirable, emotional motivation, the more we want to use it. As a therapist I always accept my client's opposite as long as it is truly an opposite. The relevant issue is whether or not the person wanting the change finds the statement to be an accurate representation of where they want to "get to."

See Chapter 11 for more examples of smoking opposites.

As will be discussed later, it really does not matter if the person seeking to change believes the new state is possible to achieve at this time. Many times the new statement is so foreign that stating it aloud feels uncomfortable and fake to the individual desiring change. This is of no consequence. The critical question is whether or not the statement is an accurate opposite for them and, secondarily, has an underlying motivating component that taps into an emotionally compelling reason to change for that individual.

The second step must be done with much attention to the detail. If care is not taken to make certain that a well-formulated opposite is stated, the entire process might backfire. Step 2 is where the dominant thought is created. Step 2 is where the power of words is utilized to properly program the subconscious mind. The discovery and creation of accurate opposites is quite fascinating and will be addressed in many forms throughout this book.

"It's not enough to say 'no.' It's not enough to simply stop a bad habit or stabilize an illness. Health is not only the ability to say 'no' to all the options and voices that are contrary to one's values. It is also the ability to say 'yes' to something so completely that all other voices and values are silenced"

Robert Johnson

Step 3: Create a Present Tense Statement That States You are Doing the New Positive Worded Behavior

When done properly, the third step may likely be accomplished with Step 2. However, it is amazing how many times people let this stumbling block weaken or extinguish the programming power of the dominant thought. In Step 3 you create a *present tense* statement stating that you are doing the future desired behavior. If you have already done this, fine. If not, check to see that the positive opposite is stated in present tense, not future tense. Note that the smoking examples above are all written in present tense. "I *breathe* clear air" not, "I *will* breathe clear air,"

Having made this point, I have to discuss the issue of tense for a moment. Just as dominant thoughts require precision, so does the tense of the statement. Let's examine the underlying implications.

As I will ardently continue to state, you must be meticulous when you want to program the subconscious. Any time you use phrases such as I "desire to," "need to," "ought to," "have to," "want to," "wish to," "hope to," etc. you are *not* programming the mind to do anything. You are simply expressing desires. Similarly, words like "will," "going to," "try," "would," "should," "could," convey only the possibility of a new behavior being implemented. There is no starting point with any of these words. These words do not initiate action. They only imply that *someday* you may do something different.

Conceptually speaking, "someday" is always in the future and never arrives. I suspect that any time you program your brain by hoping or implying that something will happen in the future the subconscious asks, "When do you want to start?" Most of us have experienced how difficult it can be to actually make changes in those difficult habits that we tell ourselves that we "need to" stop doing. Precise, meticulous wording programs and directs the subconscious to implement specific actions.

As noted, the mind is like a computer and the internal programming is triggered by the words used and not necessarily by the intention. Poorly worded mental programming statements can work against you, particularly when you want to change stubborn, ingrained habits. As I write this book my computer is able to correct misspellings of many words. However, it does not catch all mistakes and I must still proofread in order to assure correct spelling and grammar. Similarly, you should proofread your mental programming for errors in the message.

It is better to think of mental programming like you think of a URL address of a website. If you mistype one character in a URL address, the computer will not be able to take you to the website you desire. If you want to create a new future in which you live, you must program your mind with the precise "address" that you want to reach and then hit the "enter" key. Hoping or saying you should go to a certain website does not get you there. Similarly, you must tell your brain the precise place you want to "get to" and then repeat it. Understanding and utilizing precise language is vital to creating commanding mental programming.

Read aloud the examples below sensing the feeling, action, and movement each possesses. The difference is immediately comprehended logically and intuitively.

I need to stop smoking.	vs.	I breathe clear air.
I need to lose some weight.	vs.	I eat healthy, I am healthy.
I ought to get this work done.	vs.	I consistently do a portion of the job daily.
I want to start exercising.	vs.	I exercise daily.
I need to stop procrastinating.	vs.	I do now, now I do.

Understanding the differences in wording and tense between the statements in the two columns is critical to successful mental programming. Remember, you should approach this task as if you are programming a computer. What appear to be subtle shifts in language are not subtle at all. These wording nuances are strategic in transforming the mind. Such language modifications have great impact on the outcome.

Step 4: Repeat the Statement Created in Step 3 to Yourself 500 to 1000 Times a Day Consistently for Months

Mental programming takes time.

You have to repeat it. You have to repeat it consistently. You have to repeat it even when it appears unnecessary or foolish or when you don't feel like it or when nothing is happening.

There is no instant success. You are the person you are today because of years of mental programming and habit formation. Although possible, it is generally not the case that you are going to override and replace years of mental programming instantly.[3] For most of us, it is going to take time. The subconscious mind needs to be repeatedly told what you are wanting from it. Remember, the subconscious is constantly looking to the conscious mind for guidance. The subconscious is looking for and seeking patterns. The subconscious latches on to anything repeated. So, use your conscious mind to give the subconscious what it pursues and seeks—repetition of a pattern in the form of a statement.

Although Step 4 may appear easy, it is not. *Step 4 is by far the most difficult step of all* because it requires consistency across time in the midst of a mass of countering forces. There are many reasons for the extreme emphasis on consistently repeating a statement across time.

One reason that consistency is important is because there is always going to be a tremendous amount of interference from previously formed mental and environmental associations. In addition, most of us suffer from "monkey mind" in which our thoughts constantly jump from one topic to another never allowing time for a focused effort. You can add to these two forms of interference the doubt from the negative voice that almost always arises and attempts to sabotage your efforts. Without consistency these forces will destroy your efforts. Consistency is the tool that surmounts these and other sabotaging forces. These primary hindering factors will be discussed in detail in the next chapter.

> *"Spend time thinking of what you want*
> *rather than you don't want."*
> Sanaya Roman

For now, realize that creating change in humans is not like turning on and off a light switch. You are reprogramming "mental wiring" that, while reprogrammable, has a strong tendency to want to retain the status quo. This tendency is very beneficial because once rewired for the outcome you desire, you do not have to worry about the circuitry changing with every outside force or pressure that comes along. It only follows that rewiring the mind takes time because the mental programming you are doing is acting on an underlying, stable aspect of your mind.

I doubt anyone has ever made significant change by waking up and repeating a positive statement to themselves one time. Simply put, the subconscious is programmed by repetition. This cannot be emphasized enough. Consistency is paramount. Every behavior you do automatically was created through repetition whether simple or complex. **The more the conscious mind repeats, the more the subconscious will take over the action.**

Is this confirmed by research? You bet it is.

Research previously noted has confirmed that repetition is the road to automaticity.[2,4] As researchers Bargh and Chartrand so precisely summarize:

> The necessary and sufficient ingredients for automation are frequency and consistency of use of the same set of component mental processes under the same circumstances—regardless of whether the frequency and consistency occur because of a desire to attain a skill, whether they occur just because we have tended in the past to make the same choices or to do the same thing or to react emotionally or evaluatively in the same way each time (p. 469).[2]

In other words, it does not matter how you come to repeat something for automation to occur; it only matters that you repeat something. Taking this a step further, you are always repeating some things in your life. The only question is, What are you repeating? You become that which you repeat. That, that is repeated, automates. Period.

Step 4 is simply the utilization of this scientific fact. If you want to accomplish something the key is to create the built-in mental automation that sets into motion the behaviors necessary for attainment. This is true no matter how big or small the ultimate goal. There is absolutely no way around this reality. And the only route to automation is repetition. I contend that the shortest route to automation is the repetition of a precisely worded dominant thought.

The counterpart to the above wisdom was offered by Ralph Waldo Emerson who stated that "A foolish consistency is the hobgoblin of little minds, adored by little statesmen and philosophers and divines." Likewise, a wise consistency is the hobgoblin of intelligent, sensible, judicious minds. This book is all about consistency in mental programming. The question you must ask yourself is this: What am I consistently programming into my mind?

By the way, if you do not want to program your own subconscious, not to fret. There are thousands of advertisers, politicians, religious zealots, and con artists who are just dying to program it for you. Just sit back and relax. I can assure you they will work diligently to plant their thoughts in your head to manipulate you for their benefit. When you think about it you really only have two choices: You either take the time to program your subconscious to do what you desire, or someone else will do it for you for what they desire. This is a raw reality of life few want to face.

> "*Even though our lives may appear predetermined, this is an illusion. We can determine our lives by focusing on an objective, on a path, on a way of being – and following it to its natural resolution.*"
>
> Matt Furey

More Philosophical Rantings About Consistency

Absolutely nothing in this book has any impact without consistency. I told you I was going to be talking about it a lot. Well, here I go again with a bit of a philosophical rant about consistency. Skip it if you so desire.

Examine for a moment the most important things in your life—your friendships, your relationships, your physical and mental health, your financial security, your spiritual balance, your integrity, your education, the skills that define who you are and make you employable. The security you have physically or socially. In the vast majority of cases, none of these was accomplished through one-time events. The important things in life result from what you have done consistently. On occasion, someone wins the lottery and establishes his/her financial security; but this is an extremely rare event.

Universally, the most important things in life result from long-term consistent behaviors. Your relationships are not established because you did a behavior once. Meaningful, important relationships result from consistently responding to those around you in ways that build a working, respectful relationship. Even if you were born with innate talents, you were not able to use them to define yourself and make yourself employable without consistently training and nurturing these skills across time. The most gifted athletes train deliberately with consistent, rigorous schedules. No one remains physically or mentally healthy without consistently working to strengthen and enhance what they already have and thwart the forces that can throw them off course. Consistently doing the proper, necessary behaviors is the underlying factor in all success.

The most important things in life cannot be bought, worn, drunk, eaten, ridden in, looked at, or purchased on TV or the internet. Such possessions and momentary acts are not the meaningful heart of living. What you consistently do regarding some of these momentary events does give substance to life. This idea also includes giving up those things you do consistently that work against you. If you are consistently delaying important decisions, consistently not exercising, consistently eating the wrong foods, consistently spending your money foolishly, consistently doing things that work against you, your consistency is working against you.

It is only through acting judiciously regarding momentary events that life develops meaning and importance. Consistency is the essential ingredient to worthwhile, meaningful living. Consistency is the factor that separates the significant from the valueless. Consistency separates the accomplished from the unaccomplished, the successful from the unsuccessful.

Consistency is everything. Consistency is all.

Yet, consistency has become a forgotten, overlooked element in our world today. I assert that in this world of momentary, immediate, I-want-it-faster living, the importance of consistency is becoming lost. The significance of consistency does not appear as important as it once was. The emphasis on the long-term impact of consistency is being replaced with an emphasis on immediate gratification. Consistency is rapidly becoming the forgotten element of success. As a result, personal lives suffer and bad habits dominate.

We want to be able to get everything by our cell phone immediately at the push of a button. We want to quickly tweet and be on Facebook with our latest momentary, nonsensical event in hopes it will bring meaning to our life without consistent effort. We want to buy things now on credit without consistently saving first. We want to learn new things by the latest method that does not require effort. As a guitar player of many years I have to laugh at the TV ads claiming to teach you how to play guitar in a few short lessons. We want to take a pill to lose weight, stop smoking, manage anxiety and depression, and feel good without having to consistently do anything across time. We want everything to magically happen now without consistently doing anything of consequence.

I make these points here because consistency is by far the hardest part of the process. It is the part where we, as humans, are most likely to stumble. It is the part of the process that seems to fall to the wayside and fade from consciousness effortlessly. This is because there is initially no subconscious programming to maintain this part of the process. (Unless you program yourself to be consistent!) You are implanting new programming and there is no internal programming to sustain it. It must be maintained by willpower and there are many factors which naturally disrupt your conscious attempt to engrain a new thought pattern.

Frankly, what you are ultimately trying to achieve is a conscious repetition of your new mental programming until you reach the point that you automatically repeat it! Such is the circular nature of our mind.

Through conscious effort we program our mind with a new thought and the process of consciously repeating our new thought also programs the process of repeating the new thought. (Even these sentences are circular!) The point where the repetition becomes automatic is an important juncture because this is an indication that the subconscious mind is embracing and integrating the new programming.

"You must put forth effort to learn to act effortlessly."
J. Graham Disque

Remember, the mind is an amazing machine that has the unique ability to think about what it is thinking about. It can step back and "see" itself working. Stated even more figuratively, the mind can examine its "self" working. (Read the last two sentences again paying attention to the words and punctuation. Note how cleverly the mind grasps the meaning at a conceptual level through its ability to interpret and understand the message of the punctuation marks. What an incredible apparatus!) The mind has minds of its own! These minds have a circular relation to each other in learning new directions to go. Getting back to the point, consistency is absolutely critical to making changes in your life. Psychologists have long concluded that all learning is a result of spaced repetition. Note these two words, "spaced" and "repetition." All learning is a result of things repeated with space between the times when they are repeated. It turns out that both factors are essential to learning. Repeating creates and internally strengthens new neural pathways. This intuitively makes sense. The "space" provides time for new neural wiring to "grow" and be put into place.

Consistency is the forgotten element of success.

(If you haven't noticed by now, you will eventually, so allow me to point out that this book was written with the benefits of repetition in mind. Every foundational point is systematically repeated and linked with numerous concepts in an attempt to impart a clear and lasting knowledge to the reader. If you read it all, this newly engrained knowledge will likely result in your personal observations of the influence of dominant thoughts everywhere.)

Just How Long Does it Take to Form a New Habit?

One of the foremost burning questions regarding habit formation is, How long does it take to create a new habit? And while we are getting much closer to an answer than ever before, the issue is still quite complex. The reason the answer is so complex is that there are a multitude of variables that influence habit formation. So, don't expect a precise answer.

On the other hand, the research on habit formation is getting more realistic and is being helped along by the neuroplasticity research investigating structural changes in the brain. As would be expected, a fully formed habit would, by necessity, include accompanying changes in neural wiring. After all, how can a behavior be automatic without the internal mental circuitry to guide and accomplish it?

We will first examine habit formation from simply observing and studying behavior. Then we will briefly discuss some of the recent neuroplasticity research findings regarding the length of time needed to see observable changes in brain structure.

Recent Habit Acquisition Research

There has been an urban myth that, unfortunately, has been expounded by just about every motivational speaker alive (or dead) that it takes about 21 days to form a new habit. This number was first suggested by Maxwell Maltz, author of *Psycho-Cybernetics*,[5] one of the early books discussing similar concepts to those presented here. It's a great book and one that is important in laying the early foundation of mental programming. However, it appears the number was derived intuitively from Dr. Maltz's personal experience and did not have a scientific basis. I might add that those interested in personal change should read the book; however, keep in mind that it was written before any of the scientific research presented in this book was conducted and, thus, it lacks specificity in its formula for change. Yet, the general points made by Dr. Maltz still stand and his work is momentous.

Since the time of Dr. Maltz, serious research has been conducted on habit acquisition. One of the most recent studies investigated how long it took individuals to reach a state of 95% automaticity with new behaviors.[3] The results indicated that, on average, it took about 66 days. However, the variations in time were from 18 to 254 days. Mind you, individuals in the study chose either an eating, drinking, or activity behavior (such as running) to acquire. These choices as well as individual personality differences played a role in the length of time it took to reach 95% automaticity.

Of great significance was the finding that consistent repetition across time was the factor that created the habit and it increased its impact as time progressed. Specifically, the impact of consistent repetition grew exponentially across time. The more you do it, the greater the impact.

Of additional significance to this book is the fact that *failing to do the new habit on occasion had little impact on creating the ultimate automaticity.* Those who define failure as not doing the desired behavior occasionally should note and meditate on this finding. (See Chapter 8, the section entitled, "The Idea That Change Should Happen Quickly, Sometimes Referred to as Failure," for additional comments on this finding.)

I might also add that subjects in the above study did not have the added benefit of mental programming offered here. My assumption is that good old willpower was the primary force creating new habits. I suggest that effective mental programming along with willpower would have greatly shortened habit acquisition time.

Regardless, the reality regarding how long it takes to form a new habit is that it takes longer than has been previously suggested. Unfortunately, it also takes longer than most people would like to endeavor. The 21-day rule does not apply and should not be used as a measure. A more realistic time frame for automation would be around two months or approximately 66 days as a standard to assess if change is occurring. Many factors determine the ultimate outcome.

The good news is that correct mental programming can ease the strain of using direct willpower and lessen the time needed for habit formation. Participants in my lectures and other clients have reported results from mental programming from less than a week of delivering messages to their mind. One man commented that the urges to change came so quickly that it was actually frightening when he grasped how much self-control he actually had at his disposal. However, such immediate results are not guaranteed and should not be used as a standard from which to measure.

I suggest that the time needed to change is shortened significantly with consistent mental programming. The priming and ironic process research demonstrated immediate impact from brief exposure to key words, though short lived. Simply magnify this impact with a healthy dose of repetition and extrapolate the potential results.

Yet, personal motivation, level of consistency, personality, environmental variables, outside support, how deeply ingrained previous programming is, as well as the difficulty and complexity of the new habit all play a part. Clearly, the acquisition of wealth is going to take more time than switching from drinking soft drinks to water at every meal. Nonetheless, spending and saving habits can be adjusted immediately. Similarly, reaching an ideal weight will take time while dietary adjustment can come quickly. Ultimately, while small changes can occur quickly, *the world of immediate gratification is hazardous and fictional when it comes to major shifts in one's approach to life.*

Directly related to this discussion are the outcomes from the smoking cessation groups I conducted for a period of my life. Acquiring the habit of breathing fresh air after being a smoker for 25 plus years is one of the most difficult habit changes anyone can make. Members of my groups were all required to develop mental programming appropriate to their personalities and motivations. Success rates were 100% for those who seriously followed the program that covered a period of about two months. Each group members' changes were evidence that even the most difficult psychological habits that include strong physiological addictive components can be altered. At the time this book is being written, estimates are that 1.3 million people quit smoking each year. If that many people can change the smoking habit, most likely without the aid of advantageous mental programming, you have little excuse for not moving forward with your own personal change program.

In summary, the amount of time it will take for mental programming to have an impact varies tremendously depending on a host of variables mentioned above. A general, realistic average is around two months. The good news is this: If you do it properly and consistently, change is inevitable. The late Zig Ziglar was fond of saying the following that I have revised slightly by adding the word "consistently" to his words:

When you consistently change the input into your mind,
you consistently change the output in your life.
Adapted from Zig Ziglar

While the key element of the dominant thought was not included, Zig was definitely on target with his message.

The bottom line is that you must give it time. If you are not willing to commit to two months of consistent, earnest mental programming, then you are likely not realistically investing enough time and effort into the desired change. You have to get real with the realities.

Neuroplasticity: How Long Does It Take to Change Brain Structure?

Regarding the length of time it takes to change brain structure I have two pieces of information of importance. The first is that brain structure can definitely be changed and much faster than previously thought. The second is that this is a very complex area of study that encompasses a multitude of variables and, thus, the length of time for brain structure to show change varies considerably. As previously noted, the speed of structural change is influenced by brain chemistry, nutrition, amount and duration of practice, exercise, personal motivation, whether the change is a result of positive or negative events, the method used, and much more.

Another reason the answer is so complex is because researchers are measuring minute changes in extremely small things—neurons. Until the structural change reaches a state where it is large enough to measure, we know little about it. It is safe to suggest that neural changes are likely occurring before they are observable and measureable.

One area that has received considerable study relative to brain change is mindfulness and meditation. Because mindfulness and meditation are largely activities that rely on focused mental attention, they are of interest to us here. In one sense, both depend on programming the mind to attend to specific things or areas. Reviews of research have confirmed structural changes in the brain after participating in just 8 weeks of mindfulness meditation training.[1] Similarly, German researchers studied the brains of students 3 months before and immediately after taking a premed exam that required learning masses of material and found significant changes in gray matter density.[6] Therefore, measurable changes in brain structure have become observable in as little as 2-3 months.

Numerous other studies have noted brain density changes across various regions of the brain and time periods.[7,8] Yet, due to complexity of this research, readers are cautioned regarding the implications. As noted, changes reported by researchers depend on a host of factors. About all we can safely say at this point is that neural changes do occur in the brain, they occur much faster than previously assumed, and they are more likely to occur with longer periods of consistent practice.

It is interesting to note that the length of time needed to evidence neurological changes in the brain is quite similar to the average length of time needed to create automaticity in behavior.

Those interested in studying brain change with regards to broader areas of mental well-being and mental health should study the work of psychologist and author Dr. Rick Hanson.[9]

"The mind can change the brain to change the mind."
Rick Hanson

Summary

These above four steps configure the formula for effective mental programming. As you can see, they are not complicated. There is no evidence that mental programming has to be complicated. Most methods used by therapists to help people change are not that complicated. The complications of therapeutic approaches are almost always in regard to the personal motivation to follow through, not the technique. While the steps are not complicated, each must be given due attention and implemented with precision and consistency. Repetition and practice across a realistic time period result in habit formation.

Chapter 6 Key Points

- There are four steps to mental programming:
    1. Define what you are currently doing.
    2. Specifically define the positive opposite of what you are currently doing.
    3. Create a present tense statement that states that you are currently doing the new positive opposite behavior.
    4. Repeat the statement created in Step 3 to yourself 500 to a 1000 times a day consistently across time, likely 2-3 months.

- Of all of the steps, consistency is the most important. It is also the most overlooked factor in all success.

- A realistic time frame to assess movement toward automation would be around two months. The historical 21-day rule does not apply and should not be used as a measure. However, many factors determine ultimate outcomes and time frames.

Chapter 7

What to Expect: The Demons You Must Conquer and the Help Your Mind Provides

"Each person is involved in becoming that thing that his subconscious mind wills him to be...the only way to change our destiny is to change the aims of our subconscious."

U. S. Anderson

OK, it's at this point I can hear the skeptics blasting away at the simplicity of the approach. Somewhere in your mind you also may have been thinking, "If it is so easy to program the mind, then why isn't everybody doing it and improving their lives?" Or, "You're telling me that all I have to do to change is repeat a properly stated dominant thought. No way! You would have to be naïve to believe that. Personal change has to be more complicated than that." I have heard this many times before.

Let me add that I'm glad you asked. And you should ask. These questions frequently become the stumbling blocks of so much of the positive thinking and affirmation worlds. (Bear with me; I will critique positive thinking and affirmations later.) If we can solve so many problems with proper mental programming, then why isn't everyone better? Why doesn't everyone simply think their way to health and success?

The short answer is: It's not that easy.

There are factors of which you must contend and most people are either not prepared for them or don't want to have to deal with them or both. Consequently, self-improvement and habit changes are often short-lived. Unfortunately, the blame for failure often goes to the approach and not the individual. Yet, well-designed mental programming, properly applied, works. We know it works because the creation of every habit of everyone alive is proof.

With a little thought, it is relatively easy to generate positive-worded, workable dominant thoughts. If you don't want to do the work of generating dominant thoughts, I have provided a host of examples in this book. It is also easy to simply repeat the thoughts, *at first*! However, when you start delivering new dominant thoughts to your brain that are not consistent with the current, well-ingrained mental programming, hosts of backlashing dynamics emerge. If you are not aware of these demons and are not prepared to deal with them, you are likely to get thrown off course. Your repetition will slowly degenerate to nothing and you will revert back to previous programming.

This chapter explains the negative dynamics you will face and explains what is necessary to overcome them. Study it carefully, as your success is directly related to your ability to disarm the backlash. The good news is that there are positive dynamics that are very likely to emerge also. You should be well-prepared to take advantage of these dynamics and their benefits.

Demon 1: The Negative Voice

Most likely, the first thing you will experience when you begin programming your mind is that your internal negative voice will rear its head and start countering your new thought. The voice will shout out, "That's not true," "You are lying to yourself," "Who are you kidding," "You'll never do that," "What a bunch of crap," or some similar counter to what you desire. It happens to everybody. It is the natural and, interestingly, healthy initial reaction to expect.

These doubting thoughts are an attempt by the subconscious to maintain the status quo. The subconscious clings to its programming and is designed to not let its programming get disrupted. The subconscious seeks and maintains patterns and anything that attempts to disrupt those patterns will be fought against.

Because you are programming your mind with a directive that is very contrary to what you normally think and do, you may feel as if you are deceiving yourself. It feels as if you are lying and lying is against your moral character. Many times the new thoughts are so foreign and unlike you that you feel too artificial and fake to continue making the statements. In all creatures there is a strong psychological drive toward homeostasis, that is, toward keeping equilibrium and not disrupting the current state with changes. This drive coupled with previous programing creates the odd sense that you are not being legitimate and arouses the negative voice.

Thus, doubting thoughts emerge because you have been previously programmed to believe any new behavior is not part of your "self" as the subconscious perceives it. Psychologically speaking, the conflict between the new programming and negative voice is referred to as cognitive dissonance. Cognitive dissonance occurs whenever your mind is in conflict over something. You might think of it as mental discomfort or mental unrest. What you are saying to yourself is not confirmed by your previous programming and this creates dissonance.

All of this results in uncomfortable feelings. So, you stop your programming and wait. This is a mistake. You are waiting for something to happen to confirm the new programming before you continue. You might also stop in order for the momentary discomfort to go away. This is a mistake because you have put the cart before the horse, so to speak. If you wait for it to "feel" right, it will be difficult to change.

Be prepared for this.

The appearance of cognitive dissonance should be viewed as evidence of how powerful mental programming can be once instilled. Cognitive dissonance is not your enemy and should not be perceived as such. It is perfectly natural for dissonance to occur. It is simply a necessary, natural process that must be experienced, endured, and managed. Think of it as mental growing pains.

Similarly, if the change before you is difficult—one of those things that you logically know you need to do, yet, one of those things you do not want to do—you will likely experience negative feelings and emotions as well. There could be a sense of dread, a loathing of the task before you, a general uneasiness about the task before you. This is most often experienced when you have to tackle a task that is unenjoyable or requires hard work or that requires that you give up a momentary pleasure. Examples here might include dieting and giving up of sweets, exercising, doing your taxes, writing a report, or talking with someone about a difficult topic.

Again, these emotions are just your current programming fighting back at what is perceived as a disruptive and, at this moment, unpleasant change. Most of these emotions derive directly from our thinking. Everybody wishes they felt like dieting and felt like exercising and felt like doing their taxes or writing a report; but, most of us don't.

Yet, you have to be very careful not to judge anything by such feelings and emotions. The point is that experiencing negative emotions is not necessarily a good gauge of how we should lead our lives. Those who respond and react to only what feels good at the moment often end up with little accomplished and a poor self-image. For brevity, I will refer to the negative voice and emotions as the singular concept of the negative voice in this discussion.

Ironically, it is important to recognize that the stronger the feelings of self-deception, the stronger the feelings that you are lying to yourself, the stronger the feelings of discomfort and uneasiness about what you are saying to yourself, *the more likely you are on track with your new programming*. You are in the state you are in because you have never thought the thoughts you are now thinking. They feel foreign. The more awkward and foreign they feel, the more likely you need to provide these thoughts to your mind. So remember, awkward feelings are a sign that you are on track. Don't let the current programming in your subconscious fool you. Don't let it deceive you. If you are programming a realistic, doable human behavior of which you are genetically capable, you can create the new behavior you desire.

Managing the Negative Voice

The first step to managing the negative voice is to recognize that it is simply previous mental programming expressing itself. Keep in mind that the negative voice is the voice that keeps you stuck in your current situation. Yet, this is also the voice that, when trained to work for you, creates the character and habits you desire.

In many ways you should be grateful and appreciative of this voice, even though it appears to be working against you at the moment. Briefly note how strong it is and imagine how useful it will be when programmed for your consciously desired outcomes. Behold the currently negative voice with fascination, for it is an observation of the mental programming in your mind. You are observing the doorway into the code of your being. You are observing the power of the subconscious mind.

Keep in mind that the start almost always feels awkward. It is virtually impossible to begin the task of new programming without encountering some resistance. However, you cannot judge the outcome by the start. To the contrary, much of the time the more awkward the start, the more likely you are on course for a successful outcome. Cease all judgement and watch.

So, how do you manage the negative voice?

First, recognize that this is a natural reaction that is to be expected. So, expect it. Be ready for it. Know that it will happen. Know that this is the way nature intended it to be. Nothing's wrong. You mind is working properly.

Most importantly, remain calm, poised, consistent, and steady to the course. (Stated in the negative, don't get alarmed, bothered, discouraged, or frustrated.)

Now, what I am about to say may be one of the most important points of this book. The negative voice is a major stumbling block to self-change. The negative voice is notorious for impeding reprogramming before it gets a chance to have an impact. Hence, the proper management of the negative voice is critical to success in all endeavors.

So, what should you actually do with the negative voice?

Nothing.

Let it talk. Let it chatter. Let it doubt as you continue to quietly and consistently insert the new programming into your mind.

Why not fight the negative voice?

Because the more you fight the negative voice, the more the negative voice becomes your dominant thought and you set yourself up to lose the mental battle! If you let the negative voice engage you in a redundant argument, you succumb to its power.

The key is to stay focused on the get-to place and to let the negative voice die out on its own.

> *"It is your resistance to the negative thought, whether you bring it into consciousness or not, that makes it manifest in your life"*
>
> Thaddeus Golas

The let-it-die-out-on-its-own approach to the negative voice is derived directly from the ironic process research discussed in Chapter 3. If there is anything that ironic process research has taught us it is that the more we attempt to minimize the influence of negative intruding thoughts, the worse they get! The more you fight and argue with the negative voice, the louder and more predominant it becomes. Recall the golf putting experiments from Chapter 3. Even when provided with positive images that improved putting performance, subjects still reported having negative thoughts creep into their mind.[1] These same subjects reported that *intentional attempts to suppress negative putting images actually increased their occurrence* and worsened putting performance. This is exactly what we do not want to happen with ourselves.

Don't allow yourself to get sucked into an internal discussion with the negative voice. Why? Because you cannot win. You cannot actively overcome the negative voice by directly attacking it. You can only win this battle by allowing the negative voice free reign and diligently focusing on your new dominant thought. If you fight the negative voice, you lose. If you go passive, you win.

Stated in different terms, excessive focus on the negative voice does not demonstrate an understanding and respect for the fundamental characteristics of the mind presented in Chapter 4. You cannot consciously delete a thought; you can only "overwrite" a thought with another thought. This is a major characteristic of your conscious mind. The mind has a mind of its own and this mind does not allow you to delete a thought. The mind can only attend and focus. The more you consciously fight and argue with the negative voice, the more it fights back. The more it fights back, the more it becomes your dominant thought. There is no mental image of "no" or "not," only the mental image of what follows a "no" or "not" statement. You cannot consciously delete a thought; so, stop trying.

Much care should be taken to keep the dominant thought front and center. The negative must die away as a result of being overwritten by a new dominant thought. The unconscious process of "dying away" occurs over time without direct conscious control. *You have to let it happen; forcing it hinders it.*

It is here that you must call upon your willpower. Here is the place where willpower should be called upon to maintain the proper actions and attitude. Use your willpower to stay focused on what you want by way of a new dominant thought. Willpower creates the consistency of focus on the new dominant thought; the new dominant thought creates the new habit.

So what exactly happens to the negative voice? Scientists have yet to fully understand what happens to previous mental programming once new programming is introduced.[2] Some theories believe previous programming is still present in your mind, just not triggered. Other theories see previous programming as morphing into something new as alternative programming comes along. Yet, this we know, unless you take the time to create the mental programming you desire, you will default back to the previous behaviors.

In presenting this perspective, it is important that I comment on the common therapeutic practice of refuting negative thoughts. One size does not fit all and one approach may not be suitable for everyone.

Within the world of psychotherapy there is considerable attention given to promoting logical thinking. Cognitive psychologists in particular view mental problems as a result of cognitive distortions and irrational thinking. Most systems of Cognitive therapy initially focus on refuting cognitive distortions which is akin to refuting the message of the negative voice. That is, logically examining the cognitive distortions and challenging, invalidating, and rebutting them. Once refuted, the client is then helped to replace the cognitive distortions with more logical thoughts.

Yet, problems arise if too much time is focused on refuting the negative thoughts and too little time is used to create logical thoughts. This is a common error of therapists. As should be clear by now, such an approach may intensify the complications that arise when the negative voice is the focus. My personal position is that excessive focus on the negative is perilous and should be approached with maximum awareness of the pitfalls. By far the most important step is to replace the cognitive distortion with accurate logical thoughts.

Similarly, for many common habits, I assert that it is likely unproductive to engage in refuting the negative voice. The result may be that the negative influence is amplified rather than dissolved. It takes some skill and fortitude to participate in this mental battle and, because the negative voice has won in the past, you may not want to give it the opportunity to express itself at all. Without proper coaching, arguing with the negative voice may result in more unwanted behavior. The question becomes: Why give the negative voice an opportunity to defend itself? This is particularly true if you just want it to go away and don't have a compelling need to fight it. For a great many people with typical habits, arguments with the negative voice are likely unproductive, wasted time.

Yet, if you are the type that would like to seriously refute the assertions of your negative voice, be my guest. If it works for you, do it. However, one must be careful not to get bogged down in the refuting process. Some people can spend months struggling with the negative. They can wallow in it endlessly. They can ruminate and obsess with the complex issues and emotional struggles ad nauseam. I am not immune to such processes myself. To some extent, it is from noting my own behavior that I make these points.

The bottom line, you can refute the negative self-talk if you desire, but do not spend too much time there. You must remain ever aware that engaging the negative voice provides the opportunity for it to become your dominant thought. Remember, the mind can only attend. Be careful where and how you focus your attention. The real power is in creating and programming a proper dominant thought.

Regardless, in the end, the negative voice will have to die out on its own by being overwritten by new programming. There's no other way. The key is to stay focused on repeating the dominant thought and to let the subconscious mind extinguish the negative in due time.

To be thorough in this discussion, I am compelled to add an additional comment regarding the negative voice. As a mental health professional I am very aware that it is too simplistic to believe that people can just think their way out of deep-seated, traumatic experiences. And to claim that all negative emotional programming can be overcome with "positive thinking" is ridiculously naïve. Deep-seated emotional issues that stem from past trauma are not easily overcome through simple adjustments in thinking. While the above approach to managing the negative voice will be effective for many self-improvement issues such as eating healthy, smoking, procrastinating, exercising, getting organized, etc., it will not suffice for extremely serious trauma. Please refer to the section in Chapter 8 entitled, "When to Use and Not Use Mental Programming" for additional discussion regarding this point.

Another Approach to Managing the Negative Voice

A second approach to dealing with the negative voice is to make adjustments in your dominant thought. If you have set a very lofty personal adjustment for yourself that requires a significant amount of change and the negative voice is strong, perhaps you should tone it down a bit. Back off the extreme and make your dominant thought programming more acceptable and reality based. Extreme, broad, statements of grandiose outcomes are often found in the affirmation literature and are likely to arouse much negative kickback. If an outcome is just too difficult to accept, the subconscious backlash is stronger.

For example, if I repeat that, "I accept myself completely," or "I am always confident," the standard set is very high and exceptions are easily discovered. On the other hand, if I repeat that, "I recognize and use my talents daily," or "I do small, consistent actions daily to accomplish…," the backlash is surely to be less extreme and confidence will naturally follow.

By the way, you don't become more confident by saying you're more confident. You become more confident by doing things that promote a genuine sense of confidence in yourself. "Confidence" is not a good goal in and of itself. What does "I am confident" mean that you actually do? It is too vague of a directive. Confidence is a secondary outcome—a byproduct—of productive action. Program the doable and let the psychological benefits emerge naturally from a genuine experience.

While I am discussing this, to declare that you "accept yourself completely" is also a very lofty standard. Are you never bothered with some aspects of your behavior? Do you never wish you would have approached something differently? It is very easy for the negative voice to attack such claims. If you accept yourself completely will there ever be something else to improve upon?

And then there is the philosophical issue of what does "accept myself" mean? How will I know when I have done this vague thing? When you think about it, the concept of "accept myself" is very hard to define and get a firm grasp on figuratively or literally. In short, this is a vague, philosophically awkward goal that really does not explain to the mind what you want it to initiate. As a goal it invites criticism. This is a good example of why precise wording is so important when creating dominant thoughts.

In contrast, examine the directive of, "I recognize and use my talents daily." This instruction directs the mind to bring into consciousness your talents (i.e., recognize) and then find places to employ them and to do this on a regular basis (i.e., daily). This programming is much more specific and doable than "accepting yourself completely." This programming does not require the mind to figure out what the vague "accepting yourself" means. It is far better mental programming.

These ideas for managing the negative voice are related to research that observed that some types of affirmations can be psychologically harmful with some people.[3] Researchers have noted that overly positive affirmations or affirmations outside typical areas of self-perception tend to be met with resistance and rejection by subjects. Such affirmations appeared to create conflict between the perceived self and the ideal self. The more removed the affirmation was from subjects' perceived self, the more the affirmation was rejected and more negative feelings were reported by subjects. Further, subjects with low self-esteem reported feeling worse when repeating statements they did not believe were accurate. The world of affirmations is fraught with such statements. Overall, it was suggested that affirmations that are more aligned with subjects' perceived self appeared to be more accepted and are perceived as more beneficial.

Interestingly, subjects with higher self-esteem used positive affirmations more often than the low self-esteem group and reported them as more helpful.[3] Obviously, it is unclear which came first—the positive statement or the high self-esteem. Common sense and the circular nature of thinking suggest there is likely a reciprocal relationship between the two. People are not born with high or low self-esteem. Self-esteem results from recognizing and using your talents, accomplishing something, and accepting positive feedback provided by others. If anything, these research findings confirm the importance of programming the subconscious regarding the self.

I believe it is important to note that the research just cited[3] studied affirmations of the type that I believe are too broad, extreme, and whimsical to be effective. Consequently, the results should be considered with this in mind. Affirmations repeated by subjects included statements such as, "I am a lovable person," "I will win!" and "I will beat this illness." The standards set by the latter two statements are unrealistically high. You may lose and not beat the illness. While the "lovable person" statement suggests a viable personality characteristic as an objective, it is likely too general in nature. Also, as was explained earlier, the use of the word "will" implies a future tense and it assumes no immediate action is necessary. Consequently, from the perspective of this book, the affirmations used in this research were incorrectly worded to be effective mental programming. Errors of this nature abound in research and the self-help literature.

The takeaway is this: While the outcomes of this research were almost doomed to failure because of poor wording, the lessons provided about psychologically unacceptable, unrealistic goals are very noteworthy. Even with its faults, the above research relates directly to the idea that the negative voice can be managed to a degree by making adjustments in the dominant thought. The more realistic, practical, and acceptable the dominant thought, the more easily the negative voice can be squelched.

These points also shed light on the reason the priming words used in the research addressed in Chapter 1 were so impactful. In all cases, the primes were situationally fitting and, thus, there was less resistance to the influence of the prime. For example, if I am told to speak with someone and I am thwarted from the opportunity, primes triggering interrupting behavior are more likely to influence behavior.[4] And they did! When the prime was situationally appropriate, acceptance of the priming message was strongly evidenced. In other words, because the prime was not outlandish, grandiose, or outside of the world of what was reasonable relative the situation, it was more likely to work.

Similarly, mental programming that is more realistic and acceptable relative to the person and the situation is more likely to be accepted and effective. So, if the negative voice is strong, adjustments to the dominant thought are a viable approach to managing it.

Returning to the earlier example, if you like "I accept myself completely" and it works for you, then do it (though not recommended). No one size fits all. What I am saying is that, if the subconscious backlash is of such a nature that the repercussions are difficult to manage, then adjust the programming. There are thousands of words and many sentence structures available for the mind to communicate with itself.

Allow me to provide a personal example of adjusting a dominant thought in order to manage the negative voice and, actually, promote greater accomplishment.

For the most part, the dominant thought I used to write this book was, "I write the book daily." Believe me, my mind knew what "the book" meant and delivered a strong internal nudge to write throughout my day. If I did not write, I felt discomfort because this programming was delivered consistently. Problems arose when I reached a point in the writing where I was bogged down and stuck on how to move forward. When this occurred, progress was very slow and, with the strong programming to write, the negative voice became more annoying.

In the midst of one of these struggles I realized I was just fumbling along at a slow pace. Rather than fight this reality, I changed my dominant thought to "I fumble along daily." While this might not sound very motivating to you, it was just what I needed. Notice that the directive did not indicate that I stopped writing; to the contrary, the words "along daily" programmed my mind to keep me writing. When you think about it, only the rate of progress was changed. My mind was very accepting of this thought ("fumble along") and my writing actually moved forward nicely. This is a good example of toning down the standard set by the mental programming message in order to manage the negative voice while maintaining the overall goal.

The Most Important Thing to Keep in Mind

Having said all of the above about adjusting dominant thoughts in order to manage the negative voice, let me add this one final thought. **You are better off delivering some form of mental programming to your mind in an effort to change than doing nothing at all.** Even if the mental programming you repeat is not perfect—not exactly what you want—and invigorates a strong negative voice, it is better to give your mind something that approximates what you want than nothing at all. Nothing at all is sure to maintain the status quo. Do nothing and your subconscious will stay on its present course until you die. It's that powerful. It's wired that way and it will not magically change.

However…

Consistently deliver a dominant thought that approximates what you want and the subconscious will trigger associated concepts and offer up the more precise guidance needed. Specifically, your mind will start linking and moving you toward more exact wording that fits your needs. New thoughts regarding your desires will just "bubble up." You have got to try this to experience it. It's really ingenious how your mind will inevitably move you forward when pointed in the general direction desired. If you are serious about your mental programming, you will find that ideas for adjustments to inexact programming will materialize naturally. I discuss this experience in detail below.

Demon 2: Monkey Mind

The other powerful demon that you will have to conquer in order to successfully program your mind is *monkey mind.* We are all too familiar with the concept. We have all experienced monkey mind. Our mind darts and jumps from one topic or task to another. Sustained focus is difficult. In our everyday thinking, jumping from one thought to another appears to be the norm. Focused attention on one topic or one task is difficult and getting more difficult. We are now bombarded with media distractions with the aid of smart phones and computers. One recent study found that people reported their minds wandering between 30 to 47% of the time depending on the current activity.[5] This tendency also contributed to unhappiness. You can spend hours in the world of monkey mind by surfing the web and reading tweets. We might as well call the internet and social media "monkey mind world." The fact is, we are spending more time with distractions than ever before in history.

This is compounded by the host of life chores that we need to get through in our day. The distraction problem is so great we create words like "multitasking" to try to describe and justify what we are doing. By the way, multitasking is a very inefficient way to run your life. Research indicates that you make more mistakes and do a worse job when you multitask. Do not be deceived by a clever word that attempts to justify and make you feel important with an overextended schedule. Search this idea on the internet if it is of interest to you.

Remember how we noted that *all learning* is a result of spaced repetition? Well, monkey mind is a destroyer of repetition, a destroyer of focus. Monkey mind is spaced-out mental rambling. The only thing that is repeated is rambling from one topic to the next. It is amazing how easy it is to forget to plant the seeds. The long term effects of priming require repeating the focused attention across time. Monkey mind must be controlled for mental programming to work.

The solution is, first, to recognize monkey mind and, second, to deliberately take time for mental programming.

Just by becoming aware of monkey mind you begin to conquer it. Recognition of being unfocused tends to, by default, lead to focus, at least for the moment. I am not certain why this happens, but it is sort of like ironic processes working for you. Remember, no matter what you are focusing on, unexpected thoughts of an opposing nature tend to enter the mind. Thus, when you attend to how unfocused you are you move toward focus. That is, when you focus on your lack of focus, you focus. Crazy, isn't it? Awareness of monkey mind is the first step to overcoming it.

Next, deliberately set aside time to focus. Allow your mental programming to slip between the cracks of your monkey mind activities. Drop in those priming dominant thoughts any time you get a chance. While you are using the bathroom, when you can't find a song you like on your car radio, when you take that small break, as you go to sleep at night or when you awake in the morning. Just take a few moments to repeat your dominant thought. One of my favorite times is in the shower in the morning. I can do my bathroom routine in my sleep—it's subconsciously controlled. So, I take that time to drive the desired dominant thought into my brain.

This is sort of like when you wake up in the morning and hear that song on the radio that tends to play in your head all day, even if you don't like the song! Why let the radio deliver your daily dominant thought with some ricky-tick song that irritates you. (Yes, I know you might also like the song.) The point is, your well-programmed morning routine, when the necessity of conscious thought is limited, provides a great time for mental programming. The reality is you have a choice: You can either program your mind with what you want or allow some media source to do it for you. Make up your mind.

Of course, along with this you can create reminders that bring your thoughts back to the programming you want. Slip a note into your purse or wallet. Put a sticky note where you are certain to read it. Add the thought to your to-do list. I have done this for years. Many times, the first thing I write on my to-do list is my current mental programming.

Every time I rewrite the list, I rewrite the dominant thought. I very deliberately keep it front and center.

Most forms of meditation are a direct counter to monkey mind. In these meditative processes you relax and focus on one singular thought. All of those monkey mind thoughts are allowed to just drift on by with no fanfare whatsoever. If you find your mind drifting off into another thought you calmly return to the focused thought without any fuss over it. While the occurrence of mental ramblings is accepted, they are, at the same time, let go of as you return to the chosen singular thought. This is the method to focus. It turns out it does not matter what the singular, focused thought is. Whether it be a mantra, Jesus, "one," a chant, or focusing on your breath or heartbeat, it makes no difference. Returning to the singular focused thought is what's important.

Obviously, this same process can be used to program the mind. Why not make your meditative focus a short, sweet piece of mental programming to calmly deposit in your mind? While mental programming will work by simple repetition, meditative repetition enhances it. If you have never done any meditation, try it. With just a bit of consistency, you may be surprised by the outcome.

Another way to deal with the distractions of monkey mind is to talk out loud to yourself. Two recent studies have confirmed that talking out loud to yourself decreases distractions and enhances concentration.[6,7] Lots of people talk out loud to themselves, including successful athletes who are often caught on camera verbally directing their own behavior in an effort to increase focus. Albert Einstein was also known for talking to himself and the habit has been associated with intelligence. (I really like this research because my wife catches me talking to myself when I do not know I am doing it. Now I can rationalize it!)

So, if no one is around to think you are bit strange, say it out loud. Talking out loud also incorporates more senses into the process as you hear your own voice. All of this in combination appears to reduce internal and external interference and, thus, enhances focus. I really like adding this component to the process if the environment is favorable and conducive to allowing it.

Demon 3: No Instant Gratification; Nothing Happens Initially

When you first start programming your mind, expect nothing, at least, initially. You are not engaged in an instant gratification process. What! No instant gratification, how can that be! Well, that's not how mental programming works. Immediate results are not the intention and will most likely not occur. If you want instant gratification, try sex, or drugs, or alcohol, or carbs, or the internet, or Facebook, or some similar stimulating thing.

Typically the programming directive is to do what you are having difficulty doing with conscious effort or willpower. You are instructing your mind to utilize all associated words, images, sentences, emotions, etc. to move you in the direction you desire with subtle nudges and without the effort of sheer willpower. You are literally instructing the subconscious to create new neural networks that may have never existed or to strengthen those that exist and are rarely used. There are likely thousands of current micro associations that have to be re-directed by the new thought. There are many neurons that need to be rewired to accommodate the new thought.

This is quite opposite of instant gratification activities. You are presenting the subconscious with a behavior to stimulate when the situation calls for it. You very well might not be in the situation where the new behavior applies when you repeat the programming. This requires an understanding that the new dominant thought is not necessarily an immediate mental command. If you decide to do the new behaviors immediately, then by all means do so. This will surely help. However, the ultimate goal is automaticity and this takes time.

All subconsciously controlled behaviors you have acquired throughout your life took time. This process is exactly the same. You did not learn to walk, talk, type, play a musical instrument, drive with a clutch, swing a golf club, sew, or do any of a host of skills that you have acquired immediately. All complex behaviors are acquired across time. No complex behavior has ever been acquired instantly by anybody.

What is amazing is that people will practice some skills with great zest in anticipation of the time when they are done automatically, with little effort. Yet, when given the roadmap to programming the mind for breaking bad habits and creating new behaviors, many are reluctant to consistently and properly practice the same process.

Ideally, you should neither expect nor not expect a new behavior to emerge—just let it emerge. Just let the mental programming do its thing. Trust the process without expectation. Don't let the expectation of immediate results become a disappointment that hinders the natural process. Adopt an attitude much like the one you use to fall sleep.

To fall asleep, you lie down, relax, cut back on distracting stimuli, and follow a routine of which your mind is familiar and that is in sync with your physiology. You cannot command sleep from your mind. Sleep is a deeply ingrained, hard-wired biological process that is likely controlled at the unconscious level. Yet, when you let it happen in sync with your physiology and psychology, it happens every time. When you try to force sleep or when the physiological or psychological environment are not conducive to the natural process of sleep, insomnia results. You lie awake from the caffeine you drank or from the racing thoughts that were spawned by your worrying about some difficult situation that has arisen.

The underlying process for automating behavior is also automatic. While you can indirectly direct it with dominant thoughts and enhance it with repetition, you cannot force it. The key point here is to passively continue to consistently program your mind and give the process ample time.

Carrying this point further, expect delays. Many times there is a delay between when you begin mental programming and when a reaction or new behavior is observed. This phenomenon is regularly observed by those who practice hypnosis. Those who practice hypnosis know to expect delays in the effects of suggestions. Just because a suggestion does not result in an immediate response does not mean it is not effective. Sometimes, right when the suggestion is consciously forgotten the effect is seen. And so it is also when you program your mind with a new directive. Remember, there is a tremendous amount of neural work occurring outside of conscious awareness. Give your mind time. Trust the process as you calmly and passively deliver the programming.

The Overall Key is to Adopt and Embrace a Passive Attitude

A passive attitude coupled with consistent, correctly worded programming is the key to accepting results as they come and to letting go of immediate gratification needs. As has been discussed, there is a powerful drive toward homeostasis or keeping the status quo. This drive is part of what fuels the negative voice. Yet, fighting the negative voice backfires and feeds the negative voice. Similarly, fighting homeostasis creates push back from this built-in drive. The more you try to fight homeostasis, the more the mind tries to maintain it. So, what do you do? Don't fight it. Just keep the dominant thoughts coming regardless of the internal turmoil that you may feel.

As discussed in Chapter 3 regarding ironic processes, the fundamental problem that arises with attempts at the removal of a thought is that your mind must monitor the thought to see if it is there or not. As ironic process theory explains, the monitoring of a thought creates the thought regardless of your desire. Similarly, when you implant a new thought to create a subsequent automatic behavior you may have a tendency to constantly check for the new behavior. When you do this, you inevitably bring to mind the current undesired behavior from which you make a comparison. Ironically, this effort can hinder the process. The only way to avoid unproductive monitoring is to become passive about its presence or absence. This is not easy to do. Yet, it can be done.

Again, this is a foundational principle of meditation and mindfulness—both practices teach the importance of passively and effortlessly focusing on something. That is, as much as is possible. In meditation, when you find your mind wandering you do not get upset, you simply bring your attention back to where you want to focus. A wandering mind is accepted and, by accepting it, you move back to focus. Similarly, by accepting that results will not be immediately observed, you promote them. **Remember that the internal process for automation is also automatic and can only be indirectly influenced with consistency. Automation is a byproduct of the dominant thought.**

Think about this phenomenon from the opposite perspective. When you are doing a complex task that you do well such as driving or typing or knitting or playing a musical instrument, do you have to monitor what you are doing? No, you just do it. Note that the monitoring process only comes about from not doing something well. We do not monitor what we do well. The automatic pilot is in control. This is the state we seek. A state where there is no need to monitor.

So, what we are ultimately after is to consistently repeat a dominant thought that primes a new behavior without any expectation, without the need to constantly check to see if it is working. Passively repeat the mental programming without anticipation of anything. Just program the thought correctly and let the subconscious take it from there. Your only job is to identify the state you desire, create an effective dominant thought, and repeat. The only effort is in repeating the prime. No effort should be expended on looking for results. Yet, when results occur, we welcome them. What you are seeking could be described as *"effortless effort."* Wow. It's a bit weird, isn't it? It's all very paradoxical.

Keeping these ideas in mind, recall the priming research discussed in Chapter 1. The subjects of these experiments did not know they were being primed to trigger certain behaviors. Thus, they did not fight the primes and the effect of the priming was much more easily obtained. The opposite occurred in the ironic process research in Chapter 3. In the ironic process research, because there was a set task known to subjects, they had to contend with the perils of intruding, oppositional thoughts. This was further complicated, of course, by the extra pressure put on subjects to perform well. The pressure to perform works against you and reinforces the unwanted. Remove this pressure on yourself.

When you self-prime, you do not have the luxury of no competing thoughts to contend with like subjects in the priming experiments. When you self-prime you know the ultimate goal; therefore, you must manage the negative voice. However, you can allow and create the luxury of neutrality for yourself. You have to give yourself the luxury of expecting nothing. The more you can remove the pressure to do well at your new behavior, the less you have to contend with ironic processes that work against you. And, the dominant thought can be more effective. *Hence, a passive attitude accompanied by consistency is the key.*

Avoiding excessive self-monitoring is tricky business especially when you are being vigilant about repetition at the same time. However, the trick is to do what meditators do. When you find your thoughts moving away from the dominant thought simply move your thoughts back to where you want them to be. Remain calm. Remain relaxed. Remain neutral, composed, and focused. Let it happen. Use your willpower to deliver the dominant thought then get out of the way of your subconscious and let the change happen.

The Positive: Your Mind Will Deliver Better Dominant Thoughts

I really love what I am about to tell you and delight in the thought of you experiencing this phenomenon.

Another beneficial reaction that occurs when you consistently deliver new thoughts to your mind is that your mind will, in turn, begin to deliver better, more precise programming statements back to you. I have often experienced this. It is a natural reaction to priming the mind with words. Remember, each word should be thought of as a cluster of related words and concepts all linked in an endless series of connections. Each word thought creates a momentary explosion or chain reaction of associated words, concepts, images, and emotions in your mind.

All of this mental stimulation leads the mind to begin pondering and analyzing what it is you want. Remember, the fundamental drive of the subconscious is to find patterns and automate. Thus, the subconscious takes what it is given (by the conscious mind) and immediately tries to formulate the pattern of behavior you are seeking. From this internal assessment it then delivers a variety of alternative descriptors to you. Most of the time these new descriptors are refinements of your dominant thought and goal.

When this happens, tune into what your subconscious delivers. Sometimes you may be presented with a better word to describe a state you want. Sometimes you may discover a shortcut to a long phrase you are saying. With consistency, it is almost inevitable that refinements will follow. And when they do, pay attention. Study the words. Hang on to what your subconscious has provided. It has a reason for offering up these new ideas. Respect the "advice" it offers.

Note though, I am not talking about that negative voice in the back of your head that appears to completely reject any new thought. That part of you that makes you feel a bit like a fool for even making the statement that you are repeating. That voice is coming from your old programming that wants to reject anything that does not immediately fit with old thoughts. It rejects anything that does not immediately feel comfortable. As I stated earlier, simply let that voice chatter away.

You can safely assume that, at some level, your mind is already aware of what you need. Your mind is aware you need to get certain things done—eat healthy, stop smoking, exercise more, etc. You have likely thought many times about changes you need to make. So, the idea has already been pondered at some level in your mind. **The subconscious is only awaiting your instructions to begin the actions necessary for movement toward what is needed or desired.**

Perhaps your subconscious is aware that changes need to be made; yet, you are unsure of exactly what to do. You are struggling to begin the process because you lack clarity on exactly what you want. You may also have reluctance to begin the change process because of the sacrifices that you will incur. When you begin the programming process you immediately begin moving from a state of struggle and confusion to a state of clarity. This, in turn, begins to dissolve the reluctance to act. The subconscious takes what you give it and immediately tries to clarify what it is you want automated. The drive toward clarity and the whole process of refinement is automatic in and of itself. Let it happen and use it to your benefit.

Insights that recognize needed adjustments in mental programming come from another part of you—that part that recognizes possibilities. And, in recognizing new possibilities, it recognizes even better programming statements. This part accepts and enhances rather than rejects and stagnates.

When you get a new idea of a more precise way to word your programming, write it down immediately. I have found that if I fail to write it down I sometimes lose the new thought, much to my regret. Chances are the new thought is something that is quite foreign to your way of thinking. You may find yourself surprised at what emerges because it is so different from your normal way of thinking. It is so different to your mind that it is hard to remember the thought. This is why you need to write it down immediately.

Examine the new thought. Think about the message your subconscious is sending back to you. Use the message. This refining is part of the process and is always working for you. Remember, the more precisely you program your mind for a specific behavior, the more impactful the response.

A study of the mental programming statements in the last chapter of this book will quickly reveal that many are refinements of other statements. Note the wisdom in statements such as, "I am aware of what I eat and the outcome," "I nurture my body with motion and movement," or "I exploit the moment." I can tell you that all of these programming statements evolved from other self-programming statements. The mind's self-reflective nature delivered them to consciousness as a result of implementing other related self-programming.

Interestingly, refinements are often shorter, cleaner statements. Long, drawn out instructions to the mind are not necessary. Years ago I learned this lesson in a personal experience of my own. I had written an affirmation for myself for overcoming procrastination. (I refer to this as an affirmation because, at the time, I was not aware of useful distinctions between mental programming and affirmations.) It began by stating that I realized that putting things off was the language of the unsuccessful, and that a meaningful life was only achieved through accomplishment. The affirmation was actually a rather long admonishment to myself. The statement was a full paragraph and a bit long for quick memorization, so I wrote it down and carried it with me to read throughout the day. The last two summary sentences of the paragraph were: Now I do; I do now. As I look back on this I believe these last two sentences were created by my mind as a summary of everything I had written. They were an automatic refinement that subtly emerged as my mind assessed what was desired.

As I read the statement over and over, in a short time, it occurred to me that I did not need to read the entire statement. I already knew the message. I intuitively recognized that all I needed was the last two sentences. They were short and sweet and to the point. Therefore, I shortened the statement into a very concise piece of mental programming: Now I do; I do now. This entire process appeared to flow naturally in my mind. It did not take effort to refine. All it required was to pay attention to the intuitive ideas offered up by my subconscious.

For those curious, it worked very well. I have over the years moved from an unproductive procrastinator to a list making accomplisher. The first step in all of this was to let my mind know exactly what I wanted. Currently, when I have a busy day and need to get much done, I repeat, "I am an efficiency expert," to myself in the morning before beginning my day. This has been an effective time management enhancing piece of programming.

The Results: Subtle Urges and Intuitive Nudges

With consistency you will begin to notice subtle changes. Your awareness of your current behaviors may increase as will your awareness of new, alternative behaviors. Along with this awareness you may notice a new voice suggesting that you delay your old habit or begin your new habit. You may feel some internal prodding to go a different direction. You will sense subtle intuitive urges that tug at you to shift your behavior.

Now you have a choice, you can fight the new direction or go with it. This is a critical juncture and, naturally, I suggest you embrace the new. Feel and feed the new urge. If you want to fight it and sabotage yourself, that too is your choice. Yet, once you sense an internal tug to develop a new pattern, why not at least give it a chance?

Feed the new, starve the old.

The point here is that subtle feelings promoting change, and a quiet internal voice seeking a new direction is what making changes through mental programming is all about. You are likely not going to find yourself making drastic changes immediately. Yet, you may be surprised at the speed with which changes emerge. Understand that the subtle tug you feel from the inside is the result you are seeking. Accept and receive what your mind is leading you toward.

Interestingly, the results may also be quickly influential and impactful. I and others have experienced this. You may be shocked and amazed by the quickness and power of the programming you have employed. In other words, new actions do not come slowly as discussed above; they come fast and quite robustly. All of a sudden you have an awareness of how much you can control your own behavior and the responsibility for your actions is a bit overwhelming. This, in turn, may scare you. The excuses you have used in the past to rationalize not changing are no longer worthy. This can be quite unsettling if you are not prepared to experience it.

I once discussed this with a man at a training I conducted. He had started programming his mind for new behaviors and experienced the impact in a few days. He remarked how jolting it was. He said he backed off the programming because he became acutely aware of the responsibility he had for his own life. It was a bit scary for him to embrace the power he possessed to change his being. The more you are prepared for this the less you will be startled. If you expect it, you are more likely to embrace the change. Also, the more you are prepared for it, the more likely it will not occur. Life is like that.

The point is to allow the internal nudges to have a voice and a place in your life. Stay calm if these urges and nudges surprise you. Allow them into your life. Embrace what happens.

The overall fact is you should be prepared for just about anything. It is difficult to discern exactly what will happen for everyone. Some may quickly change, others may experience much inner turmoil, still others may simply gradually move away from the old and toward the new. I believe it is impossible for nothing to happen with well-stated mental programming applied consistently. So, keep an open mind and allow yourself to simply observe the results of the experiment you are conducting with yourself.

I suggest that the above reactions are the most common and the ones that you must be prepared to deal and manage. Still, there are other things that are important to understand when practicing mental programming. These are discussed in the next chapter.

Chapter 7 Key Points

- Mental programming is not as easy as it may first appear. There are reactions with which you must contend and most people are either not prepared for them or don't want to have to deal with them or both. Your success is directly related to how well you manage the backlash that is inevitable.

- The arousal of the negative voice is almost inevitable and is managed by consistency, adopting a passive attitude toward it, and adjusting the dominant thought to a more realistic, manageable instruction.

- Monkey mind must also be managed by becoming aware of it, deliberately setting aside time to focus, setting up dominant thought reminders, and talking aloud to yourself.

- The pace of results can vary considerably depending on the person and a host of factors. Immediate results are not likely. The key is to adopt a passive attitude while staying the course. Remember that the internal process for automation is also automatic and can only be indirectly influenced with consistency. Automation is a byproduct of repeated dominant thoughts.

- Be prepared for, embrace, and utilize the improved dominant thoughts that your subconscious will deliver to consciousness. Remember that your subconscious is likely already aware of needed changes and is only awaiting your instructions to begin the actions necessary for movement toward what is needed or desired.

- Accept and receive what your mind is leading you toward. Notice, embrace, and respond to subtle nudging and intuitive urges. Allow them to have a voice and place in your life. Feed the new, starve the old.

- Remember that you are better off delivering some form of mental programming to your mind in an effort to change than doing nothing at all.

Chapter 8

More Things You Should Understand About Mental Programming

"There is nothing too great of accomplishment for the man who knows the power of his word, and who follows his intuitive leads. By the word he starts in action unseen forces and can rebuild his body or remold his affairs."

Florence Scovell Shinn

Having presented the four steps and the reactions you must surmount, there are other important considerations that deserve attention. This chapter addresses a hodgepodge of issues and thoughts regarding personal change and mental programming. I have placed them together in this chapter because it is at this point that these topics arise in the minds of those interested in this subject. So, here we delve into a number of philosophical issues that often arise.

Some of these topics are addressed in response to skeptics ready to debate the method. Alternatively, these topics are discussed for those who desire to deepen their knowledge and understanding before moving forward. Because the stumbling blocks to self-change are robust and many, in some ways the following issues help to overcome stumbling blocks not addressed previously. To some degree these topics tie into issues surrounding personal motivation and the quest to sort out what is really desired and important in your life. All are points I feel compelled to address. Consequently, these topics result from a healthy inquiry and I welcome the opportunity to address and deliberate them. Accordingly, this chapter will tackle the following questions and issues:

Why and How Does Mental Programming Work?

Willpower vs Mental Programming: Partnering with the Subconscious

Sabotaging Your Own Change

The Idea that Change Should Happen Quickly, Sometimes Referred to as Failure

Positive Thinking, Affirmations, and Mental Programming: They are Not the Same

When to Use and not to Use Mental Programming

Why and How Does Mental Programming Work?

Many of us are reluctant to do anything until we understand the "why" behind the action. This is particularly true for Americans who are taught from a young age to ask why. This is partly because of a healthy skepticism and desire to not be duped, and partly because humans have an innate drive to learn and understand our world.

Fortunately, there are some very scientifically sound reasons that good mental programming works. Yet, direct, specific research on mental programming as described in this book is still needed. Consequently, we have to take a small leap from what we know about the brain and priming to the method presented.

The scientific foundations explaining why mental programming works come primarily from our knowledge about the brain and attention. Specifically, support for dominant thought theory comes from 1) the study of the Reticular Activating System; 2) findings on the salience and accessibility of thoughts; 3) what we have learned from the priming, ironic process, and neuroplasticity research; 4) basic learning theory; 5) ideas regarding the stimulation of implementation intentions; and 6) the circular nature of mental processing itself. All of these areas are strongly interlinked in their relevance. So interlinked that often we are really talking about one and the same thing from different perspectives. For clarity, I will discuss them separately. There is a mass of information regarding each of these areas of study. I will briefly address what we know relative to mental programming and dominant thought theory.

Our Trusty Friend the Reticular Activating System

The Reticular Activating System (RAS) is the part of the brain that acts as a filter regarding what is allowed into the conscious mind. In other words, the RAS is the gatekeeper for the flow of information into consciousness. It also does other things like moving us between being awake and asleep; however, these functions are not pertinent in our understanding of priming.

When you think about it, your senses are being bombarded with a mass of stimulation almost constantly. If you were to receive all of that stimulation at once, your conscious mind would immediately get overloaded. Remember, the conscious mind can only handle about five to nine pieces of information at any moment. As was stated in Chapter 4, this comes out to a maximum of about 2000 bits of information per second; many estimates are less. Relative to the total amount of information the brain is receiving and processing, this is miniscule.

Today, the constant bombardment of our senses is intensifying with stimulation from cell phones, advertisements, tweets, emails, notifications, and all of the electronic media stacked on top of the natural stimulation from the environment. Your attention is constantly being drawn to here and there and to this and that. Maneuvering the modern world requires excessive attention switching such as never before required.

So, what keeps the conscious mind from getting overloaded? The RAS. More importantly, what part of the brain "knows" what to let through to consciousness and what to filter out? The RAS. The RAS is very selective in what it allows into consciousness. It somehow figures out what you should attend to and what you should let pass by. The RAS "knows" what's important for you to know and what's irrelevant.

The RAS is that part of the brain that filters out unnecessary stuff and lets in necessary stuff.

The classic example is the fact that new parents will hear their baby crying in the night and filter out all other extraneous sounds. They could live next to a highway or an airport with the sounds of trucks and planes regularly occurring. However, the RAS "knows" which sounds to filter out and which to let through. The RAS is acutely attuned to the sound of their baby crying and lets this information enter consciousness. Thus, parents sleep like a log through all sorts of noises, but awaken almost immediately when the new baby cries. Yes, it is working constantly, even when you are asleep.

When you are driving, it is the RAS that picks up the faint sound of a siren in the distance while ignoring all of the extraneous highway sounds. It also quickly assesses if the honking horn is near you or at a distance and to which to attend. The RAS is that part of the brain that allows the sound of your name from across the room to come through all of the other chatter at a party. By the way, the RAS is super acutely aware of the sound of your name. It has been trained since birth to let this sound into consciousness.

So, how does the RAS "know" what is important to let through into consciousness? We let it know by our thoughts; primarily, by what we focus on most. It appears that the RAS is constantly noticing where we are focusing our attention. It keeps track of what we are attending to. In this way it "knows" what to allow into consciousness. It also filters based on our beliefs. If we believe people who wear glasses are smarter, we will focus on the smart things people who wear glasses do. The RAS filters relative to our prejudices, our interests, and our desires. In short, it filters relative to our regularly attended to thoughts. The RAS is acutely aware of our own systems of thinking. It "watches" what we think and responds accordingly. This should all sound very familiar to you. This is very akin to the Chapter 4 discussions on how the subconscious is constantly monitoring conscious behavior to determine what to automate.

As you can see, the RAS is that part of the brain that unconsciously, automatically makes us conscious of certain information based on what it perceives is important to us. And, although it is a subconsciously or unconsciously controlled automatic system, *it is always influenced by what the conscious mind expresses through its thoughts.*

Once again we see an example of how the conscious mind, either directly or indirectly, is the control panel regulating what the RAS is filtering and allowing into consciousness. We also see an example of how the mind is a self-programming, circular system. How amazing! If you want to change what the RAS allows into consciousness, send a message to the RAS regarding what you think is important. The RAS filter is formed, shaped, and prompted by your thoughts; change your thoughts, change your filter.

I am sure you can see where all of this is going relative to mental programming. When you repeat a dominant thought instruction the RAS becomes acutely aware that this instruction is important to you. Therefore, it allows anything related to that dominant thought to enter consciousness. It also filters out things not related to the dominant thought. What a convenient, efficient friend we have working for us. Yet, we must program the RAS in a manner that guides it to work for us. Perhaps this is a good time to note again that there is also priming research that indicates that priming one goal inhibits the activation of conflicting goals.[1] Hence, it appears that the findings of priming studies are consistent with what is known about the job of the RAS.

For example, if you are prone to procrastination and you repeat, "Now I do, I do now," to yourself 500 to 1000 times a day, your RAS is going to allow anything into consciousness that will lead to beginning and completing relevant tasks. Assuming your conscious and/or subconscious knows what needs to be done, the RAS will allow anything related to accomplishing those tasks to enter consciousness. Concurrently, distractions from accomplishing needed tasks will be blocked. In this way the RAS focuses attention in a manner that was perhaps never before thought about or utilized.

We have all experienced this in action. For example, remember the last time you needed to buy a new car. You declare to yourself that you need a new car. Your mind "hears" this. You then start focusing on cars and your RAS now allows anything related to purchasing a car to enter consciousness. You start looking at cars more. You become aware of what your friends drive. You become aware of the car lots around you. You may have driven down the same road hundreds of times, but all of a sudden you realize that there is a car lot you had never noticed before. You become aware of which cars are sitting in dealers' lots. You tune into automobile ads on TV that you previously and conveniently tuned out. A host of things previously ignored flow in consciousness. This phenomenon is so powerful that, even after you purchase a car, you find yourself still tuning into anything related to cars! This goes on for several weeks before it fades and another focus takes precedence.

This all relates directly back to the ultimate principle: *The mind moves you and your listener in the direction of the dominant thought regardless of whether that thought is stated in the positive or the negative.* The RAS controls what you attend to and the dominant thought alerts the RAS regarding what to filter in or out. The fact that we have a built-in RAS that filters input constantly *is the reason why you need* a well-stated dominant thought. Without the proper dominant thought to guide the RAS our previous mental programming will remain and there will be no filter to effectively focus attention.

In summary, the thoughts that prime your mind guide the RAS toward what to allow in or filter out of consciousness. This if very important because your life is predominantly determined by where you focus your attention. This is well-established scientifically. If you are interested in the RAS, simply search it on the internet. There is plenty of information out there explaining its function and purpose.

Salience and Accessibility

Directly related to the job of the RAS are the concepts of salience and accessibility. When something is salient it is noticeable, important, prominent, or conspicuous. Relative to thinking, salient thoughts are those thoughts you think a lot. Likewise, the more you think certain thoughts or words, the more accessible they become. That is to say, it is easier to recall words you use a lot and harder to recall words you use rarely. We have all experienced this.

In the priming research, salience and accessibility both refer to how easily an idea or concept can be accessed by the brain or how fast your brain can get to a thought. Correspondingly, they refer to how easily certain thoughts can be used to make sense of the world. Concepts and words that appear to the thinker to have broad application and which are easily "brought to mind" are salient and accessible. Salient attitudes and beliefs are often "on your mind" and frequently stated in conversations. Ideas and words you have never thought or only rarely think are not salient or accessible. If you have difficulty seeing something from a particular point of view, you can assume that the concepts and words needed to see a certain perspective are not frequently thought about and are not regularly "brought to mind."

Dr. Tory Higgins, a leading expert on priming theory, eloquently makes the point that the more salient a belief or word is and the more mentally accessible it is, the more easily it is activated and utilized in a person's life.[2] This has been echoed in other priming research discussions.[3] In other words, we filter through, sort out, and make sense of our world directly in proportion to the salience and accessibility of the ideas and words we hold in our head. Higgins defines priming as, "...procedures that stimulate or activate some stored knowledge"[2] (p. 134) and states that priming increases salience and accessibility of material and, subsequently, its use and influence. For an in-depth discussion and review of the research supporting these ideas refer to Dr. Higgins's writings.

Ultimately, priming with the proper dominant thoughts changes behavior because it increases the salience and accessibility of those concepts needed to impact your behavior. If you do not have access to and use certain words and concepts, they cannot be used to change your behavior. It's really quite simple. The four steps necessary for change through mental programming all are aimed at increasing the salience and accessibility of the precise information needed for change. This is another way of looking at the purpose of mental programming and is largely a conceptual analysis of the job of the RAS.

Brain Plasticity and the New Neural Science

Because this has been discussed previously in Chapters 2 and 6, I will be extremely brief. Several points are salient relative to recent research regarding neuroplasticity. The first point is that it has been confirmed that brain structure can be changed at the neurological level.[4] Specifically, new mental programming or neural "wiring" can be promoted through various deliberate, conscious activities. The second point is that changes in brain structure at the neurological level can occur much more quickly than previously thought. Neurological changes have been observed in as little as two months.[4] Finally, and perhaps most important to dominant thought theory, repetition is the singular, necessary, underlying ingredient for change to occur at the neurological level.[5] **That, that is repeated, rewires the brain.**

These three findings in combination endorse and provide validity for the 4-Step approach of dominant thought theory and assist in explaining why it works.

What the Priming Research has Taught Us

With all that has been said about priming thus far I will, again, only briefly discuss the major points that the priming research has revealed that explain why mental programming works. All of these were previously discussed and, as such, I will not belabor the points.

The first element that the priming research provides toward explaining why mental programming works is simply that words trigger and stimulate behavior. This is another one of those don't-make-it-complicated points. Chapter 1 provides examples of just a small portion of the research supporting this. Simply put, mental programming works because well-worded dominant thoughts stimulate preparatory thoughts that activate action.

Taking this a bit deeper, priming research strongly suggests that the neural circuits used to think about doing something are the same as the neural circuits used to actually do it.[6] There appear to be strong thinking-doing neural links in the brain. Mental programming taps directly into the thinking-doing links established in the brain. Well-worded dominant thoughts fire the neurons that stimulate action.

Directly tied to these points is the fact that it does not matter from where the priming words or images come.[6] This was discussed in Chapters 2 and 5. You can be primed from the outside world sending messages to your brain or the inside world of your own thoughts. What matters is that a dominant thought is presented to stimulate desired action.

Basic Learning Theory

Anyone who has taken an introductory psychology course has been exposed to the basics of learning theory. Learning theory offers explanations for how we learn and change. No matter which approach to learning is examined, it always comes down to one basic idea: Learning is a result of spaced repetition. All learning is a result of practicing something, waiting (space), and practicing again. This is true even for one-trial learning in which the "space" of the learning is an extremely brief, momentary event.

For most learning, the space between the practicing is just as important as the practice component. There are many studies and theories as to why putting space between practice times is important and just how much space is ideal. Suffice it to say that, generally speaking, spaced practice is better than amassed practice. The ideal amount of space between practice times depends on two things. It should not be so long as to forget what you learned or so short that what has been practiced has not had enough time to be "implanted" or "catalogued" in the brain. Modern neural science has taught us that it is likely that the space between practicing is needed for new neural growth. Thus, one reason dominant thought theory works is because it relies on the tried and true fundamentals of spaced repetition in creating new learning.

Specificity and Intention

There are also the overall benefits of specificity and intention.

Dominant thought theory is based on delivering specific, focused messages to the subconscious in a positive, to-do form. Research indicates that this is the format that is most likely to give superior results.[7] As has been explained, dominant thought theory requires very specific statements of the desired action when crafting mental programming statements.

Such mental programming statements also have very specific intentions. This is directly related to the theoretical concept called "implementation intentions." Implementation intentions specify the exact situation where actions needed for goal attainment are to be initiated.[7] It is one thing to say you want to accomplish a certain task; it is another thing to specify the exact moment where a shift in behaviors should be done in order to begin accomplishing that task.

In repeatedly delivering dominant thoughts you are forming implementation intentions that are the first step toward automation. As researchers Anderson, et al.[3] state: "Consciously deciding to pursue a goal in advance of doing so enables goal pursuit to occur outside awareness. Relevant cues in the environment will then activate the goal, triggering preexisting behavioral intentions that predict goal pursuit" (p. 153).

As you can see, when you "tell" the mind to pursue a goal, the subconscious begins preparing for opportunities that may arise for doing the necessary things for accomplishment of that goal. Thus, implementation intention moments are foreseen by the subconscious mind. This works for you because, as Gollwitzer explains, "...mental representations of the anticipated situation...become highly activated and thus easily accessible"[7] (p. 497). Here again, we see the importance of the idea of accessibility explained above.

Stated relative to the ideas in this book, repeating the dominant thoughts in the present tense prepares the brain to unconsciously recognize outside cues that activate the new behavior. This is exactly what we want to happen. The more specific the implementation intentions the better. Of course, all of this leads to automaticity.

Research by Schmitt[8] illustrates this point. Briefly, subjects had to press a button when numbers appeared on a screen and do nothing when letters appeared. All subjects were asked to respond even more quickly when the number "3" appeared. One group of subjects prepared for this by writing the number "3" repeatedly on paper. The other group of subjects prepared for this by repeating the mental programming statement, "When the number 3 appears, I will respond particularly fast." While both groups responded faster to the number "3," subjects who repeated the mental programming statement more effectively accomplished the task of responding faster.

There are two very significant points that emerge from these findings. First, the mental programming statement included the instruction of "when" the change in reaction time was to be implemented. The statement, "When the number 3 appears…," told the brain the moment the new behavior was to be implemented. Thus, the greater specificity as to when to do the behavior appeared to enhance reaction time.

Second, as asserted previously, the word "will" implies a future event and is less effective in mental programming. Although in this context it is doubtful a future tense wording was detrimental, in other contexts it could be quite detrimental because it does not imply anything is being done now. Many people are constantly telling themselves and others about things they need to do in the future, yet, never initiate action. Research indicates that only about 20 to 30% of intentions result in actual follow through with action.[7] It is clear that indicating when an action is to take place increases the chances of doing it. This component is often left out of everyday intentions.

The creation of implementation intentions is one reason why dominant thought statements are deliberately stated in the present tense. Dominant thoughts stated in the present tense logically include a message regarding implementation intentions. The message and implication is that the brain is to begin internally reprogramming the new behavior *immediately*. You could say that the mind is being told to begin making the neural adjustments necessary to change behavior as quickly as possible so that you will act accordingly when the situation arises. In this way you are prepared for all upcoming specific moments where altered behavior is called for. As noted by Andersen et al.[3] in summarizing previous research, "Implementation intentions promote goal attainment by removing the need for conscious reflection or thought of any kind at the moment of encountering the cues and initiating the action" (p. 141). This is the ultimate goal of the dominant thought approach.

If you prefer, you can add very specific implementation intention statements to your mental programming. Instead of "I eat healthy," you could state, "When I eat, I eat healthy." In the second statement the point at which the new behavior is implemented is even more specific. Regardless, dominant thought theory works because the method requires the high degree of specificity needed for the intentional creation of new behaviors at key moments.

The More Automated A Behavior, the More Likely It Will Be Repeated

Though this final thought on why mental programming works is circular in nature, it is worth noting, nonetheless. By definition, the more you implement a process of automation and habit formation the more likely it will be repeated. Stated using circular reasoning: Repeated behavior creates automation and automation creates repeated behavior. Mental programming works because it takes advantage of the circular nature of thinking discussed in Chapter 4. This notion is further enhanced by research that indicates that the more something is primed, the shorter time it takes for the priming stimulus to have impact.[1]

Correspondingly, the more you can do necessary behaviors without "thinking," the more likely you are to do them and repeat them. In this context "thinking" means two things. The first is you have to consciously remember to do them. The second is that "thinking" often refers to behaviors that take effort and are willed by the conscious mind. Unfortunately, the more unsavory the task at hand, the more we feel as if willpower is needed to accomplish it. For too many, "thinking" often implies that we have to force ourselves to do a difficult task. Automation eliminates the need for willpower and prompts us to do the challenging things needed to succeed with much less effort. Ultimately, the more we automate, the more we repeat what is necessary to accomplish goals with minimal effort.

The bottom line is this: **If you want to get yourself to do something, automate it.**

Similarly, if you are trying to accomplish a large, complex task, automate the smaller habits that are necessary for its accomplishment. Success at any endeavor is a result of repeating a number of necessary smaller behaviors that, in total, result in larger accomplishments. Personal automation is the key to accomplishing all large, complex tasks.

Mental programming works because, by definition, it creates repeated behaviors. Mental programming works because it is the shortest route to automation available.

"We are what we repeatedly do."
Aristotle

Willpower Versus Mental Programming: Partnering with the Subconscious

I want to take a few minutes and discuss the difference between using pure, raw self-discipline to enact personal change versus using self-discipline to reprogram your subconscious and, thereby, piloting your subconscious to generate the change from within. I believe there is a tremendous difference in the amount of internal, gut-wrenching effort required to change when using pure willpower than when you focus your efforts on inducing the subconscious to instigate the change.

When most people make up their mind to break a bad habit and form a new one they typically approach this undertaking using sheer determination and self-control. There is nothing wrong with this approach as it has served many of us well when we have mustered the willpower to follow through and conquer the forces that must be faced. With such an approach we are, literally, challenging the subconscious head on. You might say we enter into direct battle with the subconscious and all of its commanding internal programming. Some likely enjoy the challenge.

Unfortunately, not everyone is successful at taking on the subconscious directly. It is quite powerful and does not easily submit to change. As we all know, lots of good intentions never culminate in change. As mentioned above, only about 20 to 30% of intentions result in actual follow through with action.[7] Further, follow—through to the point that an old habit is completely extinguished and a new habit is firmly in place is even more difficult. Of course, this is highly dependent on the type and strength of the established habit and a host of other personal and social variables.

I submit that one reason habit change is so problematic is that directly fighting the subconscious is a difficult, arduous task. Your subconscious is the most powerful force shaping your life. If you don't believe me just experiment with going against a well-ingrained habit and experience the power it has in directing your life.

Having studied habit change and mental programming for years, I **would argue that the much easier way to change is not by fighting the subconscious, but rather, by simply reprogramming it. Instead of using your willpower to fight it, use your willpower to consistently deliver the programming message you desire to the subconscious and let your subconscious activate the change. Don't fight the subconscious; recruit it to do the change for you.**

Please note that I said "easier" not "easy" way to change. You must still deal with the backlash from the subconscious; however, you do not enter into direct battle with it. You merely continue down the path of consistent mental programming while maintaining a detached attitude toward the backlash. With mental programming you move from forcing it to happen to letting it happen. You avoid the fight. Your only exertion is in consistently staying the course and detaching from the backlash. When you do this, you don't force change, you germinate change. You shift your subconscious from the position of opponent to partner. Test it. I believe you will find this to be a much easier way to create winning habits.

I learned this the hard way many years ago when I stopped smoking. Back when I was a smoker, I would return home to visit every Christmas and encounter old friends, all of whom had quit smoking. I very much wanted to quit smoking but, at that time, I was very unskilled at how to go about breaking such a strong habit and addiction. By the way, by far the greater part of smoking cessation is habit and not addiction. The physical addiction components of smoking are over long before the deeply ingrained psychological associations are extinguished.

One Christmas I was absolutely determined to stop smoking—to become a fresh air breather. However, at the time the thought of "fresh-air-breather" did not exist in my mind. I had no mental programming ideas to move me away from smoking and in a new direction. Yet, I had become so terrified that I would never be able to beat this habit that I used this fear to motivate me and I made up my mind to quit one night.

As it was, the next night I went to the same bar, sat at the same seat with the same smokers and used pure willpower to fight and overcome the urges to smoke. This was a formidable task. As I recall, I did not tell anyone what I was doing. I just sat there battling the overwhelming urges to smoke. I had no knowledge of mental programming to aid me in the internal war I was experiencing. I did stay in touch with my internal desire to break this habit and this was what probably got me through the night successfully. I went the entire night smoke free and, to make a long story short, eventually quit. However, this was not before weeks and months of follow-through that consisted of an uncomfortable and difficult state of living. In many ways I am still amazed that I did it.

I used pure willpower and self-discipline to break this habit. Needless to say, I wish I knew then what I know now. Today, I know this is the hard way to break a habit. You do not have to suffer such a war within yourself. You will have some degree of internal struggle, but it does not have to be so ferocious and strenuous. Now I use mental programming for implementing the simple to the complex. I have accomplished more than I ever dreamed. To get this book written, I programmed my mind. This book was also written so you can mold yourself into the person you desire while avoiding such arduous internal battles. This book was written to provide a road map for creating lasting change in your life while minimizing agonizing struggles that require maximum willpower. There is another way.

In summary, **the easiest way to change is to use your self-discipline to reprogram your subconscious and let your subconscious generate the changes you desire at its own pace.** The only thing you have to use your willpower for is to consistently repeat a well-worded statement. When you directly reprogram your mind, you greatly diminish the struggle with internal urges and impulses that tug at you. Instead of using willpower to fight subconscious impulses and urges, you simply stimulate *new impulses and urges* to guide you elsewhere. Remember, it's your mind and you have the ability and tools to program it. You also have the choice of the method you use.

Sabotaging Your Own Change

If you are a generally oppositional person who tends to argue against things, who tends to not go with the crowd, who tends to find the flaws in approaches offered, who fights against anyone telling you what to do, and you allow your oppositional characteristics to burst forth and sabotage any new idea that you encounter, then I have nothing for you. I am almost certain that you will sabotage your own mental programming and proclaim the approach as unreliable, fraudulent rubbish.

Such sabotage is quite easy to do. I know, because I am, to a large degree, this sort of person.

I appreciate and search for those thinkers and writers who take issue with the most commonly offered clichés and explanations, and seek the closest thing we can get to raw truth. I am the sort of person who reads the new age, positive thinking, affirmation mumbo jumbo and declares it won't work. This book was written because of my skeptical, oppositional approach to examining hard facts and data—a characteristic sorely lacking throughout our culture.

So, if you are this type of person and you let your oppositional personality take control before you seriously test the method, I can assure you, you will succeed in failing to change.

Sabotage is easy. In fact, it is beyond easy. Just don't take the time to consistently think a thought. Just let your everyday monkey mind wander and never receive a clear statement of precisely where you want it to guide you. Or, only give your mind brief moments of precise programming and then simply allow yourself to return to an unfocused mental state of everyday life never to receive the effective programming again. Allow all of the massive media chatter that we are bombarded with daily to fill and dominate your thoughts. Just keep hoping without acting. Just keep expecting some mystical force to do it for you. Just keep doing what most people do.

I guarantee nothing will change.

I guarantee your current behavior will continue or be gradually shifted by the consistent input you are receiving from outside stimulation and information.

You see, you have to really desire to change. At least, you have to really want to change enough that you will consistently follow through with the method across time. If you half-heartedly want to change and you half-heartedly repeat your dominant thought for a few days and quit, don't expect anything. It will not work.

If you do not follow through, your thoughts cannot follow through.

Allow me to remind you again that research indicates that the influence of the prime is increased when it is perceived as important to the task at hand[2] and the impact of repetition increases the more it is done.[9] I am aware this is rather commonsensical when you think about it. Simply put, if you repeatedly prime yourself regarding something relevant in your life that you really want, it has greater potential to produce results.

The really-want-it component is the part that is solely dependent on you. No one else can do it for you. Others can support you, but you have to do it. This is a pure inside job.

"Nothing happens until something moves."
Albert Einstein

There are many ways to sabotage yourself of which the easiest is to fail to follow through. Another way to sabotage is a bit more indirect. It is simply this: You can create ludicrous, unrealistic dominant thoughts that demand that others or the world change while you do nothing. For example, "I am in perfect health," "My body heals all ailments," "I will win the lottery," "My spouse will always love me," "My kids behave everywhere we go," "The universe provides me great wealth," and the list goes on.

As an extreme example, I can repeat, "Pigs can fly," from now to the day I die; however, I have no confidence that this will result in pigs flying. Moving a bit more toward reality, I can repeat, "I am rich," for years; yet, this does not remotely assure wealth is certain or the inevitability of anything. This is especially true if the users of such techniques have been sold a mindset that repeating such statements is *all that is necessary* for riches to magically materialize in their life. Such wishful thinking escapes reality to an absurd extreme. If you embrace such thinking be prepared for disappointment.

If you do not create practical, realistic programming that you can readily begin doing, you can easily set yourself up for failure. Now, I hate to say this because of those who will take it as an excuse to not attempt realistic change; but, there has to be a practical awareness of genuine physical and mental limitations also.

I am a thin, six-foot, 165 pound man who has never had a strong physique. I have been this way my entire life and it is largely genetic. You could say I am a stereotypical Ichabod Crane college professor type. I am never going to be the center on a football team no matter what I do or say to myself. Yet, I most certainly can go to the gym, lift weights regularly, practice yoga, and greatly improve my physique and health. However, there are physical limits that make some goals unreachable. The same is true for almost everyone in some area of their life.

Many people do not have the mental capability to do certain jobs and tasks. Most of us could never manage the memorization required for completion of medical school or the complex mathematical understanding necessary to be a theoretical physicist like Einstein. While the greater problem is people underestimating themselves, we all do have our limits

I hate to bring this point up because most people are significantly underestimating themselves and I do not want to provide another excuse for stagnation. Most basic habit control is well within the abilities of the vast majority of people. Most people are not using their potential to the fullest. The mindset instilled by society, parents, schools, and a host of other social systems is much more likely to be the culprit holding people back from countless achievements. Yet, there has to be some awareness of practical limitations.

Another painless way to sabotage yourself is to ignore or fight the subtle urges that will surely arise when new thoughts are repeated. Dominant thought theory is not a hit-you-in-the-head-with-a-hammer approach. It is not a will-it-to-happen approach. It is much more subtle and relies on you allowing the subtle shifts in behavior that tug at you to have a chance. You have to give way to new impulses and promote their aspirations. You have to let it happen. If you fail to let it happen, it will not happen.

Returning to the main point, you have to really want it. If you find that you are not succeeding, perhaps some reflection as to how much you really want it is warranted. If you don't really want it, I've got nothing for you.

The Idea that Change Should Happen Quickly, Sometimes Referred to as Failure

Here I am again forced to use a word I would rather avoid because of all of the things it brings to mind. Yet, I have come to realize that many people have unrealistic and unhelpful ideas about the concept of failure. With this realization, I am compelled to address the topic.

If you are consistently properly programming your mind with a realistic dominant thought and you find yourself doing the things you do not want to do, it should not be framed as failure. It simply means that the current mental programming is, for the moment, still doing its job and you did not use pure willpower to override it. As long as there is a realistically accomplishable goal, there is nothing in this situation that constitutes failure.

No momentary action is the final outcome. The outcome is a result of thousands of small actions in total. This takes time.

Not doing a new habit on occasion is not and should not be labeled as failure. This was substantiated in the research previously mentioned regarding how long it takes to create a new habit.[9] A subsequent finding of this research was that failing to do the new habit on occasion had *little impact* on creating the ultimate automaticity. It was consistency *across time that was primary* in creating automaticity and its impact *grew exponentially* as time progressed. Can we say enough about consistency?

Those who are successful at accomplishing things are well aware and accepting of momentary setbacks. Such occurrences are common to their life and well-accepted as part of the process. That is, people who are successful at anything are accepting of mistakes along the way. They embrace the process of self-correcting and going at it again.

When professional athletes miss a shot, do they give up and call themselves a failure? When pro golfers hit the ball out of bounds, do they consider it a failure? If you make a wrong turn are you a failed driver? I am an extremely poor typist. I mishit keys at a phenomenal rate, particularly for someone writing a book. Yet, I never declare my typing a failure. I just correct and keep pecking. If I don't exercise one day is my entire exercise program a failure? If I eat crap food at one meal is my entire diet a failure? If I make an inappropriate statement am I always a bad communicator? If I smoke one cigarette has my movement toward breathing fresh air completely failed? If I miss a day at work am I not putting forth enough effort? If I take a break from an arduous task am I giving up? Absolutely not.

Unfortunately, there are those who frame undesired momentary behaviors as failure. To make matters worse they sometimes compound the reaction by saying that they will never change and might as well give up. This is sometimes referred to as the "what-the-hell effect."[10] It is the kiss of death for those desiring change. With the what-the-hell effect momentary setbacks are used to justify larger setbacks. It is most commonly seen with those dieting. I am not sure why people allow this to occur in one area and not another. That is, they practice their golf swing or their cooking skills or their art skills or their music skills with great acceptance of momentary mistakes and, yet, give up on their diet after the first piece of chocolate cake.

Psychologically-minded readers are probably saying that, in such cases, people do not really want to change and that they are using a momentary unwanted behavior as an excuse to give up. Or perhaps the labeling of one instance as failure is used to relieve them of the effort required to change. (By the way, the effort is not that great if they use their willpower to program their mind and let their mind direct their behavior.)

To counter such faulty thinking, the first idea that must be understood is that the ultimate goal is the goal, not any singular momentary action. The road to behavior change is rarely straight; it is paved with detours and self-corrective actions. A capsule on the way to the moon is off course 93% percent of the time; but, by constantly correcting its course, it reaches its destination. A plane flying from New York to Los Angeles is said to be off course 98% of the time; yet, through small, consistent adjustments it reaches its destination. All successful change is a winding road to an ultimate outcome. Just because you do not proceed in a perfectly straight line does not mean you have failed. As long as a generally reasonable amount of momentary actions are moving in the direction desired in a generally increasing rate, that is success. It does not have to be perfect, only moving in the desired direction overall.

Thus, **successful change requires that you accept the fact that your degree of success is directly related to your tolerance for being off course momentarily.** Your tolerance for momentarily not doing what you desire is directly related to your ability to reach your objective. Successful people realize this.

And so it is with mental programming.

You don't put a thought in your mind one time and assume instant, lasting change will occur. One setback is not failure because this is not an instant change system. So, rid your mind of such thoughts, they are of no benefit. If you want instant change, try hypnosis or extreme willpower. Both of these may get you to realistic goals when used properly.

From the perspective of this book, failure occurs for several primary reasons. One is that the dominant thought is not realistic or something you can genuinely control. Another is that you are not consistent with your new mental programming. The third is that you do not manage the demons and kickbacks the subconscious hurls at you. And finally, you do not embrace the subtle nudges and urges that are cultivated. With this in mind, failure takes on a whole new meaning. The subconscious mind is programmable, period. As long as the goal is realistically attainable, failure is only defined by not doing the things necessary to program the mind and not managing the roadblocks the mind will hurl at you.

The idea that the subconscious fails is a bit ridiculous. Beyond what is genetically wired into your brain, the subconscious only does what it is programmed to do. You cannot "blame" it if it continues in its job of consistently maintaining what it has been programmed to do. That's precisely what it is supposed to do. You have not failed either. You have simply not delivered new programming to the subconscious to the point that old programming is overwritten and the new programming dominates.

This will not happen overnight or in a short period of time. While the subconscious can change instantly under the right circumstances, it usually does not. This is a slow, persistence-based, deliberate change system. It you are one of those quick to declare failure, perhaps you should reconsider your definition of failure.

Positive Thinking, Affirmations, and Mental Programming: They are Not the Same

I want to make two important distinctions at this point. This book is not about positive thinking or affirmations as they are often discussed. This book is about mental programming—literally, the programming of your mind-computer. And there are distinctive, scientifically-based differences.

Positive Thinking

Positive thinking is a broad, general concept that is given more credit for success than is justified. Unless it includes careful attention to dominant thoughts—which it often does not—it is not going to magically change your life or a bad situation. Positive thinking is not going to stop it from raining or snowing or keep you from getting the flu or magically change your spouse or the president or a host of other things that are not controlled by thoughts.

One of the problems with positive thinking is that it often assumes good things will happen because you look on the bright side. Such ideas are naïve and unrealistic. In this sense, positive thinking is often portrayed as a thing that will miraculously lead to better results. While a pleasant and positive attitude can greatly enhance work relations and accomplishments and meeting room results, it will not, in and of itself, fix difficult complications and circumstances. While a pleasant and positive attitude will often guide the mind to behaviors that result in beneficial outcomes, it is not going to solve all your problems.

Don't get me wrong, I am not against positive thinking as long as it is contextually understood. The great motivational speaker Zig Ziglar, whom I had the pleasure to meet before his death, would often say that positive thinking will not help you do anything, but it will help you do everything better than negative thinking. This is true to a large degree, particularly if it is used to muster up a "can do" attitude and move you to approach problems and tasks with a focus on how they can be resolved or accomplished. Such an attitude directs the mind toward possibilities and end solutions. This is the great benefit of positive thinking.

However, positive thinking is not going to magically change a bad situation. Positive thinking is not going to change your mate or make criminals behave or result in congress not being in the pockets of big business. You cannot bring back the dead, change the past, and make someone love you with positive thinking. Incorrectly applied, excessive optimism can lead to a lack of awareness of potential problems. Unfortunately, positive thinking is sometimes used as a reason to avoid taking action and just hope for the best.

The truth of the matter is that things do not always work out and you have to be acutely attuned and prepared for potential problems to attain successful outcomes. I have seen exuberant positive thinking lead to a lack of attention to detail. "The devil is in the details" is a very insightful quote that has emerged from instances where details are not addressed and focused upon because of too much reliance on simply assuming the bright side.

The overall problem with the concept of positive thinking is that it is not specific enough to precisely guide your mind and actions. Also, just because you are positive does not mean you are directed to act. I can be positive about a host of things; but, if my mind is not directed to take meaningful action it is unlikely that anything is going to change in my life.

The hard core, scientifically-confirmed truth is this: Successful people obsessively focus on the negative and what can go wrong. They are always planning how to manage situations when things do not work out. They are not excessively positive; they have a disproportionately negative focus in an effort to accomplish the positive. Please do not fall prey to commonly accepted, cutesy, socially appropriate assumptions about life that do not endure in the real world.

For those interested in the power of the negative thinking and the power of focusing on and managing the negative, I have two suggestions where you can start reading. Julie Norem in her book, *The Positive Power of Negative Thinking,*[11] addresses the importance of "defensive pessimism" and the benefits of tending to the details of what can go wrong and being prepared for it. Similarly, Roy F. Baumeister et al. in their article, "Bad Is Stronger Than Good,"[12] review a host of areas and confirm the overwhelming impact of bad events. They ultimately espouse that being attuned to the bad things is a critical survival mechanism and should not be discarded but promoted. All of these authors provide a hard core, reality-based look at what is important and what actually works for success in the real world.

If you want to be positive about something, be positive about the fact that your mind is programmable when the proper procedures are applied consistently. Use your positive attitude to motivate consistency in your mental programming.

Affirmations

Of equal importance, this book is not about affirmations. At least not some of the types of affirmations that are found throughout the new age literature and on the internet. I am personally quite amused by some of what I read. The repeating of general, vague affirmations as a key to success is phenomenally overrated. Such notions are often found in the new age world and suffer to even a greater degree than positive thinking from making rash generalizations about magical fixes. If it were so easy, we would all be successful. Everybody could just affirm their way out of poverty, bad relations, poor health, nasty neighbors, and a host of other issues of which we must contend.

Below is a discussion of the primary characteristics of affirmations and mental programming with an emphasis on where differences emerge. Because so much of this is self-evident, I am only going to briefly address these points.

An affirmation is defined as, "The assertion that something exists or is true," or "A statement or proposition that is declared to be true." While this is ultimately what is desired, merely declaring a generalized truth does not bring it into existence, particularly if the desired outcome is about general circumstances and not something that can be controlled by an individual. Affirmations too often credit accomplishment to some mystical force such as the universe or nature or some "universal creative force" (Whatever that is?) or to things just "flowing" into your life without effort. Regardless, the theme is often that the metaphysical forces of the world are in control and magically make things happen.

Mental programming, on the other hand, defines personally controlled and individually achievable end states for the mind to direct action toward or, better yet, specific actions to be taken in order to reach intended end states. Well-stated mental programming focuses and directs the mind toward specific, desirable action that is caused by and accredited to the individual doing the action. There is no metaphysical mysticism here. Mental programming does not assume the universe is just going to give you a miracle without some effort on your part. All results are co-created between the person and his/her interaction with the world.

There are similarities between some affirmations and mental programming. Affirmations and some approaches to mental programming both declare a state of existence to be a point of fact or to be occurring. I once had a student who lost 20 pounds in four to six weeks diligently repeating "I am healthy, I am thin" to herself. Upon declaring her life to be as such, she told me that she felt and responded to those intuitive nudges and mental insights that naturally and logically emerged. She found herself taking the stairs instead of the elevator. She started drinking water rather than sugary soft drinks and started eating salads and not burgers. Affirmations of this nature that declare specific states of being which are clearly within an individual's control can be very effective in programming the mind.

Yet, beyond this similarity, differences emerge.

Many affirmations declare extreme conditions to be true, lack specificity in their wording, and veer off so far into the mystical for solutions that they lose their potential to realistically direct the mind. The differences are found in the wording subtleties. Let's examine the components of these differences in detail.

Affirmations are sometimes so grandiose in what they declare that they are drastically unrealistic and foolish. Such affirmations abound and I will not delve here extensively. By the way, I searched the internet and found all of the examples below in minutes.

Unexpected money simply falls into my lap. How convenient! Are you really sure if you say this it will magically happen? I would not bet on it.

My ability to conquer my challenges is limitless. Or, my *potential to succeed is infinite.* Wow, you have no limits! Infinite? I've never met a person with no limits. There is *nothing* you can't do? Have you not determined that there are some things at which you may have limits in doing? Then why aren't you in a much better position in life? Why are your grades not straight A's? Why don't you play the stock market and get rich quick? And success at what? Nice thought, but, this is so vague that the mind has no goal to move you toward.

I see only what I choose to experience in my life and nothing else. I really don't feel like commenting on this one. Is there any reality in this person's life? Is denial a healthy state to seek? Do you really want to affirm your way into la-la land?

I am a powerhouse; I am indestructible. I've never met an indestructible person. Are you impervious to injury, illness, or accidents? The next time you stub your toe take some time to evaluate the reality of this affirmation.

This is akin to the popular expression "No Fear" which may be one of the stupidest expressions ever created. Show me a person with no fear and I will show you someone completely out of touch with reality. Have you not seen the multitude of stories and videos about how people die and get seriously injured from doing dangerous things? Such expressions are often quoted from race car drivers and others who risk extreme sporting activities. If racers have no fear then why are they wearing a helmet, and a $2000.00 fire suit, and spending thousands of dollars on roll bars?

I raced stock cars on a hometown short track for five years of my life. Before my very first race I asked an old timer about being afraid in the race car. He replied something to the effect, "You should always have some fear when racing, if not, you do not have an understanding of what you are doing and you will get into trouble on the track." That's the kind of thought you need to keep in mind when racing and it came from a genuinely experienced person.

How about this piece of mental programming for the race car driver: *I drive with precision, accuracy, and maximum speed, constantly aware of my surroundings, the limits of my car, and safety.*

Affirmations too often declare a broad, general state of existence to be a point of fact. Accordingly, they lack specificity and do not focus the mind to attend to anything. Similarly, while mental programming specifies to the mind a personal, individual goal state, affirmations often declare a condition of the world or universe of which the individual is included and stop there. Regrettably, such affirmations fail to stimulate action on the part of the individual declaring them. The primary fault of vagueness in such statements leads to the secondary fault of a failure to foster specific action.

I possess the qualities needed to be extremely successful. At what? Can you get more vague? This may be true, but what are you going to *do* about it. What action are you going to do?

I am aligned with the energy of abundance. OK, just where is this "energy of abundance?" What are we talking about here? And just what does it mean to be "aligned" with this ever so vague thing? So, you are aligned, now what are you going to do?

Something amazingly awesome is going to happen today. Sounds like a fortune cookie.

Abundance flows into my life with ease and grace. Isn't it nice you don't have to work at anything!

The most detrimental aspect of some affirmations it that they assume the source of change is the universe or some metaphysical, mystical, magical force. They do not directly assume any personal action or effort is necessary for their accomplishment. The credit for change is not personal and the issue of personal responsibility is sidestepped. Isn't this convenient! I do not have to do anything to be successful, break my bad habits, or change my life. This is further compounded by the fact that such affirmations lack any instruction to the brain regarding where to focus or what to do. There is no direct or indirect call to action, I can just sit back and wait for a miracle.

As noted, related to this aspect and those above, affirmations often focus on circumstances that are beyond individual control. Perhaps people rely on the affirmation because the situation is truly beyond their control and there is comfort in such statements. Examples abound.

My efforts are being supported by the universe; my dreams manifest into reality before my eyes.

The universal creative force supports and empowers me to successfully fulfill my life's purpose.

I am guided in my every step by Spirit who leads me towards what I must know and do.

The universe is for me and with me and responds to me in positive and constructive ways.

Money comes to me easily and effortlessly. Wealth constantly flows into my life.

A river of compassion washes away my anger and replaces it with love.

My obstacles are moving out of my way; my path is carved toward greatness.

I trust in divine timing, the universe always has my back. Timing toward what? When things go wrong, what happened to the universe guarding your back?

Wouldn't it be nice to not have to think for myself, struggle with my bad habits, and do anything! I know many people still waiting for some spirit to move them. I have to admit I have waited for the spirit to move me many times. Eventually, if it got done, I took action. I sometimes think the spirits are sitting there wondering what I am waiting for. (Please note that I am not suggesting the absence of a deity. I am only suggesting that the deity most likely wants *you* to take action for *yourself* and not sit and wait for divine intervention.)

The movie and CD entitled *The Secret* emerged as a best seller a few years ago. I truly enjoyed both the CD and the DVD. I listened with a keen interest and great enthusiasm as the writers delivered eloquent quotes that held within them profound ideas and idioms about success. The quotes were all generally accurate and relayed important points about life.

Yet, I began to sense it was all presented as just too easy. It was not that the quotes were wrong that was so disappointing. The quotes all contained wisdom and seeds of great truths. I thoroughly enjoyed the messages presented. The problem was that nowhere in the messages was there anything that implied a person had to *actually do something* to acquire success! I know this because I listened to the entire CD again with a focus on what actions were needed for all of the great accomplishments to occur. Other than simply believe it would happen, no specific personal actions were ever deemed necessary. The series strongly implied that all that was necessary for success was that I think and believe the generalized quotes about success. All I would have to do is sincerely believe that the universe will bring me success and it would somehow magically happen.

Sorry, it's just not that easy. (Really, I'm not sorry. If it were that easy, life would be dull.)

There are many people who *think* about being rich, having better relationships, smoking cessation, becoming healthy and fit, studying a subject, but who do nothing. There are people who regularly *say* they are going to start saving, they are going to start eating healthy and exercising, or they are going to start a degree program; yet, they do nothing. The point is this: **If the words you use do not stimulate personal action there is little assurance of a mystical fix.** You must repeatedly think about it in a manner that creates focus, perceptual awareness, and action toward an ultimate objective that is well-defined to the mind. Ultimately, effective mental programming maximizes the potential for neurological change. There is plenty of anecdotal evidence that random thoughts and talk alone do not, in and of themselves, create change.

Finally, there is the error of bringing to mind an undesired dominant thought. This is the most basic of errors in programming the mind and it occurs throughout the affirmation world. This error fails to understand ironic processes and inadvertently brings to mind unhelpful concepts.

My fears of tomorrow are simply melting away. Why mention "fears"?

I am superior to negative thoughts and low actions. Why bring to mind "negative thoughts" and "low actions?"

Today I will not stress over things I can't control. Why mention "stress?"

I inhale confidence and exhale doubt. Why mention "doubt?"

I let go of all negativity that rests in my body and mind. Why bring up "negativity?"

Your life is not ruled by the universe or the success gods. You are an independently functioning organism that is controlled by the mental programming in your brain. It is true that random events change and influence our lives. Completely random events are beyond our control. Yet, in the midst of the randomness of life, we have been provided the ability to control and mentally program our mind. Through this programming we spawn the actions that maximize the potential for better and desired outcomes. And this is where we should focus our attention.

This is why I study mental programming and not affirmations. Mental programming has a practical, down-to-earth quality that involves everyday behavior and attention to everyday events. Mental programming has the built-in assumption that we are personally responsible for ourselves and our actions, and are capable of directing our own behavior. Good mental programming defines and clarifies what behavior patterns you want programmed into your subconscious.

Recognizing that there is a wide range of styles and approaches in the world of affirmations, there are likely those who would argue against these differences. To those in this camp I would agree and respond that, in a sense, a well-stated affirmation may become effective mental programming. Likewise, poorly worded mental programming statements are likely to sound like fanciful affirmations.

At the risk of offending someone, I will briefly comment on an excessive dependence on religious deities to fix all problems. I truly do not write this as a criticism of any religious or spiritual beliefs. I have my own religious and spiritual beliefs and believe there is much more to life than what we see and experience at this level of existence. However, the practice of accrediting everything that happens or will happen to a deity as if we have no personal responsibility for what we do is akin to the reliance on the universe or some mystical force to change your life so often found in the world of affirmations.

Having said that, I do encounter people who appear to excessively give responsibility to their god to fix everything without personal effort. Sometimes this is done as an expression of faith. Sometimes it is done when it is clear we do not have control of a situation. At other times it is done as an excuse for not taking personal responsibility for one's own actions. This last situation is the one to which I am now addressing.

Frankly, this is in direct contradiction to religious teachings. Speaking from a purely Christian perspective of which I am most familiar, there are numerous statements in the Bible indicating people are responsible for their decisions and their behavior and that they have to take action themselves if things are to improve. I am certain other religions are similar in their writings. The Bible indicates that we all have been given free will and are responsible for our decisions and actions. If you think that God is going to fix all your problems without any personal contribution, I suggest you contemplate the research and ideas in this book. You have been given a programmable brain that you can control through proper consistent thinking. Inevitably, we are responsible for ourselves to a large degree.

When to Use and Not Use Mental Programming

While mental programming can be helpful in every area of self-improvement and therapy, as noted earlier, there are situations that I do not recommend reprogramming as the sole or primary method for dealing with difficulties. In my opinion, problems that include strong, deep-seated emotional trauma are best dealt with through therapeutic techniques that deal directly with such complexities. Loss of a loved one, childhood and adult abuse, divorce, family of origin issues, etc. are typically such problems. It is my experience that it is a mistake to try to "fix" emotionally laden issues with logic and mental programming alone.

With deep levels of emotional trauma and the resulting negative programming, counseling may be necessary for resolution. It is beyond the scope of this book to address the multitude of treatment modalities for trauma. Suffice it to say that, if you are dealing with painful trauma, counseling is highly recommended and counselors have a host of effective approaches that can be employed to aid in resolving the negative influence in your life.

Yet, mental programming can be an aid and adjunct when dealing with any type of problem, emotional ones included. For example, many times we avoid dealing with emotionally laden issues because they are painful. To avoid the pain we avoid the issue. Meanwhile it festers and continues to disrupt our life. Hence, we continue to feel bad, be unproductive, and stagnate in our growth. Mental programming can be used to move toward addressing issues. Also, once critical emotional components of an issue are earnestly addressed, a thoughtful adjustment in your dominant thoughts can greatly speed your healing and return to growth.

In order to get yourself to deal with the issue, you could use programming such as "I deal with my issues" to move you toward the necessary steps for resolution. Consistently stating "I deal with my issues" to yourself will inevitably program your subconscious to lead you to taking the necessary steps for resolution. The interesting thing is that taking-the-necessary-steps will likely sneak up on you. After consistently programming your mind with "I deal with my issues," you may one day hear a friend mention another person's beneficial counseling and all of a sudden you find yourself gravitating toward making an appointment. The influential forces are present, but subtle. This is the way much change occurs.

A few other examples of statements that may lead toward facing and releasing the pain of emotional issues follow. If you recognize that you have emotional baggage that is negatively influencing your life, read each statement and assess your own internal sense of the need to begin talking to someone about your issues.

I discuss my issues openly & honestly with those who understand.
I talk about my issues and problems.
I am aware that I must work to resolve my problems.
I trust enough to talk.
I face and talk about my emotional concerns.
I take responsibility for my actions and their consequences.

I talk and release my emotional baggage.
I take responsibility to address and manage my emotional baggage.
I create the opportunity to approach and deal with problems.
I put forth the effort to address and move through all issues.

Note that the directives here are focusing on talking and taking action rather than the negative, unproductive actions of shutting down, wallowing in, and avoiding responsibility to resolve problems.

At a more moderate level of psychological concern, there are those times when you are worried and upset over an issue that is quite disconcerting. Perhaps you were treated unfairly, have a health concern, have concern over a loved one, worry over a job, or the well-being of a child, for example. For most people it is quite difficult to just "think" away difficult, worrisome momentary situations and "think" your way to peace of mind. In such instances, typical attempts to be rational and logical fall short of providing serenity. I have had emotionally upsetting events in my life in which it was extremely difficult to simply let them go and not ruminate.

In such situations, defining dominant thoughts that are realistic, acceptable, and accomplishable can be of great benefit. For example, "I work on what is accomplishable at the moment," can lead to productive activities. Or, "I recognize and accept what I can control and maintain a realistic perspective," may lead the mind toward a reality-based acceptance of concerns.

I once had a client whom I had counseled for over a year about a host of problems, most of which stemmed from a difficult childhood. We had spent hours discussing the horrible childhood this person experienced. In fact we had discussed childhood issues to the point that the discussion of them had become a hindrance rather than a benefit.

Recognizing this, I made an agreement with the client to not discuss childhood problems but to only discuss possible problem resolution strategies. I recognized that we needed to focus on action rather than past trauma. From our discussions it became evident that the client was blaming the difficult childhood for all current life failures, and, in order to create movement, the client needed to begin to take responsibility for her current actions and not continue to dwell on and blame every life difficulty on childhood events.

From our discussions it became apparent that the client did not take responsibility for her own actions. So, I instructed the client to say repeatedly, "I take responsibility for my actions and their consequences." Interestingly, this was an entirely new thought for this person. The results were amazing. Within two weeks the client began taking definitive action to change her life. For the first time, she stated on her own that she had been using her horrific childhood as an excuse to not move forward. In her own words, she recognized that she had used her childhood to maintain a ready-made victim status. This insight resulted in a major shift in her thinking. Recognizing her own role in current difficulties, she got a job and made a number of definitive decisions about the direction her life was going.

I am not saying that this new mental programming was the sole reason for the significant change or that this should be a singular approach. Absolutely not. This client had done considerable emotional work in counseling prior to introducing this thought. I have no doubt that the timing of the new thought was important and that it would not have been effective if it had been introduced before emotional issues were well addressed.

What the programming did was implant a genuinely new thought that, in turn, led to a major insight at the subconscious level. Once this insight was made, her subconscious mind delivered it to her conscious mind and she had a jolting "ah ha" experience. The result was a major shift in thinking and how she approached her difficulties. I have no doubt that consciously and deliberately introducing the new thought and repeating it was a critical catalyst in moving this person forward. The changes that followed were so dramatic that I was a bit overwhelmed even after seeing such results many times! I can remember commenting to my wife how astounded I was that my own approach was substantiated so emphatically.

This case provides an excellent example of how well-stated, mental programming can be an adjunct to therapy for emotional issues. It also demonstrates the powerful influence that repeating a properly worded, new thought can have on the direction of one's life.

Even though sound mental programming may not be adequate for complete resolution of significant traumatic events, it can be a powerful tool for leading the mind to those factors needed for resolution. The concepts presented in this book can be a powerful adjunct to counseling and should be employed where beneficial.

Chapter 8 Key Points

- Mental programming works because:
  1. It guides the RAS toward what to allow in or filter out of awareness and, thereby, controls mental focus.
  2. It increases the salience and accessibility of those words and concepts needed to trigger behavior.
  3. It utilizes and builds on our knowledge regarding neuroplasticity.
  4. It stimulates the thinking-doing neural links and, thus, it stimulates the preparatory thoughts that activate action.
  5. It builds on the tried and true fundamentals of spaced repetition in creating new learning.
  6. It uses present tense statements to specify the exact situation where actions needed for goal attainment are to be executed and, thereby, it creates implementation intention awareness within the subconscious.
  7. It takes advantage of the circular reasoning power of the brain in creating repeated behaviors and automation.

- Mental programming harnesses the power of the subconscious by making it a partner in change. This is a much easier way to change because you avoid the arduous task of fighting the subconscious directly with pure willpower.

- Sabotaging your own change is beyond easy. If you don't really want it, I've got nothing for you.

- No momentary action is the eventual outcome. The outcome is a result of thousands of small actions in total. Mental programming takes time. Your degree of success is directly dependent on your tolerance for being off course momentarily. As long as you consistently return to productive action, momentary lapses have been shown to be insignificant relative to ultimate outcomes.

- The subconscious only does what it is programmed to do. If the mental programming is realistic and doable, failure is a result of a lack of consistency and patience.

- This book is not about positive thinking or affirmations as they are often discussed.

- Mental programming is not recommended as the primary method for dealing with problems that have strong, deep-seated emotional components that are best dealt with through therapeutic I interventions. However, it can be a beneficial adjunct.

Chapter 9

Using Dominant Thought Theory in Psychotherapy: Applications for Mental Health Professionals

If you do not want to learn to use words carefully and accurately you should probably consider another profession.
Bryan N. Baird

As a psychologist and a person who has taught counseling theory and techniques for over 20 years, I feel compelled to include this chapter in this book. This chapter is written specifically for mental health professionals to explain and demonstrate the many ways that priming and dominant thought theory can and *should be* incorporated in the therapeutic dialogue, or be used as a therapeutic technique in and of itself.

Of course, the same benefits can also be used by anyone in everyday conversations, work settings, conflict resolution efforts, speeches, letter writing, advertisements, as well as any form of communication and media. Thus, while the focus will be on mental health professionals, the concepts can be applicable to many professions and will likely benefit anyone.

If this is not of interest to you, skip this chapter.

Interestingly, the application of the priming research and dominant thought theory to therapeutic dialogue has been addressed directly by only a handful of trainers in the field. Other than my own writings, I have yet to see the concepts taught in the theory and techniques books used in classrooms.

However, the ideas are addressed indirectly or under different labeling throughout the mental health literature, particularly in approaches using hypnosis. Good hypnotists are always cognizant of the thoughts being introduced in clients' minds and are always leading clients in desired directions, either directly or indirectly. When clients are open to new ideas, dominant thoughts are accepted and prime clients toward new behaviors. Yet, there is still not enough emphasis on the importance of these concepts to the therapeutic dialogue.

There are two general ways in which dominant thought theory can be used in therapy. The first is to indirectly influence clients by stating dominant thoughts that plant seeds in the minds of clients regarding concepts that would be helpful in their counseling. For example, positively worded deficit statements can be tagged on to the end of empathic statements, embedded suggestions can be utilized in therapeutic responses, and descriptions of desired outcomes can be stated in the positive. In general, there is a conscious effort by therapists to use their words to plant seeds that "move" clients *toward something* as opposed to *away* from something.

These approaches are particularly useful with resistant clients who counter by giving "Yes, but..." responses to suggestions of solutions. Through the use of indirect suggestions, clients are not provided anything to resist against. When this approach is employed consistently, clients often find themselves thinking about solutions in new ways without conscious awareness of the thoughts introduced and proposed by therapists' use of words.

The second way to use dominant thought theory is to directly teach the concepts to clients and utilize the theory as a technique in and of itself. Many clients enjoy learning and applying the ideas to their lives.

I will address priming and dominant thought theory first as it applies to the therapeutic dialogue in general, next through its application in specific areas of the therapeutic dialogue, and, finally, as a direct technique. Of course, there is considerable overlap in the separate areas addressed; yet, there are so many applications of the theory that some sort of organizational breakdown is necessary.

Back To Basics: The Therapeutic Conversation

When you remove the psychological complexities, therapy is basically a conversation. It is a conversation between a person with a psychological problem and a person who possesses the linguistic skills to aid in the resolution of the psychological problem. Thus, therapists are those people with the skills to aid in the resolution of psychological problems through conversation.

At its most basic level, the therapeutic process is repetitive. The client says something, the therapists says something. The client says something, the therapist says something. Over and over this is repeated. **What therapists say and how they say it *is the therapy*.** Don't make it complicated.

Therapy does not take place in "theoryville." It does not take place in the writings of the textbooks and the words of trainers and theoreticians. It does not occur simply because you run through the motions of doing a specific technique. Techniques do not work in and of themselves. Therapy occurs because of the skillful application of techniques in the current moment supported by the context crafted by the therapist. Techniques without the surrounding therapists' words are useless. To be effective they always require skillful wording from therapists delivered in a highly attuned, relational context. Therefore, therapy occurs in the moment-to-moment interactions between clients and therapists.

What the therapists say and how they say it either moves clients toward resolving their problems, keeps them in the same state, or makes matters worse (increases resistance). How the words are spoken—the tone, the pace, where emphasis is placed, the facial expressions, etc.—is referred to as paralanguage and is absolutely critical to a successful dialogue and outcome. However, for this discussion I will be emphasizing the words used only. Please refer to my other writings on resistance for a more in-depth discussion of the vital importance of paralanguage.[1]

Continuing, each therapist statement is very likely priming clients in some manner. **Each therapist statement has a dominant thought that is leading clients' minds and planting seeds of new ways of thinking and responding to the world and their situation.**

It only follows that the fundamental, primary question every therapist should ask themselves with each statement they make is this: *In what direction am I priming my clients with the dominant thoughts I am saying?*

The reasons for this have been repeatedly demonstrated throughout this book: The mind can only attend. Every word you say is triggering related words in clients' minds regardless of whether stated in the positive or the negative. From the study of priming we are left with the inevitable conclusion regarding the therapeutic conversation: You cannot, not manipulate. When you say a word, you are, by the inherent nature of words, manipulating. All therapists should be cognizant of this.

Although it is not conventional or kosher to describe therapy as manipulative, it is. The job of the therapist is to acquire an understanding of clients and use this understanding to manipulate clients into doing the difficult tasks they desire or need to accomplish. Often, the fundamental benefit of the (priming) dialogue is to aid clients in resolving the internal struggles necessary for goal accomplishment. This is followed by a dialogue that primes clients with preparatory thoughts for new and different actions. Any way you look at it, therapists manipulate clients into accomplishing goals through providing a dialogue that primes new thoughts and actions.

The idea of manipulation is frequently not used in conjunction with discussions of therapy because the term often carries negative connotations. This is a result of the term being commonly associated with self-serving agendas. However, we do not manipulate for our benefit; we manipulate for the client's benefit. Oh, but we do manipulate.

We have no choice. Not to understand that therapy is manipulative is naïve. Because we cannot, not manipulate, we must constantly be aware that we are manipulating and learn to actively manipulate for clients' benefit. Thus, the question is not: Do we manipulate? The question is: In what direction and in what manner are we manipulating?

Some of the most ineffective and dangerous therapists are not cognizant of these points. They go about their craft unaware that they are manipulating constantly, whether they want to or not. Their lack of awareness leads to a haphazard, deleterious use of language that promotes resistance and may even make problems worse. Those who realize that you cannot, not manipulate, understand that language is a primary force that creates realities and moves people in one direction or another.

A careful choice of words is the cornerstone of effective therapy. Effective therapy primes appropriately; ineffective therapy primes poorly, or worse, detrimentally. Effective therapists are meticulous and precise in the words they speak because they are ever aware that they are triggering a host of related words in clients' minds and that those words create movement. There is no way around this.

Further, the influence of our words is magnified by a number of factors inherent to the therapeutic environment. One such factor is clients' foremost emotional needs, which are usually quite high as is evidenced by their seeking counseling. Another is the physical environment—usually a rather neutral room, in a private setting, with few distractions. In addition there are the rules and content of the conversation. For example, the conversation is held in strict confidence and is usually highly focused on emotionally burdening issues. Thus, the therapeutic environment is one in which the manipulative power of words is augmented by the nature of issues and the context in which they are discussed. The therapeutic environment is designed to be one of the places where words have greater influence. In therapy, the fact that we cannot, not manipulate is amplified.

Words are the primary tool of counselors. Regardless of whether you are doing Gestalt therapy, cognitive therapy, reality therapy, Rogerian therapy, behavior therapy, drama therapy, art therapy, or zip-a-dee-doo-dah therapy, words are always the vital, fundamental tool used to guide the client in the therapeutic experience. All theoretical perspectives rely on your linguistic skills to some degree. Most approaches are highly dependent on linguistic skills. Your success as a therapist hinges on your ability to use language as a tool to create change. Your linguistic skills—your words and paralanguage—create the therapeutic interaction and it is this interaction that results in change and healing.

Ultimately, clients are paying you for a conversation. **The value of your conversation is directly related to your ability to plant seeds through priming with dominant thoughts.**

Having watched thousands of counseling sessions I can tell you that too many counselors are not maximizing the potential in their therapeutic conversations and are just too sloppy with their language. Regrettably, I also find this to be true in the training videos I am sent that are supposed to represent models for how to talk to clients. Some of the demonstrated dialogues are so poorly executed that I have used the videos to demonstrate how *not to talk* to clients.

I have also taught these ideas to thousands of mental health professionals in hundreds of trainings and, from the reactions and examples I have received, I am quite concerned that the practice of precise wording with clients is inadequate. There is simply not enough awareness of the impact and implications that our choice of words has. Unfortunately, haphazard wording also contributes to resistance and poor success rates in counseling.

Let's apply these ideas to the management of depression as an example.

First, if therapists continually use the word "depression" in the dialogue with clients, every time therapists say the word, they are triggering all of the associated words and ideas. No word stands alone in the brain. All words are defined by other words. If you will recall, the priming research has confirmed that, when a word is stated, all associated words are more quickly assessed by the brain.[2,3] As previously noted, you should consider each word spoken as a cluster of words. The question becomes, What cluster of ideas am I bringing forth in the client's mind? How many times have therapists made statements such as, "My, you are so depressed," "We need to see what we can do about this depression," and "How was your depression this week?" Depending on clients' internal associations, here are just a few of the words that might be triggered by the word "depression."

> Unhappiness, despair, sadness, hopelessness, helplessness, misery, dejection, stagnation, stuckness, sorrow, discontentment, melancholy, anguish, despondency, gloom, impossibility, desperateness, inactivity, inertia, sluggishness, immobility, unproductivity, regret, disgruntlement, downheartedness, torment, idleness, etc.

When you consider the thoughts that might be stimulated by the word "depression," it is a bit frightening. Clearly, you are not stimulating thoughts that lead toward mental health.

Please note that I am not saying you should never use "depression" and the related words. I am simply pointing out that we should be very judicious with the use and limit it to those times when it might be of benefit only. In order to display understanding and empathy, the emotional states of clients should be initially stated as clients experience them. However, once rapport has been established, therapists should gently move away from using words that stimulate unwanted states and consistently use words that stimulate wanted states. In other words, after you use the negative word to establish rapport, then use the positive opposite to prime toward resolution and mental health.

This understanding now leads to a search for words that are the opposite of depression which can be used as dominant thoughts to prime clients to move away from this state. We are so accustomed to talking in the negative you may initially find yourself struggling to conjure up antonyms of "depression." Try it. Here are some ideas and possibilities.

> Contentment, meaningful, hopeful, pleased, activity, engagement, productivity, satisfaction, pleasure, gratification, movement, moved, substantial, important, expectant, encouraged, commitment, fulfillment, enjoyment, creative, heartened, invigorated, stimulated, exhilarated, success, amusement, inspired, gladdened, energized, restored, delight, attainment, motivated, etc.

Note how each of these words represents some component of the opposite of depression. Yet, how often are they inserted into the dialogue in order to prime clients? Of course, the use of such words is highly dependent on the client's world view, timing, and a host of factors regarding the appropriateness at the moment in the dialogue. In the midst of these words, it is easy to see how the overuse of the word "depression" and all of the associated words offer little benefit by way of a dominant thought.

As an aside, please note that the word "happiness" was not offered as an opposite of depression, and it should not be. Happiness is a momentary emotion that is too often sought by clients and people in general. Therapists should not create the false impression that it is a consistently obtainable state. It is frequently overused and misunderstood and we do not want to mislead clients with its use.

From this exploration into the complexities of the word "depression," it is easy to see how therapists need to have an arsenal of words opposite of those so commonly used in the world of mental health. Take some time and make a list of words that could possibly be used in lieu of commonly spoken mental health terms such as "anxiety," "fighting/arguing," "drinking and drugging," "dependent/dependency," "isolated," etc.

Here's a hint at how to find them. First, use your computer to search for synonyms. Typically, the thesaurus will also provide a few antonyms. Then search the antonyms provided and, in turn, for synonyms of them. Continue by searching each new synonym for other synonyms. This is a great exercise in exploring language possibilities.

Of course, the concepts above are true for all conversations regardless of whether they are taking place in business, social situations, personal relationships, public speaking, classrooms, or politics. Whether intentionally or unintentionally, the person speaking is always triggering thoughts and priming listeners with dominant thoughts.

Let's take a look at some specific applications in therapy. If these ideas are appealing to you, they are all discussed in detail in my book, *Effective Techniques for Dealing with Highly Resistant Clients.*[1]

Enhanced Empathic Responding

One of my favorite examples of the use of dominant thought theory and priming is to consistently augment empathic statements by including an acknowledgement of what the client is currently lacking or seeking at the end of your response. Such statements are referred to as "deficit statements" because they clarify what the client is *deficit of* at the moment. Deficit statements implicitly recognize what clients are lacking and explicitly state what clients need at the moment.

By adding deficit statements to empathic statements, therapists bring to the forefront of the conversation what is needed in clients' lives. In this way the deficit statement primes clients for direction, movement, and goal creation. Yet, when added to the end of empathic statements, the priming effect goes completely unnoticed by clients (consciously that is!). When stated with an air of concern, clients never experience the ideas presented as being imposed or forced upon them. Effective therapists understand and take advantage of this feature as it circumvents the resistance created when possible solutions are presented directly.

The construction of such statements is formulaic. You start with a well-worded empathic statement that should include recognition of the content of what the client stated. This is then coupled with a clarification of the emotions the therapist understands are present and/or the deeper meaning behind the client's statement. To this you add the deficit statement in an effort to prime the client toward change. Let's quickly review.

The content is merely the facts of the situation. Recognizing the feelings associated with the content or the meaning for the client displays deeper understanding by the therapist of the client's world at an emotional level. This also brings to the forefront motivators for change. Content, emotion, and meaning stated together create a full understanding of what is occurring and results in empathy. The addition of deficit statements carries this impact even further by recognizing what the client is missing and needing at the moment in his/her life. Such complete statements can be very therapeutically powerful. If nothing else, they are the foundation of rapport.

The construction of deficit statements is presented below. Simply attach a phrase similar to those presented below to the empathic statement and follow this with a statement or suggestion of what is needed in the client's world.

Empathic statement + ...and what you're looking for... + deficit
...and what you need...
...and you are searching for...
...and what you want is...
...and what you require is...
...and what you desire is...
...and what you wish is...
...and what you crave is...

Examples of empathic statements that include content, emotion, and/or meaning, and the additional component of a deficit component might be:

"You are very distraught over the divorce from your wife. The marriage in which you have invested nine years of your life appears to be coming to an end, and you are *searching for a way to make some sense of what has occurred.*"

"You are at your wits' end with your children and are experiencing much anger at your husband for reinforcing their misbehavior. *You strongly desire a way to obtain support from your husband and to develop more effective methods of discipline for your children.*"

"You have tried to have a child for quite some time and are experiencing much grief at the moment over the possibility that it may not occur. As you talk about it now, it appears you are *looking for a way to begin resolving the enormous dissonance this causes in you.*"

If you are correct in your perception of the current deficit, such statements will provide direction and open the door for a discussion of how to go about acquiring what is needed to begin resolving problems. They also plant the seeds for goal setting. If you are wrong in your perceptions, clients will likely correct you and clarify what they view as their deficits themselves. If corrected, empathize and clarify the new need, then proceed toward a clarification of goals.

Of course, a well-worded deficit statement is also priming the client for new behaviors. Notice how the last statement in the examples above uses the words "...to begin resolving...." Ideally, the word "resolving" will trigger other related words and concepts and trigger approaches taken by the client used in the past where "resolving" has been accomplished. Also, the prime was to only "begin" resolving. The client was not primed to "completely" resolve, just "begin." This wording is used because the client is more likely to accept the suggestion to "begin" as opposed to "fully resolve" which may appear too difficult at the moment.

Another wording note is warranted here. While it is very important to grieve and to allow the opportunity to grieve, grief should not be framed as a continuous state. Grief is a tool used to reach resolve. Hence, the word "resolve" may be needed to subtly shift the focus toward movement as opposed to stuckness. Therapists need to be aware that they are framing clients' problems with the words they use.

If the therapist speaks of grief as a permanent state and not a momentary state, they may be inadvertently creating psychological stuckness. Thus, the example above includes the phrase "...at the moment" implying that the grief is temporary. When the linguistics of this statement are studied in detail, readers will recognize that many messages are being conveyed to the client, all with the intention of priming the client toward creating a goal to be reached. In this case, the goal is to resolve the dissonance. Later in the conversation the word "dissonance" should be replaced with words such as "harmony" or "congruence" or "resolve" in order to prime in this direction.

It is important to note that deficit statements should always be worded in the positive with a keen awareness of the dominant thought. An example of a very unproductive, possibly harmful, deficit statement follows.

"Your situation is quite irritating to you and you are *lacking the guts to speak out.*"

A much better statement would be:

"Your situation is quite irritating and you are *searching for the best words to say in order to have a significant impact.*"

Although the first statement above does recognize a deficit, it is critical of the client and triggers unwanted ideas. Conversely, the second statement leads the client toward considering the right words to say in an effective manner. In this statement, there is no mention of a personal shortcoming. Obviously, the second statement primes the client to consider making an assertive statement.

Empathic statements are powerful therapeutic tools. The use of empathic statements that include a deficit component is a characteristic that separates the average from the truly skilled. Deficit statements are a wonderful example of the application of dominant thought theory and priming in the counseling dialogues.

Embedded Suggestions and Commands

My other favorite example of the use of dominant thought theory and priming in therapeutic dialogue is with the use of embedded suggestions and commands within responses to clients. In this instance, a priming message is delivered to the client by including it as a component of another statement. The client is not consciously aware of the dominant thought presented and that they are being primed toward future behaviors.

The hypnosis literature is filled with examples and uses of embedded suggestions. I have long advocated that all therapists be trained in hypnosis techniques; yet, not necessarily for using hypnosis per se. The main purpose of such training would be to learn the eloquent use of language in and of itself. Ideas related to priming are found throughout the hypnosis literature; yet, rarely are they tied directly to the priming research.

The following are example statements that show how a typical statement might be made to a client and how the same statement can include embedded suggestions or wording that attempts to move the client toward change or a goal. Note that the first statement merely describes the situation in terms that offer no direction. As you study the responses note that each implies a certain reality. This phenomenon is inevitable when you use language. All language implies realities. What realities are you implying with your wording? Of course, the suitability of a statement is always dependent on the particular situation with the client.

Negative Suggestion: "You really are *stubborn*."
Positive Suggestion: "At that point in time, you struggled to…*be open to other options*."

Negative Suggestion: "As you stated, when you *attempt to say* something about the situation, the *cowardly part of you emerges*."
Positive Suggestion: "As you stated, when you *start to say something* about the situation, you find yourself searching for a way to…*bring forth the courage to follow through*."

Negative Suggestion: "You are *hanging on to your grief*."
Positive Suggestion: "You are trying to…*discover the best way* for you to…*move through your grief in a healthy way*."

Negative Suggestion: "It is hard for you to not *let your anger take control* of you."
Positive Suggestion: "You are seeking to *find a means* by which you can…*remain composed in these situations*."

The application of dominant thought theory and priming to the therapeutic dialogue adds a level of depth and sophistication not typically encountered.

How to Talk Positive to a Negative Person without Them Knowing It

The following is a specific application of an embedded suggestion. Even though a bit long, the title does a very good job of describing what you are doing with the technique. It is entitled, "How to Talk Positive to Negative People without Them Knowing It" because it is typically used in response to a despairing, despondent statement from clients and it plants a positive, alternative thought to consider. Its uniqueness lies in the linguistic formula that is always used in creating the opportunity to state the suggestion. The formula is this: Make an empathic statement and then follow it with a statement of how difficult it is to do, or imagine, or comprehend, or consider the very behavior the client is having difficulty doing or facing.

When done without any special attention or inflection given to the suggestion, clients rarely realize that the new dominant thought or prime has been introduced. Clients also do not negatively react to what is being suggested. Personally, I have never seen a negative reaction from clients. When stated at appropriate moments throughout a session, the thought is re-seeded and the impact grows subtly.

Now there is an interesting thing that may happen. Many times clients will introduce the suggested idea after a period of time has passed with no awareness that it was previously suggested indirectly by the therapist. This phenomenon has been discussed in various therapy books over the years. Veteran therapists are very aware of how clients state something as their idea even though the therapist has mentioned it previously. Of course, credit is always given to the client for the insight! Below are some examples of responses using this formula.

"I can tell you're deeply hurt by the loss of your boyfriend, and it's at times like these that it's so hard to...*imagine other men available to date.*"

"You've wanted to divorce for a long time, but it's hard to...*comprehend reestablishing yourself away from your current partner.*"

"You're so angry with your ____ that you could really give him/her a piece of your mind. It's at times like these that you struggle to...*imagine sitting down and having a mature conversation about this situation.*"

"At this time it appears that you get very nervous before a test, it's hard for you to...*see yourself sitting there calmly taking a test.*"

As with most of therapy, timing is critical to the success of techniques. If you suggest something that is too far removed from the client's mind, you will likely have minimal impact. Attempts to move the client too far too fast are more likely to create resistance. However, if you suggest something that appears close to what the client is already considering, you are very likely to influence the client toward discussing the suggested idea. Below are some dialogue statements regarding a hypothetical case in which a client needs to have a difficult conversation with another person. As you read the therapist's responses, notice how the suggestions move from the general to the specific in small increments. This is done in an effort to match the client's current position in the deliberations.

"As you sit there and assess your situation, it is hard to...*imagine yourself doing something different.*"

"Right now, you are struggling to...*consider if a conversation could possibly impact the situation.*"

"As you...consider possibilities of how to handle this situation, it is difficult to... *hear yourself saying an assertive statement.*"

The idea that you are priming clients with dominant thoughts should be applied throughout therapeutic dialogue. Whenever clients state concerns or desires in the negative, time should be taken to discover and state the positive opposite. From then on, you should speak only in terms of the positive side of the concerns and desires.

Goal Setting

The establishment of a mutually agreed upon goal is a primary factor in forming effective client-therapist relationships.[4] Hence, one of the most obvious applications of dominant thought theory is in effective goal setting. The above uses of priming and dominant thoughts all lead to the creation of goals for clients either directly or indirectly. Therapists should be aware that many statements they make are setting the stage for creating and implementing effective goals.

Goals should be stated with an awareness and use of a dominant thought that primes the client for desired behavior. Goals should never be stated in the negative as they will only bring to mind the undesired.

It is the therapist's job to make certain goals are formed with an appropriate dominant thought. Unfortunately, clients simply will not initially grasp and understand the importance of the dominant thought. Clients rarely offer well-worded goals and, if the therapist does not tend to this aspect of goal setting, the odds are goals will be poorly worded and mostly ineffective.

This stems from the fact that clients almost always present problems in the negative. That is, they tell you what they do not want, instead of what they do want. This is, in part, one of the reasons they are stuck in their present state. They do not have dominant thoughts that move them away from their current state and lead in new directions. Most likely, their current dominant thoughts are priming undesired behaviors and keeping them stuck in their current state.

Remember, clients' dominant thoughts are priming their behavior. By carefully listening to the words clients use to describe problems you can immediately discern what ideas their mind is promoting and in what direction they are moving. Having studied and observed dominant thoughts for years, I have reached the point that I am immediately aware of how clients' words reveal core roots of problems. With a bit of awareness and listening practice, therapists can quickly determine the dominant thoughts of clients and the problems they are fueling.

Hence, most of the time when you inquire, "Tell me what you want," clients will tell you what they don't want. They tell you that they don't want to be depressed or anxious. They will say they need to stop drinking or smoking or worrying or obsessing or fighting with their children or partner. They say, "I don't want to be alone," or "I need to stop giving in to everyone." On rare occasions they state what they want. For example, they state that they want to learn to be more assertive or to stand up to people or to make a career change or to get a divorce. These are much better objectives but still need much specificity.

When clients respond in the negative to what they want, I suggest that you kindly explain that they are only telling you what they don't want, not what they want. You might then try asking a client what is the opposite of their current state. Most often, they simply put a "no" or "not" or "shouldn't" or "wouldn't" or "don't" or "won't" in front of the negatively worded desire. For example, if you direct a worrywart client to, "Tell me the opposite of worrying for you," they will most likely say, "Not worrying." Ask an alcoholic the opposite of drinking and they respond, "Not drinking." Ask those seeking a healthy weight what they desire and they often state something to the effect, "Stop eating so much junk food."

As has been explained and you can readily see, the dominant thought is the same when "no's," "not's," etc. are used. Remember the lessons from the ironic process research. When "no's" or "not's" are used, all thoughts remain focused on the undesired and do not lead to a desired behavior. Clients that use such language enter counseling already "trapped" by their linguistic framing of their problems. Have you ever had a worrier tell you that his/her goal is to be relaxed, poised, and calm in the midst of stressful uncertainty? Have you ever had a smoker declare that they wanted to consistently breathe fresh, clear, clean air? Have you ever had a depressed person tell you they are seeking contentment and movement through engaging in meaningful activity? It just does not happen.

When goal setting, while it is always beneficial to empathize and use words that mesh well with clients' descriptions of problems, it is not beneficial to continue to discuss problems in the negative as clients most often present them. When you continue to discuss problems in the negative, you are inadvertently setting clients up for failure. You are not moving clients through the pain of the internal struggles; you are maintaining a focus on the struggles in an unproductive manner. In order to create therapeutic goals, it is always beneficial to take time to reframe and clarify clients' desires in the positive. In doing this you provide words and language that creates new images and dominant thoughts that trigger new motivations and directions. Most of the time you will literally be introducing words to clients' dialogue that they are not accustomed to hearing or using.

For example, the goal should not be to "stop fighting." The goal should be to "remain calm and speak with a soft voice," or "wait five seconds before speaking," or "talk only when in a calm state." The goal should not be to "stop drinking." The goal should be to "remain clean and sober," or to "maintain a healthy body system." The goal should not be to "lose weight." The goal should be to "consistently move toward health with each meal," or simply to, "eat healthfully." The goal should not be to "stop yelling at the kids." The goal should be to "speak with a calm, firm voice." The goal should not be "relapse prevention," but rather, "recovery enhancement."

I suggest all therapists review goals with clients and determine if the wording is beneficial or not. Simply observe the dominant thought offered by the goal and adjust as needed. Also, don't rely on insurance company reviews to comprehend these concepts and suggest changes. It is rare that they understand what I am saying with any depth.

Using Dominant Thoughts to Manage the "I don't know..." Response

Many times when you inquire, "Tell me what you want," clients will honestly reply that they do not know. This "I don't know..." is very significant because, if clients do not have a dominant thought that is leading them in a desired direction, they will inevitably remain in their current state. "I don't know…" is likely the most commonly encountered three words in therapy. How you manage it is very important to therapeutic outcomes.

I consider the "I don't know…" response to be one of the most critical junctures in the therapeutic dialogue and a place where therapists should be meticulously careful with their wording. The "I don't know…" response and the state of "not knowing" is quite complex and wise therapists are judicious when responding. While I do not want to delve into the complex dynamics in-depth here, responses to "I don't know…" should be respectful of the not knowing state while delving into an understanding of the meaning behind the response for the particular client. Often, through this process solutions emerge.

Briefly, the safest response to an "I don't know…" statement is to simply embrace and honor clients' "not knowing." Chances are they truly do not know. They have no ideas that appear viable for resolution or solutions. Frequently, the "I don't know…" response is an indirect statement of unresolved conflicts either internally or externally. After respecting and empathizing with the "I don't know…" response, delve into the meaning behind the response for the client. After this, carefully help the client form and clarify what is needed to move away from "not knowing." During this process therapists should be planting seeds of possibilities through their general language and with embedded suggestions that prime beneficial dominant thoughts.

For an in-depth discussion of the management of "I don't know…" responses please refer to my earlier book, *Effective Techniques for Dealing with Highly Resistant Clients*,[1] which includes a detailed chapter exploring the "I don't know…" response along with numerous techniques for managing it. Below are some suggestions for responding to "I don't know…" statements. The formula is almost identical to that used with the examples above. An emphasis on the priming statement through subtle paralanguage accents can aid in planting ideas.

"It is very difficult for you to *see a way to deal with this,* currently."

"You really cannot *think of a possible approach that you can take* that appears better than what you are doing."

"Currently, it is very difficult for you to *see a way to deal with this.* You are searching for *new ways to approach this quandary."*

"It is difficult to sort out these philosophical struggles. You really want some *peace of mind and balance in your life."*

"Right now, it is difficult to *imagine saying or doing something different* in these situations."

Let's analyze the components of some of these example responses so we can fully appreciate what is being communicated to the client. Words such as "right now" and "currently" convey that the current state of not knowing is only temporary. These words also suggest that, at a future point in time, things could be different. Thus, we are indirectly suggesting and planting the seed of the idea that the current stuckness is a momentary state. Similar suggestive words would be "at this moment…" or "at this point in time…" or "as you are talking about this now…."

Next, note that the dominant thought is always suggesting something for the client to do. Embedded suggestions of "…deal with this…," or "…to think of a possible approach…," or "…imagine saying or doing something different..." all prime the client to move toward solutions.

In addition, there is also recognition that the task is "difficult," thus, empathy is shown regarding the client's struggle. Yet, "difficult" does not imply "impossible" or "unsolvable" or "undoable." The message to the client is that the task is doable but will require some work.

Combined, these components create a therapeutic response with much utility. Foremost, such statements do not bring to mind or prime stuckness or unproductive behaviors. While the stuckness inherent in the "I don't know..." response is recognized through embracing the difficulty of the situation, no permanence is given to the state. This is all done indirectly through the use of language. When done this way, clients do not fight the therapist and resistance is avoided.

Direct Application as a Technique

Taking all of this a step further, it can be very beneficial to directly explain dominant theory to clients and the steps for change offered in this book. None of this is a secret. The formula for change is easily explained. Also, through an open discussion clients understand what you are trying to do with your inquiries and approach. Clients become aware of how the words they choose are limiting and how important it is to clearly define a "get to" place.

Therapists are welcome to provide clients handouts of the examples of dominant thoughts offered in Chapter 11.

I have found that motivated clients who enjoy the counseling process and the world of psychology love this approach. It is also applicable for those clients seeking practical, down-to-earth approaches. Such clients may not be enamored by the often intuitive, psychodynamic discussions in which therapists are prone to engage.

While many therapists fall into the category of being intuitive in approaching problems, many clients are not. Most people and clients are sensory and approach problems at an immediately observable level. Consequently, the assessment and analysis of interpersonal dynamics do not always fit with clients' worlds. In such cases, once explained, a more direct mental programming approach may be fitting. It is easy to discuss dominant thought ideas and see if clients are attracted to them. Clients often take the lessons and concepts with them and begin applying them to many areas of their lives. Thus, dominant thought theory can be taught directly when clients appear inclined to embrace the process.

In order to apply dominant thought theory directly, it is best to offer a bit of explanation of the process along with why it is so important. Handouts explaining the process can be provided that briefly explain the process along with what can be expected. Once the theory is explained to clients, the first steps in using the approach are very similar to that of goal setting. That is, time is spent determining which dominant thoughts meet client needs. This in and of itself is of enormous therapeutic benefit. As noted, research indicates that a well-formulated, mutually agreed upon goal is most important to a working therapeutic relationship.[4] Once this is clarified and agreed upon, clients can form a present tense statement to be repeated for mental programming.

Therapists should also explain the natural reactions that are to be expected and methods for overcoming them. Chapter 7 addressed the demons that will arise that should be addressed in sessions and on handouts. Therapists can discuss with clients the results of repeating the dominant thoughts and possible adjustments. Progress can be assessed for client benefit and recorded for formal progress notes for insurance monitoring. The entire process will undoubtedly open up a host of discussion.

Please do not underestimate the practical application of this approach. The steps are very basic and easily grasped by even less insightful clients. Even if follow through by clients is weak, the process of addressing the language and dominant thoughts used in this change system is sure to result in insights that may stimulate change by another means.

Summary Thoughts

I hope these ideas are beneficial to therapists. **The bottom line for therapists is simply this: Therapy is priming.** The two are inseparable and, therefore, we should always be acutely aware of the dominant thoughts we use in the therapeutic dialogue.

Unfortunately, I also must mention the other conclusion I have reached from years of observing dominant thoughts: **The current**

language of mental health is, by and large, bad for your mental health. It is time we actively change this through a conscious focus on beneficial dominant thoughts.

As noted, these approaches are also applicable to any interaction and conversation regardless of the context. Those in the business world are certain to realize the benefits to applying the theory. Parents whom I have taught the theory have told me that they have completely turned around the atmosphere and behavior in their family by changing the wording used within the household when talking with children. It is hard to imagine a place where the concepts are not applicable.

Chapter 9 Key Points

- A careful choice of words is the cornerstone of effective therapy. Effective therapy primes appropriately; ineffective therapy primes poorly, or worse, detrimentally. Effective therapists are meticulous and precise in the words they speak because they are ever aware that they are triggering a host of related words in clients' minds and that those words create movement. There is no way around this.

- You cannot, not manipulate. We have no choice. The only question is: In what direction and in what manner are we manipulating?

- Empathic statements that include deficit statements are a wonderful example of the application of dominant thought theory and priming in the counseling dialogues.

- With embedded suggestions a priming message is delivered to the client by including it as a component of another statement. The client is not consciously aware of the dominant thought presented or that they are being primed toward future behaviors.

- Goals should be stated with an awareness of dominant thoughts that prime clients for desired behaviors.

- It can be very beneficial to directly explain dominant thought theory to clients and the steps for change offered in this book. As clients become aware of how the words they choose are shaping their life they can use words to change their life.

- Therapy is priming. Unfortunately, as it is frequently used, the language of mental health is bad for your mental health. It is time we actively move to change this.

Chapter 10

Concluding Thoughts and Previous Contributions

The general themes and ideas in this book are not new. They have been written about for years in various forms by a broad range of writers from scientists to self-help writers to success-promoting speakers. People have been talking about this stuff for years from an anecdotal, instinctive perspective. It is as though writers have intuitively known that thinking, self-image, and visualizations have a great deal to do with accomplishing goals and successful outcomes for almost any endeavor; yet, they have not been able to provide a research-based formula for the application. I see my contribution to these ideas as providing a scientifically based foundation and a much needed level of refinement to the formula for mental programming.

This contribution is now possible because recent research has provided substantiation and validation of the general ideas previously advanced by so many writers. This research has been repeated across a number of domains and, for the most part, has provided strong support for the idea that words (and other stimuli) influence and control behavior. Further, often to the surprise of those conducting the research, the manipulative power of words on behavior has been much more influential than previously imagined. The research of the last 20-30 years has blown away any suggestion that the impact of words is of little consequence. To the contrary, the impact and power of words has been judiciously confirmed.

This research is important because more and more people want to understand why something works before they are willing to try it. Hopefully this book has offered a healthy dose of scientifically based "why" to satisfy this need. To this end, I also have endeavored to remove the mystical, magical, metaphysical mumbo jumbo that often surrounds discussions regarding the impact of thoughts on success and life. If I have succeeded, the reader will be left with a practical, workable system for augmenting change through an understanding of the concept of dominant thoughts.

This system has also been distilled and refined to its basic elements while removing previous inefficient, fruitless components. It does not promise miracles without consistency. It makes no bones about necessitating the management of the mental backlash that is inevitable. While direct and basic in the methodology, there are no claims of easy, effortless results. This system parts ways with those approaches that mystically promote change without steady personal effort.

I feel compelled to give credit to those who have contributed to the understanding of mental programming regardless of the terms used to describe the process. Those interested in this topic will likely find pleasure in reading previous works. I certainly have myself.

Another reason I feel compelled to note previous work on the subject is to thwart criticisms from those who will say this has all been said before. Much of this has been said before; however, much of what I am saying has not. As noted, new research has led to refinements in our knowledge regarding how behavior is influenced and a more refined understanding of the factors that trigger preparatory thoughts in the mind. Thus, while the general themes have been generally discussed previously, the specifics have been lacking.

Below are just a few of the more popular, well-known writers that have written about approaches related to mental programming in one form or another. There are too many to include them all. I simply cannot read or keep up with the plethora of people writing about the topic. They are all over the internet and all over the board in their methodologies. Most of those below are classics in the field or some that I happened upon in my life. All can be searched and learned about on the internet.

William James, considered the father of modern psychology, wrote about the "principle of ideomotor action" as early as 1890 in *Principles of Psychology*.[1] The basic idea was that thinking about doing something stimulates the actual act of doing it to some degree. James's ideas are perhaps the earliest scientific deliberations leading to the concept of mental programming.

Psycho-Cybernetics,[2] written by Dr. Maxwell Maltz in 1960, probably spawned as much discussion on the topic of mental imagery as any book. Maltz realized the impact of positive visualization on desired outcomes and his work has inspired numerous self-help authors over the years.

Creative Visualization: Use the Power of Your Imagination to Create What You Want in Your Life[3] by Shakti Gawain has been another popular book on this topic that has survived the test of time.

Dr. Joseph Murphy wrote *The Power of Your Subconscious Mind*,[4] first published in 1963, that alluded to the idea of mental programming. Murphy mostly discussed affirmations and saw a strong link between the subconscious, spirituality, and religion. He went as far as to say that the subconscious was our link to God.

One of the premier books on the topic and an all-time best selling self-help book that has sold millions of copies worldwide is Norman Vincent Peale's *The Power of Positive Thinking*[5] that also strongly argued for the power of mental attitude on outcomes.

Many years ago I read Joe Karbo's *The Lazy Man's Way to Riches*[6] that was sold through ads in magazines that promised great wealth. He termed his system "Dyna/Psych" and suggested "Daily Declarations" be made to oneself. Karbo did not view his approach to be about positive thinking but rather about *positive action* that was promoted through the use of what he termed "super suggestions." Numerous books with similar approaches to achieving wealth have been and are still being published.

Shad Helmstettler wrote *What to Say When You Talk to Your Self*[7] in the early 1990's which elucidated the importance of internal self-talk on personal health and habits. Many other books have been written along these lines that borrow from the field of cognitive therapy.

One of the most recent forays into the topic is The Secret[8] by Rhonda Byrne mentioned earlier in Chapter 8. This quite mystical approach attributes success to the popular "Law of Attraction" which is kindled by attitudes and thoughts. The Law of Attraction strongly relates to ideas of mental programming and has been discussed by many.

These writers and a multitude more have endeavored to promote what research appears to be confirming: **The mind moves you and your listener in the direction of the dominant thought regardless of whether that thought is stated in the positive or negative.**

May your dominant thoughts guide you to much contentment and success.

Chapter 11

Implanting New Programming for Specific Habits

To learn to think is to learn to live.
Dan Custer

I realized the problem was me and nobody could change me except myself.
John Petworth

This chapter provides suggestions for dominant thoughts to program your mind for various goals and habits. From studying and understanding each of these sections, you should easily be able to develop dominant thoughts with which to prime your mind for virtually any behavior or habit. The steps are always the same. Identify what you are doing. Define the positive opposite for you. Make a present tense statement that you are doing the positive opposite and repeat. Once a realistic, functional dominant thought is formulated, the outcome is solely determined by consistently feeding the programming to the mind.

As a quick review, remember to think in the present tense and convey to your mind that the programming is to begin immediately. Avoid terms such as "should," "will," "going to," "need to," or any reference to doing action in the future. Of course, always think about what is desired and avoid the negative.

Having just said to avoid the negative many of you will note that in this chapter I veer from my own admonishments. Unfortunately, in order to describe and connect with the reader regarding what is desired and the habits we want to change, I have to momentarily leave the positive and refer to the habits in the undesired negative. For the obsessive readers, I am aware that I am doing this. It is just that the negative is such an ingrained aspect of our language that it is easier to communicate using common expressions and linguistic norms. Thus, in order to describe bad habits, I initially present them in the negative. When you become acutely aware of this aspect of our language, you begin to see what a detriment it is.

Before providing some examples of mental programming regarding specific habits, perhaps a discussion regarding realistic programming statements is appropriate.

Creating Realistic Dominant Thoughts: Understanding What We Can and Cannot Control

When creating viable dominant thoughts, it is important that you are clear in understanding what you can and cannot control in your life. No amount of mental programming is going to change things of which you have no control. Below is a brief discussion regarding what we cannot control. Without this understanding, you may be needlessly frustrated.

For simplicity's sake and because I believe this is a good source for this discussion, I am borrowing from William Glasser's Reality Therapy. Glasser's approach to therapy is extremely focused on taking specific actions that are evaluated by the client to have a chance of generating the changes desired. In his experience, Glasser discovered that many times the goals and changes that clients desired were unrealistic because they required that someone or some situation other than the client change. To deal with this, Glasser outlined goal areas that were unrealistic and unacceptable within the approach so that clients could realistically assess the viability of their goals within reality. Hence, acceptable goals are those created around specific actions that are within the clients' control and avoid areas outside of the clients' control.

Glasser noted that there are three primary areas of life that we cannot control: genetics, accidents, and other people. I will discuss each briefly.

One of things that we currently have the least control over in our lives is our genetics. While it appears that in the future this may change considerably, it goes without saying that there are considerable genetic abilities and limitations with which we are all born. We have little choice over the genetic hand we are dealt. Your basic physical appearance, height, hair color, etc., as well as potential abilities in various areas is determined at birth. Some people are naturally more muscular, some are born with perfect pitch, and some are born with a proclivity for math, while others appear to have artistic talent. Some are born with debilitating diseases and deformities while others possess great physical stamina. The variations are endless.

Interestingly, we live in a culture that has created a multitude of ways to alter physical appearance. These ways cover the gamut from clothing, to makeup, to hair color, to diet, exercise, to weight lifting, to plastic surgery. Most of us know someone who has markedly altered their physical appearance and provided a lesson as to what is possible.

Mentally, we also have enormous possibilities for change. Through serious study and practice, your mental capabilities can be nurtured and developed. Educational opportunities abound in our modern world. The decision to use these opportunities is up to you. Yet, some are born with serious deficits in their mental capabilities. Although your genetic makeup is the hand you are dealt at birth, it's up to you how you play that hand. Regardless, there are genetic limitations with which we must learn to live and realistic dominant thoughts must consider them.

The question of dominant thoughts changing genetics is quite interesting and beyond the scope of this book. Suffice it to say that there are a multitude of anecdotal examples of people changing physical problems with their mind. The degree to which the changes actually alter genetics has yet to be determined. Yet, it is clear that people have changed the physiological reactions in their body through practiced mental focus. It is difficult to determine the limits in these situations.

Accidents happen to all of us and we have little or no influence over their occurrence. You drive your car to work and run over a nail resulting in a flat tire. The flat tire may result in being late to work or a serious automobile accident. For the most part, you have little control over such events. You did decide to drive a car and, therefore, must be prepared to accept the possibility that you may have a punctured tire and the consequences. These possible consequences come with the decision to drive a car. You do have the choice to wear your seat belt, drive defensively, and obey the traffic laws. But even when you take precautions, accidents beyond your control occur.

In all areas of life you are to some degree at the mercy of randomness or fate. You do have the choice to take precautions and use good judgement in what you do. But, regardless of all efforts, we are all at the mercy of random events. Regarding accidents, dominant thoughts can instill behaviors that lessen their chances of causing harm, but no amount of mental programming can assure accidents will not happen.

The other thing that we cannot control is other people. However, that we can influence people is a possibility. It is important to recognize the difference.

We say we cannot control people because we recognize that people have free will. A person can choose what they will do. Even when given dire choices, people choose which direction to go. You can threaten a person with firing them, grounding them, beating them, or killing them; yet, even with the threat of death, people can choose for themselves. People are free agents. And, if they are willing to suffer the consequences, they cannot be made to do anything they do not want to do.

Yet, although we cannot control people, we can and do influence people constantly. In the above examples I described threatening consequences that influence people to do certain things. But, this is not the type of influence I want to discuss here. We also influence people in much more subtle ways. The primary way we might have influence on others is through what we say, how we say it, and what we do. Thus, if you want to potentially influence another to change, you must change what you are doing also. And, even if you do change your behavior, there is no guarantee that others will change.

There is an old expression, you can't change the past, you can't bring back the dead, and you can't make someone love you. Recognizing and avoiding unrealistic objectives is important to creating effective dominant thoughts. This is particularly true with regards to others. When you state your dominant thoughts make certain that they are directing your behavior and not expected to change something that is out of your control.

In summary, dominant thoughts should always be focused on things that are within the control of the individual stating them. Dominant thoughts should focus on small changes in doable behavior or end-goal states that are genuinely possible. Dominant thoughts that focus on others changing are of little value. Dominant thoughts that attempt to change the randomness of life are futile. Yet, dominant thoughts that guard against or utilize the randomness of life can be beneficial.

Therapists are welcome to and are hereby granted the right to copy the following specific sections only and use them as handouts for clients.

Mental Programming for Healthy Eating

I thought I would start with the one concern that is so prevalent in our culture—dieting. So, this section is written for those desiring ideas on mental programming for dieting and healthy eating in general. Because mental programming regarding eating teaches us so many lessons regarding words and language, this section will be given extra attention.

I am not going to discuss what foods you should eat or not. I am not going to discuss the underlying dynamics of your upbringing and the deep seated psychological dynamics fueling your eating habits. I am not going to discuss our ever-present social obsession with food or the incredibly stupid foods we eat. None of that. This section is about the mental programming necessary to eat in a healthy manner. You can analyze and ruminate over the above issues all you want; yet, until you reprogram your mind to eat healthy, nothing will change.

I also realize that there are metabolic imbalances that result in weight gain for some and of which mental programming may be of limited value. With this understanding, I approach this discussion with recognition of what we know we can change through mental programming.

Before delving into mental programming for healthy eating, let's examine eating from the perspective of the mind. Because it is so easy to eat without conscious thought and because there are so many priming cues in place to stimulate eating, eating is clearly a subconsciously controlled habit. You don't have to think to eat. We are so good at it, we can be eating and not even be consciously aware of it. You can eat while you do a host of other behaviors. We can eat and not even remember eating. Just like driving to work. Who has not had the experience of sitting in front of the TV eating a bag of potato chips then suddenly the bag is empty and we wonder where they all went? Oh yeah, this is one habit the subconscious is well-programmed to do. So let's begin here.

The foremost issue that must be dealt with in order to begin healthy eating is the mental programming in the subconscious.

Read that sentence again and meditate on it for a few minutes.

Don't make it complicated; unhealthy or healthy eating is undoubtedly a result of mental programming. And that's the good news. It's programmable. It's changeable. This is evidenced by the fact that millions have changed their eating habits and millions are in the process of doing it right now. Excessive, unhealthy eating is not some deep-seated genetically driven compulsion that is beyond human control. To the contrary, it is very controllable. The fact that eating habits vary tremendously between people and cultures is evidence of this.

The remedy is to consistently deliver the right thoughts to your mind and then allow the intuitive urges that follow to guide you. Empower yourself and welcome the empowerment into your life.

Let's take a moment and discuss eating from the perspective of priming cues and common attitudes.

The priming cues to eat are abundant. We are primed in social situations where food, often sweets or other less healthy food, is offered. When a fellow employee unexpectedly brings cake to work and offers it to you, the triggers are fired. When you sit down at a restaurant and see all those high quality, perfectly posed pictures of food on a menu and begin to desire items that you know are not good for you, you are likely being primed. When you come home from work and see the brownies on the counter that you had forgotten all about during your work day, those eating neurons are stimulated. You can also be primed by simply sitting down to watch TV or entering the kitchen or even the presence of certain people. In most instances you had not even thought about eating until something was offered or seen.

We are also primed to eat by psychological states such as boredom and loneliness. Any negative feeling can quickly become associated with eating when eating is used as a momentary "fix" for the emotion experienced. This is sometimes justified by labeling what you eat as "comfort food."

The same is true for positive feelings. We also use eating to celebrate life's momentary successes. However, none of the above states have anything to do with hunger; they have become tightly linked with eating and, if not held in check, lead to poor health and obesity.

In the situations just mentioned, we often conceptualize food as something that is controlling us. We think of food as something that has power over us. It is almost as if the food is giving off a cosmic force that is drawing us to it. Such conceptualizations are wrong and are psychologically and physically unhealthy. We are deceiving ourselves if we believe that a food substance has control over us. We are attributing a power to food that does not exist. This is because *the source of the strong urge to eat is your mind.* Food is only a trigger that sets off a series of previously programmed internal signals and urges. **The forces you are experiencing are internal, not external. They are in *your* head. The force is previous programming and such forces can be reprogrammed.**

Simply recognizing this fact can be helpful in controlling eating. The more you think in terms of raw truth—in terms of what is actually happening—the more capability you provide yourself in managing your life. Life is full of little deceptions that lead to unhealthy conceptualizations and unhealthy living. Understand what is actually occurring and manage the behavior at the source of control. This is the purpose here.

Years ago I would eat my morning cereal with a coating of sugar across the top. I would carefully load a spoonful of sugar and take care to coat the cereal such that each spoonful I ate included some sugar. The idea of eating cereal without sugar was extremely foreign to me. How could anyone eat plain cereal? How dull could a food get? Then, for some reason I do not specifically recall, I experimented with eating my cereal plain—no added sugar at all. Someone had said something about the evils of sugar or about getting healthy or some other combination of ideas that culminated in my willingness to try an alternative eating style for breakfast.

I can still recall how absolutely foreign the initial idea and experience was. Yet, I practiced eating dull, sugarless cereal for several weeks. Notice I used the word "practiced." I choose this word because that is what I was doing. The dictionary explains that when something is "practiced" it means "to perform or do repeatedly in order to acquire skill or proficiency." That is what I was doing. I was repeatedly eating my cereal plain in order to acquire proficiency at eating my cereal plain. Don't make it complicated. What resulted was very surprising to me.

After about two weeks of practice I had no desire to add sugar to my cereal. I liked the cereal just as it came out of the box. (It was very likely pre-loaded with sugar!) Now, the idea of eating that much sugar on my cereal was repugnant. I could not imagine going back to the "old way" of eating my cereal. I have never eaten cereal that I have coated with sugar since. I would estimate that to be for over 40 years. Two weeks of practice for a change that lasted over 40 years. That is an extremely high return on my efforts.

The point of this story is that it was not the sugar that controlled me. It was my mind. What changed was my mental programming. I changed the internal by changing the external and practicing. It should also be noted that it took about two weeks for lasting impact. We must allow time for the mind to rewire itself. Instant change is rare (but possible!). All new learning is a result of spaced repetition. The initial feelings, sensations, thoughts, and urges were to add sugar to my cereal. These were all temporary perceptions and had little to do with where I ended up. It is often quite difficult to see beyond the powerful signals and urges we have internalized. This is particularly true if they bring us pleasure, no matter how temporary and deceptive. With food, we create our own reality with regard to our needs through our mental programming. **With all food the critical change is internal. Reprogram your mind; change your mind's reality.**

Another topic that deserves discussion is diet plans. It is unlikely that you need to continue in search of the perfect diet plan. There is a new diet plan published monthly in newsstand magazines—they must have a positive impact on sales. Books touting the latest diet plan are abundant and continue to be published. Diet plans are abundant and many will work if you remain loyal to the program. While certain diet plans may work better or be more suited to your liking, consistency is likely more important than the plan you adopt. Setting aside the influence of medications, in the end it always comes back to the same fundamental scientific question: Did you eat more calories than you burned? Keep it simple and keep a clear perspective as you look beyond the hype.

Furthermore, you know what you should and should not eat for the most part. If you do not have good knowledge regarding quality, low calorie food, the series of books entitled *Eat This Not That*[1] and *Cook This Not That*[2] by David Zinczenko and Matt Goulding are excellent places to start. Undoubtedly, your brain already has a very good idea of what you should eliminate in your diet—sodas, french fries, desserts, and simple carbs are prime foods to start with.

Diets do not fail because the diet is not viable. Diets fail because of a failure to consistently follow the plan. (You should be thoroughly familiar with this consistency theme by now!) The primary component that is lacking in diet plans is a simultaneous change in mental programming. **Diet plans should be viewed as tools for the reprogramming of the mind.** Diet plans that do not ultimately change the mental programming regarding eating are of little value once stopped. Diets are only successful to the degree that those dieting adopt a new approach to food and eating for their entire life. If you follow a diet plan for months, reach a healthy weight, but never change your mental programming and assume you can return to your old habits, you will return from whence you came. Unfortunately, you have spent a lot of time on a short-term, short-lived solution.

The error those seeking a healthy weight continue to make is that they view the diet plan as the solution. Diet plans are not solutions. Diet plans are tools for enhancing a reprogramming of the mind—the real solution. Unfortunately, in order to increase sales, diet plans are marketed as solutions. Typically they are promoted as the ultimate solution to your weight problems. Do not be deceived; understand the benefits of diets and their limits. Use diet plans within the context of their benefits and accept them for what they are—an aid to new thinking. Do not expect more from a diet plan than a diet plan can give. If you perceive a diet plan as a solution, you are likely to fail in your endeavors. Use tools to your benefit recognizing that they are only vehicles to reach a goal of a lifestyle change.

In summary, **you do not need another diet plan; you need a mental programming plan to maintain healthy eating in a culture that promotes obesity.** Healthy eating is about more than just weight loss. The material offered here provides many ways to program the mind toward healthy eating.

I have yet one other comment regarding movement toward healthy eating. This is in reference to numerous myths and misconceptions about the benefits and need for food, and regarding genuine hunger. I have often heard people say they are tired and immediately link it to a need for food. This not necessarily the case. I had a student once tell me that he walked across campus and felt tired and needed something to eat. I doubt food was the issue considering his excessive weight. In many instances, this is just another false association. Every momentary negative feeling is not a result of a lack of food. To the contrary, many are just as likely from poor eating habits. Myths associating negative feelings to a lack of food are abundant. See through them.

Related to this is the issue of hunger. Most of us have never experienced genuine hunger. I am talking about the hunger experienced by those in countries where people are literally starving—a genuine physiological need for food in order for the body to function. You would likely have to not eat for many days in order to reach such a state. I personally have fasted for five days drinking only minimal liquids and did not even approach genuine hunger.

The "hunger" typically experienced by most is a result of pure habit strength and a result of primed associations. It is not physiological, it is psychological. Remember Jarod, the guy who lost weight eating Subway sandwiches prepared with very basic ingredients? He was once asked if he did not get hungry on his diet plan. His answer was exceptionally insightful and profound. He stated that, yes, he got hungry, but that he just assumed that being hungry was a part of dieting. In other words, he accepted that he was going to experience psychological feelings of hunger. However, he did not believe they were bad and necessitated eating more. He did not fall prey to the myth that all hunger urges required that he eat. To the contrary, he associated hunger with success. If I am hungry and not responding to it, I am being successful in my endeavor.

I personally believe that adopting a similar understanding and attitude is critical to successfully moving to a healthy weight. Not responding to psychological hunger as well as some hunger pangs is a positive to be embraced and is key to successful dieting.

Eating Word Binds

Similar to the world of smoking where you are either a "smoker" or "nonsmoker" and your dominant thought includes the concept of "smoking," the entire food and dieting realm has some interesting word binds also. Take for example the phrase, "I eat healthy." Not bad, but it includes the word "eat" which has to link to an enormous amount of unwanted behaviors. Would "I am healthy" be a better statement because it leaves out the idea of eating entirely? You will have to decide what fits your needs.

Yet, it is very difficult to move away from words associated with eating when programming the mind to move your body toward health. The way around this is to include words and themes such as "healthy," "sound," "appropriate," "sensible," "levelheaded," "balanced," "conscious," "mindful," "fit," and "aware" (Since we often eat unaware of the ultimate consequences), when doing your programming. Therefore, some of the mental programming toward a long healthy life, by linguistic necessity, may include words of questionable and conflicting value.

There is one word, however, that I believe we can and should avoid in our new mental programming. This word is "lose." Let's delve into this word as it provides a great lesson in understanding the importance of being precise and detailed when choosing words to program your mind.

Think about the word "lose." Virtually everything you lose you want back, except weight—another tricky word. If you lose your wallet, your purse, your password, your car keys, your dog or cat, etc. you want to get them back. It is difficult to think of something you lose that you do not want back. Except weight. The point is, the word "lose" has built into the meaning a need and yearning to get something back, *except in the almost singular case of weight.*

From this analysis of the underlying meaning of the word, it only follows that many people lose weight only to gain it back. Ironically, the gaining back of the weight lost is built into the meaning of the word they chose to describe what they wanted. When you say the word "lose," your mind most likely assumes you want something back! Very few understand the word bind in which they have placed themselves when using the word "lose." This notion is once again based on the premise that every word should be thought of as a cluster of words all with underlying additional associations and meanings. The cluster of words associated with "lose" most likely attach to the concept of "getting back."

I have found that the most common phrases used with regards to movement toward health are something like, "I need to lose some weight" or "I ought to lose some weight." Unfortunately, such statements are fraught with linguistic perils. First, as has been pointed out previously, the words "need to" and "ought to" are future tense. They only communicate to the brain that this is something that needs to be done and, worse, it only needs to be done in the future. No instruction of what to do *now* is submitted to the brain. No mental programming is offered. The only thing provided is a statement of fact without a summons for action. The use of the future tense is worthless with regards to getting anything done in the realm of mental programming.

Secondly, the word used to describe what is needed in the future is "lose" which comes with the built-in meaning of "getting something back." This is the very thing not wanted when dealing with fat. Further, the sentence uses the word "weight" which, in this context, is also what is not wanted. Such statements are quintessential examples of bad wording and horrible, unproductive dominant thoughts.

Please note that there may be contexts in which the word "weight" is useful, but not here. Only use this word when you are certain that it is in a context that benefits. For example, "I am a healthy weight." Similarly, words such as "eat," and "calories," should be considered with acute attention to context.

Getting out of such word binds is a bit tricky; you have to think out of the box so to speak. For years I have offered a unique and somewhat humorous statement of mental programming in my trainings that cleverly circumvents the above problems. The mental programming statement is this.

I shed pounds daily for no apparent reason.

Let's examine the advantages and power of this wording. First, the statement is present tense and instructs the brain to perform the action daily. There is no reference to the future. You should understand the practicality of this by now. Second, the sentence uses the word "shed" to describe the action desired. No mention of "losing" and all of the accompanying pitfalls. Shedding is the natural process of getting rid of something and *does not include the built-in meaning of getting anything back.* Think about it, do you want back that which you shed? (Well maybe, perhaps a bit of hair.) Now you're doing some real mental programming. What a beautiful, precise word to describe exactly what we want!

In addition, the sentence includes a statement recognizing that eating is an automatic, subconsciously controlled process. You do not have to think to eat and, most likely, your mind already knows how to eat in a healthy manner. Basic healthy eating approaches are commonly known. So, when you say, "...for no apparent reason," you are sending a message to your mind to eat in a healthy manner using the same subconscious control you formerly used to eat in an unhealthy manner. Note that the statement does not say that there is no reason for your shedding the pounds; it only states that the reasons are not "apparent." It only implies that you do not have to be consciously aware of the reason—that you do not have to be consciously thinking about what you are doing. The statement relinquishes control to the subconscious assuming it has the knowledge of how to eat in a healthy manner. However, if your knowledge of healthy eating is limited, this may not be an appropriate statement for you.

For the above reasons, this bit of mental programming is clever and powerful. This is a beautiful example of how to use language and words to program the mind with a dominant thought that focuses on what is wanted exclusively. Remember, the mind can only focus, it can only attend. So let's provide the mind with programming that only attends to what we want. Such pure programming statements are rarely heard by most. Get out of the box by putting such statements into your vocabulary.

Now let's get to some suggestions of effective mental programming regarding healthy eating. Many of these mental programming statements can also be used directly or tweaked for use with other healthy habits such as exercise, breathing clean air, etc. Statements are in no particular order.

I shed pounds daily for no apparent reason.
I eat healthy at all meals.
Everything I eat turns to health and beauty.
I am conscious of what I eat.
I am aware of what I eat.
I consistently recognize the relationship between calories and health.
I am aware of what I eat and the outcome.
I make a habit of eating a balanced diet.
I eat a balanced diet.
I consistently eat a balanced diet.
I eat appropriate portions.
I eat in a balanced manner.
I am acutely aware of fullness and walk away.

I walk away before fullness.
I walk away before full.
I leave the table early.
I drink healthy.
I respect my body.
I honor my body.
I appreciate my body in all I do.
I act to live a long life.
I eat to live a long life.
I act to be present for my children and grandchildren.
I eat to be present for my children and grandchildren.
I eat to benefit my body.
I eat to honor my body.
I eat to fuel my bodily functions.
I stay healthy.
I keep in mind staying healthy.
I focus on health.
Health is my ever present focus.
Balanced, healthy eating is my focus.

Exercise

Since we started with healthy eating, I thought I would follow up with exercise. It goes without saying that exercise and movement of just about any kind is better than sitting around stagnating. Many of the mental programming dominant thoughts in the section on eating can be tweaked to apply to exercise.

Incorporating exercise into our lives is just like everything else. It is largely a matter of planning, habit, and, initially, a bit of willpower. Good mental programming brings these elements to the forefront of your mind to fuel this habit. Your mental programming should be such that it makes exercise something that comes to mind when you are at those points in your day where you are not certain what to do next. Let's briefly examine some ideas that can feed and nurture exercise.

The word "exercise" may be a bit of a stumbling block for some. While the idea of exercise is delightful for some, to others it could bring to mind pain, ineptness, weakness, embarrassment, struggle, humiliation, and a host of other negative associations. There is no need to bring to mind such associations. One of the beautiful attributes of language is that we have a host of words to use that circumvent ineffectual mental links. To get around this you might use words like movement, action, stretching, nurture, motion, etc. that may have a more positive connotation and feel less threatening. Use your synonym finder in your word processing program to find the words that ring useful for you.

Another key to incorporating more movement into your life is to make it appropriate for your own level of fitness and to let the growth of your abilities come to you at your own pace and physical strength. The idea of pacing may be something you need to program also. There is no need to make it painful. The idea is to just grow into it gracefully—but to grow into it. Interestingly, those who exercise routinely in their life quickly reach a point where it becomes essential to their day, similar to brushing your teeth.

Perhaps a bit of self-exploration and self-examination are needed to find those particular areas regarding exercise that you need to tend to in your mental programming. The above ideas are just some of the places to start. As previously stated, start with something and, if it is not exactly fitting for you, the mind will morph it into what you need. Trust the process. Do the process.

Here are some ideas on what to program.

I exercise daily.
I recognize the benefits of exercise.
I recognize the benefits of movement.
I recognize the benefits of motion.

I recognize and act on the benefits of exercise/movement/motion.

I nurture my body with exercise/motion/movement.

I honor my body with exercise/motion/movement.

I appreciate my body and nurture it with exercise/motion/movement.

I feed my body with exercise/motion/movement.

I respect my body and exercise daily

I walk.

I walk daily.

I walk every hour. (For those sedentary in their work.)

I stretch.

I stretch daily/hourly.

I plan exercise/motion/movement daily.

I incorporate exercise/motion/movement into my life daily.

My day always includes exercise/motion/movement.

I exercise at my level.

I exercise with respect for my body.

I exercise and honor my body.

I grow in my exercise/motion/movement skills.

I cultivate my exercise/motion/movement skills.

I foster my exercise/motion/movement skills.

I pace myself as I exercise daily.

I exercise with an appropriate pace.

Movement is medicine.

Movement is my medicine.

I move because movement is medicine.

Breathing Clear Air*
(*Also known as smoking cessation.)

While we are on this health kick, let's take a look at breathing fresh air.

As someone who smoked for six years and later ran a smoking cessation program, this habit is one of which I am very familiar. Early in the smoking cessation groups I would always spend at least an hour of time having members define their personal opposite of smoking. The lessons learned from this exercise were foundational in forming the theories in this book. Why did it take an hour? Because no one who came to the group had ever thought about it! Defining your personal opposite of smoking was completely new mental territory for the members.

Inevitably, when I asked, what is the opposite of smoking? I got "not smoking" or being a "nonsmoker." When I asked, what is the opposite of smoking without using the word "smoke," people were always initially stumped. They had no positive opposite of smoking in their mind. They had not formed a well-worded dominant thought to move toward. Ultimately, a number of absolutely wonderful opposites were discovered. These were formed into mental programming and motivational statements by the group members.

The beauty of smoking cessation is that the body really does not like smoke. It does not want smoke in its lungs or in its system. It sent very strong signals to you about this when you first tried to smoke and found yourself coughing and gagging. Those who successfully overrode the negative reactions of the body became smokers. They were successful at overriding the innate programming regarding smoke and training the body to tolerate it. This does not take long because the addictive properties of nicotine quickly hijack the brain and convince it that it needs more nicotine containing smoke.

The wonderful thing about becoming a fresh air breather again is that there are parts of your body and brain that crave clean oxygen. These parts love getting back to health. Once the movement toward long life and fresh air is begun, there is a part of each of us that wants this badly and the cravings for smoke will diminish at an ever increasing pace. The longer you go without smoking, the urges to smoke arise less often, are shorter in duration, and become easier to wait out. Eventually, most people reverse. That is, you will not want to be around smoke. You will not like the smell of smoke. You will not be able to imagine that you ever desired cigarettes. Many habit changes include a similar reversal phenomenon, but few as strongly as smoking. You will only want to breathe clean air and have fresh breath.

As with all habits, mental programming is an essential ingredient in an effective smoking cessation plan. However, this habit is so powerful that other techniques and approaches should be employed also. In the groups we utilized behavioral techniques, family support, medical support, group support, financial incentives, and anything possible that could aide in the quest. For those wanting to live a long life of breathing clean air, I recommend you go at this habit with every tool at your disposal. And there are many wonderful, effective approaches available. Study what is available. Learn from the millions before you that have beaten this habit. As formidable as it may appear, it is very doable. Literally, millions of people have become fresh air breathers and every one of them initially wondered if they would be able to do it.

I will tell you one of my favorite mental programming stories regarding smoking. There was a man who struggled to define a meaningful smoking opposite. He thought and thought and, finally, he looked at me and said something similar to this. "I am a control freak. I control every aspect of my life except cigarettes. Cigarettes tell me when I have to smoke them. This is what upsets me about smoking." From this statement we concluded that the opposite of smoking for him was being in control. With this knowledge, his new dominant thought became, "I am in control." When he said it aloud, he noted that this had the precise feel of the state he wanted to create. The point of this story is that your opposite and someone else's opposite may be completely different concepts. You have to find what works for you. Start with the best thoughts you have, repeat them, and let your subconscious hone from there.

Below are some wonderful mental programming thoughts for those desiring long life and health. As noted, the programming for health and exercise are easily adapted to apply here.

I begin with a beautiful example of a well-worded mental programming statement for smoking cessation: *I breathe clear air*. This is one of my favorite dominant thoughts regarding this habit. It is simple, direct, and a pure opposite. It is rarely thought; yet, serves its purpose superbly. It was developed by a student of mine after considerable pondering.

I breathe clean air.
I am a good model for my children.
I save money.
I am in control.
I have fresh breath.
I am a good kisser.
I live long.
I am a long liver!
I take care of this body temple I am in during this phase of existence.
I live a healthy lifestyle.
I appreciate the fresh air I breathe.
I show appreciation for my body and lungs.
I promote a long life.
I care for my body.
I smell clean.
I appreciate health.
I promote my health.
I support the health of my family.
I honor my body with clean, clear air.
I respect my body with clean, clear air.

I show love for my body.
I show love for my lungs.
My car smells clean.
My house smells clean.
I desire to live a long life.
I act to live a long life.
I take care to live a long life.

Fingernail Biting

I feel compelled to include fingernail biting in the book. This is because, after presenting hundreds of trainings and keynotes on dominant thought theory for over 30 years in which I worked with audience members regarding their habits, this is one of the most common habits encountered. So, let's give it some attention.

Interestingly, fingernail biting is another one of those concepts that common language simply does not provide a positive opposite word or phrase to describe. You either bite your fingernails or you do not bite your fingernails. The struggle to find a positive opposite dominant thought is so convoluted that I am stuck with having to use the word "biting" in order to begin the discussion. As you know, this is a word I most certainly want to eliminate from the mind. Unfortunately, for the moment I surrender to the pitfalls of our language. But only initially, for the sake of beginning the discussion!

When working with those who desire to stop biting their fingernails I always ask, "What is the positive opposite of biting your fingernails for you?" I almost invariably encounter either, "Not biting my fingernails," or "I don't know." Then I leave them for a few minutes to search their mind for an opposite. It is easy to see the internal struggle. I am convinced that one of the reasons the habit is so hard to break is that there is simply no easily accessed, positive opposite dominant thought. Think about it. Have you ever in your life encountered a word or concept that clearly defines the positive opposite of biting your fingernails? From the perspective of this book, you will always move in the direction of the dominant thought regardless of whether it is stated in the positive or the negative. The linguistic bind is very strong here.

In searching for a positive opposite two questions arise. The first is, What would the outcome be or look like when the old habit is obliterated and a new habit is formed? The second is, What would I have to do in order to avoid doing the habit? From these answers we can begin forming positive opposite dominant thoughts.

Let's start with the first question, defining the outcome. If you did not do this habit you would have long, extended, fingernails; healthy fingernails; beautiful, attractive fingernails; natural fingernails, etc. (You could also describe cuticles similarly if desired.) Below are dominant thoughts based on these concepts.

With regards to the second question, the behaviors necessary to form a new habit, you would have to keep your hands down or keep your hands low. Or perhaps keep your hands relaxed and calm. Obviously, you cannot bite what you do not have near your mouth.

This leads to a third approach. Is the fingernail biting associated with nervousness, indecision, anxiety, or a similar emotional state? If so, perhaps statements such as "I am calm," "I am relaxed," "I am poised," offer an opposite state.

Before leaving this topic I want to relay an experience regarding this habit. For years I was the guest speaker at a local leadership group's annual Communication's Day. Dominant thought theory was always my topic. One year a young woman in the audience wanted to work on her fingernail biting habit. After the usual process of getting her to define the positive opposite of the habit she came up with, "I have long, beautiful nails." Several years later I returned to my regular annual presentation and upon approaching the front desk a young woman thrusts her hands in my face and exclaimed, "Look!" Having had no immediate, specific memory of the past presentation, I had no idea what I was supposed to see. This was quite obvious and she then stated, "You don't remember me do you?" I apologized for my poor memory and she reminded me of the training several years back as she displayed her long nails to me of which she was very proud. She then expounded on the process and how well it worked when she simply delivered an effective dominant thought to her mind.

Based on these approaches to finding positive opposites, below are some ideas for dominant thought programming in order to grow long, healthy, beautiful nails.

I have long, beautiful nails.
I attend to my nails.
I file my nails.
I care for my nails.
I manicure my nails with care.
I maintain my nails with care.
I have healthy nails.
I show appreciation to my nails.
I appreciate and honor my nails.
I have long nails.
My nails extend to an ideal length.
My nails are attractive.
I have attractive nails.
My nails are natural and well-manicured.
I keep my hands down.
My hands are relaxed.
I am calm and relaxed.

Being on Time

Here's a habit that, when cultivated, not only helps you but others as well. To be late—a word we want to eliminate—on occasion is understandable; however, there are those who have cultivated the habit of tardiness—another word we want to omit. Consistently not arriving on time is one of the habits of which others quickly take note and genuinely despise. So, for those who have been reprimanded and scorned for their consistent lack of punctuality and want to do something about it, or those who just want to make things run a bit smoother, this section is for you. By the way, if you fit this habit category, check your brain and vocabulary for words like "punctual" or "early" or "prompt" and assess if they have a foreign feel to them. This is your first clue.

The benefits of being punctual are numerous. So, let's begin by focusing on the benefits of arriving early that will naturally lead to the words and phrases that describe the ultimate objective and mental programming desired.

Very few habits are more disrespectful of others as habitually not arriving in a timely manner. Frankly, it's rude, arrogant, inconsiderate, thoughtless, self-centered, impolite, and bad-mannered. Now there are some words that should arouse some uncomfortable feelings that may motivate needed action. Such a habit is disastrous for relationships and is a good way to not get invited or to find yourself frequently driving alone in order to catch up. It only follows that the benefits of punctuality and promptness are respectfulness, kindness, consideration, thoughtfulness, politeness, and being well-mannered. Ultimately, these characteristics lead to better relationships. So, these words give us really good dominant thought end points.

Another benefit to punctuality and promptness is a reduction in personal stress—another word we would rather not bring to mind. (Why do we always mention "stress" when we are trying to reduce it and create poise, peace, and calm?) On the short list of things people can do to bring poise, peace, and calm into their life, being prompt is always beneficial. The rush of being late is a great stress creator. If you want to de-stress your life one of the simplest things you can do is arrive a bit early to everything. Try it. It is amazing how much better things go with this simple adjustment. In addition, the extra space you create in your life provides time for unexpected delays and interruptions further creating that poise, peace, and calm so needed.

Being on time requires planning. Planning is a necessary component to promptness and punctuality. Do you plan? You need to plan to be on time. Without planning, promptness is quite difficult. So, perhaps the idea of planning is something you need to incorporate into your mental programming relative to punctuality. A bit of self-examination quickly reveals the needed words for your new dominant thoughts.

Below are some mental programming dominant thoughts for creating calm, peaceful, poised, respectful, considerate, punctuality in your life.

I am punctual.
I am prompt.
I respect others by being punctual.
I respect myself by being punctual.
I tend to myself by being punctual.
I respect others' time.
I arrive early.
I always arrive in a timely manner.
I plan my time and arrive early.
I remain poised by arriving early.
I calm my life by arriving early.
I get there with time to spare.
I appreciate others' time needs.
I respect others' time needs.
I am respectful of others' time and my time.
I tend to others by arriving early.
I safely get there.
I plan for safety in my travel and movements.
I bring poise and calm into my life by arriving early.
I bring peace into my life with punctuality.

I honor my friendships by arriving on time.
I honor my relationships with punctuality.
I am well-timed in all my arrivals.
I plan my schedule respecting myself and others.
I plan with awareness.
I plan.

Getting Things Done

"It's amazing how long it takes to complete something when you are not working on it."
R. D. Clyde

OK, for clarity I am going to say one time what we are talking about here: procrastination. That's the word everybody uses and that's the word we do not want to say ever again. If you want to experiment with yourself, note all the associations you have with that word. I bet most of them are bad and unhelpful. So, drop it from your vocabulary if you want to become an accomplisher.

Now, think of all of the things associated with getting things done. Words like starting, completion, acting now, efficiency, and time management. These are the concepts you need to feed your mind.

I don't need to lecture here, but we are talking about one of the primary factors that determine success, happiness, contentment, and an overall meaningful life. Enhance your ability to complete things and you change your life. If you need to work on yourself in this area the list below is a good place to get some ideas to feed your mind.

One of my absolute favorite quotes of all time comes from Einstein. He said, "Nothing happens until something moves." The depth of this quote is extraordinary. It is true at all levels from the world of physics to our everyday lives. Meditate on this. The opposite of procrastination is "focused movement" or "focused action." How often do you say that dominant thought to yourself? Probably never. So, get focused, get moving. Get efficient with time.

Now I do, I do now. (I used this one myself for years!)
I start and finish.
I act now.
I act today.
I act meaningfully.
I use this day fully.
I move into action now.
I do what needs to be done now.
I start, I complete what I start.
I use now.
I complete.
I complete today.
I accomplish now.
I do, I complete.
I am doing what needs to be done.
I exploit the moment.
I use my minutes.
I endeavor now.
I act in the moment.
I work now.
I am an efficiency expert. (Another personal favorite.)
I use time efficiently.
I use time effectively.
I am efficient with time.
I accomplish now.
I am a model of focused movement.
I am a model of focused action.

Getting Organized

Similar to being punctual and getting things done, getting organized is one of those rather simple, mundane achievements that can have a tremendous impact on your life. Because of the complexity of living in our modern world, our lives are often an endless stream of chores and tasks. Pay the bills, cook the meal, feed the pet, keep a list of phone numbers, send the cards, get gas in the car, sort email, sort the mail, recycle the recyclable, wash the dishes, check on the laundry, do the homework, do the housework, get dressed, get undressed, sort the drawer, and on and on the list of daily tasks goes. Many times even the most mundane tasks such as getting dressed become taxing because clothes are not sorted in a functional, organized manner.

The consistent act of organizing has much more impact on our lives than many realize. Those who are organized get more done, have less stress, and more free time than the disorganized. They also likely have better relationships because they do not waste other's time with their disorganization. How many of you have disorganized friends that regularly infringe on your time as a result?

If you are one of those people who constantly finds yourself walking all over the house or office, or backtracking in order to get things done, this may be an area that needs some mental programming.

The good news here is that the most common term to describe what is needed is a positive term—"organization." Organization is the opposite of unorganized, which beneficially, includes the word "organized." For the sake of studying unproductive dominant thoughts, opposites of being organized or organization would include chaos, muddled, messy, disorderly, sloppy, and careless. Do you ever use these words to describe your life? If so, drop them.

Related to being organized we have a wonderful list of related terms and concepts. These include being prepared, planned, ordered, systematized, structured, methodical, sensible, functional, consolidated, arranged, categorized, managed, and coordinated to name a few. Note your mental and emotional responses as you read these words; there is information in these gut feelings and reactions. It is very easy to create mental programming from this list.

Getting organized is really a matter of focusing on creating an efficient, structured, systematic environment around you. Those lacking this component in their life have simply not tuned into and focused on these matters. They do not approach life with attention to function. In order to get organized, the first step is to direct your mind to attend to functional, organizational aspects. You do this by directing it to focus its attention toward issues regarding the words listed above. Then, when an organizational adjustment is need, you do it.

With the rapid accumulation of things in our world today, remember that discarding the unnecessary is just as vital to organization as sorting and categorizing. Many times, deciding what to keep and what to discard is the critical component or first step needed for organization. As such, some of the mental programming directives below include these notions.

I am organized.
I organize daily.
I create a place for things.
I put things in their place.
I organize efficiently.
I organize for efficiency.
I create an efficient, structured, systematic environment
around me.
I am systematic.
I am structured.
I am methodical.
I categorize.
I make the time to organize.
I plan in a systematic way.
I organize for utility.

I organize for success.
I organize to remain calm.
I organize to move efficiently.
I consolidate when possible.
I eliminate the unnecessary.
I exclude the unnecessary.
I eliminate when needed.
I eliminate excesses.
I treat waste as waste.
I eliminate waste.
I gain from eliminating the unnecessary.
I gain from eliminating the superfluous.
I put like things in one place.
I place needed things conveniently.
I store needed things conveniently.
I plan my day.
I plan sensibly.
I write lists.
I create lists and follow the lists.
I consult lists for efficiency.
I organize to create free time.
I structure to create free time and calm.

Building Savings and Wealth

The accumulation of money is a rather common goal, particularly in American culture. Yet, with all the books and programs on how to get rich, it is amazing how few people really do it. Mind you, people do it. However, the data on the accumulations in American's savings accounts is dismal.

Take a moment and think about the underlying attitudes and behaviors necessary in order to accumulate savings. You should study money, study what the wealthy do (Also, study what the poor do and do the opposite.), read books on money, understand compound interest whether working against you or for you, respect money, save money whenever you can, spend wisely, use coupons, look for economic ways to live, conserve, plan, keep good financial records and check them regularly, always balance your checkbook, be frugal, never buy in haste unless you absolutely know it is a bargain, be measured, calculated, slow in all purchases, investigate all purchases fully, be very leery of too-good-to-be-true offers, very rarely take the first offer, live below your means, seek wise counsel and make sure the counsel is wise, and invest time and money in educating yourself for a rewarding career, to name a few.

On the "don't do" side of the equation, don't gamble, don't play the lottery (My state's lottery is referred to as a "tax on ignorance" by one of my state's congressmen.), don't lend money without solid collateral, don't buy impulsively, don't live beyond your means, don't invest in things you do not understand fully, don't hang on to losing stocks, don't buy cars you can't afford or don't need, don't let compound interest work against you, don't avoid facing your financial reality, don't delay dealing with money issues, and on and on. In *The Millionaire Next Door*, authors Thomas J. Stanley and William D. Danko also point out that you will not be wealthy by being a welfare system for your family. This book is excellent reading on the subject.

If wealth or just better savings is your goal, take a look at the lists of wealth building ingredients above, pick one that is applicable for your needs and current weaknesses, and begin programming your mind. Start somewhere.

Remember, there are millions of people who dream and think about wealth and never get anywhere. At the most basic level, they do not think the correct thoughts and do not take effective actions regarding money. Yes, at the broad, basic level it is just that simple. The details get more complicated.

Before going any further with this discussion, I must comment on the effects of environment, genetics, family, randomness, luck, etc. in the accumulation of wealth and much of your success and life's direction. Without going into an extensive analysis on the subject, I am very aware that a multitude of random factors make up your life's course. If you believe that success is not determined in part by random events, you are patently wrong. Recent research on success has confirmed that random events play an enormous role in determining one's success and life's course. Random events influence our lives much more than the average person is aware and much more than the success gurus selling their books and DVDs are ever going to admit and tell you.

On the other hand, serious practice across time, formally known as deliberate practice, also plays a significant role in your life. Serious study, continuous effort at the right thing, effort in and of itself, trying things, and "going for it" also plays a significant role in your life's position as well.

To think that life is determined solely by randomness or by personal effort exclusively is incorrect. Your life's outcome is a combination of these two broad ingredients. Unfortunately, even with your personal efforts, it may not work out. On the other hand, you may find that a significant number of things work out in your life from luck and you wonder why you are so fortunate.

The bottom line is this: **If you attempt nothing, there is a greater probability that nothing will happen; if you attempt much, there is a greater probability that something will happen.** Life is largely random, but, the more chances you give yourself the better the odds. The more you try, the more likely something will work out. There is a general truth to the common motivational theme that success is a result of lots of failures. Yes, if you do not find yourself successful, you probably have not made enough mistakes. This should more accurately be stated as you have not made enough mistakes, *learned from them, and made appropriate adjustments*. Hence, if at first you don't succeed, try again, either with a different method or at something else. It is also beneficial to keep this in mind: If the horse is dead, dismount.

Mental programming is about increasing your odds in a random world. Mental programming is about controlling the aspects of life you actually can control. Mental programming is about creating direction in the midst of randomness by programming your subconscious to do things and respond to things in a manner that increases your odds for success. You cannot control the random events that affect your life. You can absolutely control your own mental programming and your own behaviors. Mental programming gives you greater control in areas that are controllable.

Perhaps a bit of a side note on the psychology of acquiring wealth is appropriate here. Anthony Robbins[3] noted in one of his earlier books that you cannot become that which you resent. This is a very serious and deep psychological truth. If you resent the wealthy, if you continually make negative comments about those with money, you are sending a message to your subconscious to avoid becoming wealthy. Through continuously demonstrating such an attitude, your subconscious will lead you toward decisions and actions that avoid the accumulation of money. You must show a respectful, positive attitude toward the wealthy to have wealth. There is nothing about the accumulation of wealth, in and of itself, that is inherently bad or negative or unworthy.

Many years ago when I first read Mr. Robbins' observation I contemplated the meaning for months and realized, if I wanted to have more, I needed to make an internal attitude shift. At this later point in my life I am absolutely confident that moving from a position of resentment to a position of respect was a necessary factor that led to the financial stability I now enjoy. Effective mental programming will bring forth similar values and attitude struggles that may need to be adjusted for goal attainment to occur. Perhaps a statement such as, "I respect wealth," is needed?

Below are some mental programming dominant thoughts from which to begin your financial mental programming. Pick one that best suits your needs and hone from there. Read the list noting which words stimulate your internal voice. Grab those words that are meaningful to you and make your own dominant thought. Note that all statements direct personal actions. No statement depends on the universe or metaphysical forces for the magical attainment of wealth. No statement assumes wealth from positive thinking only. If you want to try to wish for wealth, be my guest, but don't bet on much happening.

I look for and act upon potential money making opportunities.
I seek, study, and judiciously act upon money making opportunities.
I seek, study, and prudently act upon financial opportunities.
I save regularly.
I study money.
I study wealth.
I respect wealth.
I respect money.
I review my financial status monthly.
I am aware of where my money comes from and goes.
I appreciate and use money wisely.
I study the actions of the genuinely wealthy.
I respect the wealthy.
I learn from the wealthy.
I seek wealthy models.
I spend wisely.
I research all purchases.
I plan, I conserve.
I read books on money management.
I keep accurate, up-to-date financial records.
I always balance my check book.
I am frugal.
I plan for the long term.
I live below my means.

I recognize and enact wise spending habits.
I cultivate wise spending habits.
I cultivate the habit of saving.
I observe and adopt the habits of those with money.
I save.
I invest in my education.
All of my actions demonstrate respect and appreciation for money.
In all of my actions I am financially prudent.

Writing a Paper, Book, Thesis, Dissertation, Report, Etc.

As you may suspect, this is an area of mental programming that is especially dear to me. I have struggled with the burden of writing for years. Even after numerous articles, papers, and a book, I still struggle to move myself to complete writing endeavors. Yet, I have gotten it done and have developed a number of ideas on what is needed to get things written.

It does not matter if you have a book, article, dissertation, thesis, report, term paper, blog, newsletter, or personal letter to write, the essentials are the same, you have to sit at the computer and peck. Nothing writes itself. The key is systematic action. Thinking or worrying or stressing over such work does not get it done.

Because this is a topic that is dear to me, I am going to approach it a bit differently. Rather than discuss unproductive thoughts per se, I am going to offer some tips regarding writing that address the thoughts that so often lead to stagnation. In this instance I am going to note some simple tips and approaches that you should keep in mind when it comes to writing. Related ideas can be found throughout the internet. From an understanding of these points you can build the appropriate dominant thoughts for yourself.

First, to make the task easier, start with what you know has to be written and let the, as yet, unknown components sit by the wayside for the moment. Too often, people delay writing because of concern over the parts they are not sure of. They have a clear picture of one aspect to be written, but are in the fog on other aspects and, thus, delay. This is a completely incorrect approach. Always start with what you know and later move to what you don't know. Even if the part you know appears minor and insignificant.

For example, if you are writing a dissertation or thesis and know you have to type up the references, do them. Don't say to yourself that part can wait. Do what you know and let the other components grow in time. Interestingly, when you start writing the known components, almost inevitably, an aspect of the previously unknown component will clear up and you will know what to do. In this way, you piecemeal forward.

Second, write down any part of anything you know you will have to write. One of the beautiful and powerful aspects of the personal computer is that you do not have to write linearly. You can write in a completely random order and cut and paste things together later. Get anything "on paper" or, in actuality, in a file. So, if you have merely one sentence or one thought that you know you want to state, put it down. Thoughts always link to other thoughts. Anything always leads to something. Let it happen.

Third, allow and appreciate a sloppy first draft. Getting something written poorly is much better than nothing written at all. With the computer we can edit with ease. So, not only do you not have to write linearly, you don't even have to write clearly and pretty. Just slop down the thoughts and edit later.

Years ago as a college professor I was required to publish to get tenure. I had an idea for an article but no refinement. What I did was so effective I amazed myself. I simply wrote the ideas down in the most absolutely basic, crude language and got them on paper. I wrote the ideas in the simplest, everyday language that would never be acceptable for publication. Then I converted the sentences to acceptable language. Then I used the computer's synonym finder to replace unsophisticated language with "academic" sounding terms. (Unfortunately, academia likes to think that complex, run-on sentences with fifty-cent words has something to do with knowledge.) The article was immediately accepted for publication.

In writing the article, a phrase such as "This whole thing started when..." was later refined to "The origins of...." A sentence such as, "It's really a bunch of crap to think that it's going to work if you blab to parents about what their kids tell you," was later refined to, "It is central that counselors remain cognizant of the need for confidentiality when working with preadolescents." I am sure you get the picture. Write, then refine. All good writing is a result of good editing.

Fourth, never worry about your opening or closing. Worry over how to start is often a roadblock to getting things written. Relax about the opening. As was just noted, write the parts you know and let the opening and closing come to you later. I have seen many a graduate student fail at finishing a thesis or dissertation because of a lack of understanding of these first four principles.

For those in graduate school working on a thesis or dissertation, here's a helpful tip. Write something, anything and give it to your chair or committee member. They will tell you what to do next. They have been through the process so many times that they will readily know what needs to be done. So, let them guide you. If you do not hand them something to read, they cannot guide you to the next step. Tell them you know it is not perfect and what is ultimately needed, but that you wanted to get something written to get an idea of what to do next. Let them do the hard thinking. It's really easy for them to sort through this stuff.

Fifth, don't set deadlines; set work schedules and dates. Deadlines are threatening, work schedules are doable. Don't require that you have to complete a section or component by a certain time. Simply set times when you will write regardless of the amount. For example, make an appointment with yourself to write for one hour each morning. Set aside times for writing with no expectations regarding the amount done.

Amounts are burdensome; getting small bits accomplished is fulfilling and easy. The famous science fiction writer, Ray Bradbury, said he was successful because he had a habit of writing 1000 words a day. That was his daily goal and he recommended programming this habit into your life. Search the internet on his approach and tips if interested.

How did I get this book written? My primary dominant thought was, "I write the book daily." I also wrote this on my daily to-do list, except, I shortened it by removing the vowels. I wrote IWRTHBKDLY on my to-do list. I am not sure where I got this tip, but, I liked it. It planted the dominant thought I wanted. As I mentioned previously, when I was stuck and fumbling I repeated, "I fumble forward." Study the words. I gave myself permission to write bits and pieces without a clear sense of the ultimate outcome. Yet, note that I said "forward." The thought was that I was always making progress—I just allowed myself to do it haphazardly. This way I motivated myself to continue even in the midst of uncertainty. And it worked. The thought was so present in my mind that I felt an internal drive to write almost constantly.

One final thought is of the utmost importance and deserves serious attention. With all tasks there is a period of time where you transition from what you are currently doing into the work at hand. With no task is this truer than with writing. That is, in order to get your writing done you must understand, accept, embrace, and provide for transition time. You must allow for the gradual shifting of attention. It is a natural process. There is no way around it; therefore, you must move to a position of complete acceptance of transition time.

Complete acceptance means you allow transition time to have its space. You must accept that you move into doing the task rather than instantly start. Those who do not embrace transition time will find it to be a mental and physical barrier to accomplishment. This must stop if you are to get any writing done. By the way, one of the characteristics of successful people is that they understand and embrace transition time. Successful people do not fight it; they learn to effortlessly live with it naturally. Dominant thoughts for the acceptance and management of transition time are provided below.

Remember, consistency is the key. Everything ever written was written one letter, one word at a time. Here are some dominant thoughts to get you started. Read them and tune into those that strike you. Mix and match thoughts.

I write daily.
I write the (book, thesis, dissertation, paper) daily. (IWRTHBKDLY)
I fumble forward.
I appreciate editing.
I write what I know needs written.
I write something, anything; but I write.
I always write the parts I know first.
I write what I know.
I write what I want to say.
I embrace a sloppy first draft.
I appreciate a sloppy first draft.
I honor a sloppy first draft.
I write, then edit.
I appreciate and utilize editing.
I honor writing.
I love the sound of the keyboard peck.
I sit and write.
I write, then refine.
I peck daily.
I appreciate my chance to edit.
I edit.
I appreciate the writing process.
I love the writing process.
I embrace the writing process.
I allow my subconscious to provide the writing ideas.
I note all ideas immediately.

I write all ideas immediately and later refine.
I put it down.
I peck it down.
One peck at a time, consistently.
One word at a time, consistently.
One sentence at a time, consistently.
I feed the writing process.
I support the writing process.
I comfort my writing.
I placate my need to write.
I nurture my writing.
I embrace transition time.
I nurture transition time into writing.
I gracefully move through transition time.
I respect and honor transition time.

Moving Away from Worry, Anxiety, Stress

Take a look at the title of this section and the word "worry." For the word "worry" only, try to write a title that considers and examines worry without using the word "worry" and that accurately conveys the message. It is very difficult, but not impossible. Just what is the opposite of worry without using the word "worry?" We actually do not have a word that is the direct opposite of "worry" in our language. Similar to smoking, we have many words that convey states opposite of worry, but no clear, specific antonym. No wonder people have so much trouble eliminating this habit.

I, too, am stuck in this word bind. So again, forgive me for initially using the very words I want to eliminate.

Because the concepts of worry, anxiety, stress and other similar negative states are related, I am going to lump them together in this discussion. However, I am going to give worry the greater attention. It appears to be a core ingredient in many undesirable emotions. As before, we will begin with a discussion of the concept and, from here, build ideas of positive opposites from which to construct dominant thoughts.

Filling Voids with Negatives

My favorite approach to understanding worry stems from the idea that worry is filling voids with negatives. Let me explain. Whenever you have an event or situation that you do not know the reason behind what is happening or the outcome, or an outcome of which you have no control, you experience a psychological void in your life. Your lack of an explanation or control can be very uncomfortable. You have a space where there is no knowledge to comfort you as to what has happened or a space in your life where you do not have control. Consequently, you feel helpless and this fuels worry.

For example, your friend says she will meet you at 3:00 pm; however, she does not arrive. As the clock moves farther past 3:00 you have a void in your knowledge of why she is not there. You do not have an explanation for what is occurring. Now here's the interesting thing. What do we almost inevitably begin to fill that space with in our mind? Positive, pleasant explanations or negative, worrisome explanations? Almost inevitably, the less you know regarding why she is late, the more likely you will fill the void with negative explanations.

This is when you start wondering if she was in a car wreck, or had a health problem, or got held up in bad traffic, or forgot all about you, or that she stood you up and doesn't like you anymore, or some other catastrophic explanation that your mind is so adept at conjuring up. When you examine worry closely, it is almost inevitably the act of filling of psychological voids with negatives. The same applies when you do not have control over a situation and your lack of control results in you thinking of all of the negative things that could occur.

Such instances are foundational for the creation of worry. The fundamental component is not knowing something or not having control and the ability to change the situation.

Mind you, as explained earlier, realistically preparing for potential complications and snags is a key characteristic of successful people. I am not against planning for negatives. It is important to understand that there is a big difference in planning for potential negative events and simply filling voids with negatives. In fact, preparation for possible complications is one antidote for worry.

Filling voids with negatives when there is no available explanation and when all the thinking you can do would only be unproductive guesswork is the road map to infertile thinking otherwise known as worry. Similarly, thinking that producing a plethora of negative outcomes in your mind will change a situation of which you have no control is the essence of the formula for worry.

This tendency toward the negative is likely biologically ingrained. Dr. Rick Hanson is an expert on this topic and discusses the problems that arise from it in his latest book, *Hardwiring Happiness: The New Brain Science of Contentment, Calm, and Confidence.*[4] He notes that we detect and process negative events faster and that we store more of them in our memories. Further, our negative bias not only increases the negative, it decreases the positive. This is not an easy process to overcome. However, with practice, the positives in our lives can be brought forward to a much greater degree. Dr. Hanson explains methods to do this in his book. Similarly, if you work to overcome filling voids with negatives, you can diminish worry. Yet, if you do not do the work, I can assure you nothing will change.

One of my favorite examples of filling voids with negatives that has happened to me personally occurs when the boss calls you in the morning and asks if you could meet with him/her at 2:00 that afternoon. Of course, you agree and the conversation quickly ends with you having no idea what the meeting is about. You now have four or five hours of mental thought time to assess the purpose of the meeting. What happens? You almost inevitably think of every negative thing you have done and every negative outcome that could occur. Did they discover that I stole a ream of paper for my home use? Did he/she hear about the negative comments I made about his/her partner at the office party? Has he/she heard something about my private life that makes me a liability to the company? Am I going to be fired or moved to another position? By the time of the meeting you are in a minor panic. When you get to the meeting it turns out to be something of marginal importance like planning a birthday party for an office member. You hate planning parties but are so relieved to discover the meeting was not about the tumultuous worries you conjured up, you immediately agree! Your skill at filling voids with negatives has resulted in you agreeing to do something that you find quite annoying and unpleasant. Ouch!

Similarly, anxiety is the highly skilled ability to fill voids with negatives. Stress has some of the same qualities along with various other components like poor planning, being out of your comfort zone, as well as facing unknowns, and having a lack of control.

From this perspective of worry, anxiety, and stress it becomes apparent that the positive opposite we seek is acceptance of the unknown. Wow, that's not so easy. Yet, if you do not program your mind to accept what you do not know and cannot control, you will inevitably fall into the filling-voids-with-negatives trap that stimulates worry.

So let's talk about accepting the unknowns that happen so often in life. This is not a new idea. Life is full of unknowns. In fact, more of life is unknown than is known. Philosophically, the existentialists call this resulting struggle "angst" and point out that it is an unavoidable part of life that everyone must face. There is no escaping the angst of the unknowns of life. These unknowns create and are the result of the random events that so often determine our life's course. Life is full of random events which are more prevalent and controlling of our lives than known events. Those seeking to delve into this area might read the writings of Nassim Taleb who expounds on these ideas in his books *Fooled by Randomness*[5] and *The Black Swan*.[6] However, be forewarned that this is not easy reading by any stretch of the imagination.

At this juncture we all have a choice: Either worry about the unknowns or accept what we do not know and focus elsewhere where we do have knowledge and control. In summary, the essence of worry is a lack of acceptance of the things we do not know about or control. And it is here that we begin forming insight into the real opposite of worry—acceptance of the unknown.

Building from this understanding we can begin developing mental programming that moves toward acceptance and flowing with the unknown and the emotional states that follow such as calmness, peace, good cheer, trust, contentment, etc.

If you are one who is prone to excessive worry, I am almost certain that the mental programming statements below will be uncomfortably foreign to you. You will read them and experience a sense of impossibility. Or perhaps they will appear impractical in your world of concern. Nonetheless, there will be a strong sense of rejection to the ideas put forth. If this is the case with you, then this is also a sure sign that your current mental programming needs adjusting. Frequently, the more foreign the new mental programming thoughts appear and the more rejection that arises as you read them, the more you need to embrace them. Ironically, rejection of the ideas reveals a need for the ideas. Read them daily until some sense of practical use emerges in your mind. Start with what you can embrace partially and build from there.

I flow with life.
I accept all aspects of life.
I accept the unknowns of life.
I embrace the unknowns of life.
I move forward in all circumstances.
I act upon that which I can and let go of the rest.
I let go.
I let go where appropriate.
I am at peace with life's uncertainties.
I move with life's uncertainties.

I flow with life's uncertainties.
I flow with the unknown.
I accept the unknowns of life.
I am fully aware of the randomness of life.
I embrace randomness.
I remain calm in life's unknowns.
I remain calm with life's uncertainties.
I only hang on to what I can impact.
I only hang on where I can control.
I am calm with uncertainty.
I am at peace when I walk with the unknown.
I influence only where I can.
I align with life's uncertainties.
I align with the unknown.
I align with randomness.
I progress in spite of uncertainties and unknowns.

Test Taking

As an academic and licensed professional, I have had to take many tests. Thus, similar to writing endeavors, this is a topic that is dear to me. Therefore, I am going to approach this topic by immediately moving to the necessary ingredients for effective test taking and limit discussion of the host of negative mental programming statements that often accompany testing. From this understanding you can construct appropriate dominant thoughts for yourself. There is limited benefit in focusing on the negative and, by now, you should have a good idea how to build opposites from your own ineffective programming.

Being able to remain alert, poised, focused, deliberate, and appropriately calm during test taking is a skill. It is a learnable skill that requires practice at the right things. In order to practice the right things, it is helpful to mentally program your mind to focus on and be alert to the elements necessary to have good test taking skills. Let's look at a few.

No amount of mental programming is going to give you information you have not studied. Likewise, I doubt the universe or mystical forces are going to put knowledge in your head either. So, you have to study. Remember, all learning is a result of spaced repetition. This means you have to study, give it a rest, and study again, over and over. If you get it the first time, great. However, it never hurts to double check on your knowledge level if you want to consistently do well. If you are not willing to use spaced repetition to acquire knowledge, your chance of success at test taking is greatly diminished.

In addition, when you study you must practice the exact skill that will be required of you when you take the test. That is, recalling and applying the information. One of the biggest mistakes students make when studying is to over and over again put information into their brain without practicing pulling it out—recall. When recall is not practiced, students often take the test and cannot retrieve and apply the information needed. They often say they knew the material but could not bring it forward for the test. The reason this has happened is that they have not practiced recalling the information when studying. The process of putting information into the brain and the process of pulling information out of the brain are different. You will only be good at the one you practice. So, when you study, you must practice recalling the information. By the way, if you practice recall, you are automatically practicing input. Yet, if you only input information, you have not practiced recall.

Another rudimentary element of successful learning is to learn the meaning of the words you are reading. That is, look up the meaning of each and every word you do not understand. Do not skip over words thinking that the material will make sense without them. It won't. In fact, the avoidance of learning the meaning of the terms necessary to understand the material you are studying is another primary, fundamental error of students. I know this well myself, as I used to not look up words. Today, I constantly seek the meaning of words I do not understand and, boy, it makes learning so much easier!

When you break down the basic components of what you are required to do for high school, college, and so forth, the largest portion of what you are required to do is learn the terms used by a discipline. I believe that it could readily be argued that the greatest extent of what you are required to do to get a degree is to learn many sets of terms associated with the areas you study.

L. Ron Hubbard was an egotistical, radical, cult-creating eccentric. Even though he did write about concepts somewhat related to what I am presenting in this book, it does not appear to me he ever presented a coherent theory. He did, however, offer a wonderful insight into the process of learning and the importance of learning the meaning of words. He wrote, "When reading a book, be very certain that you never go past a word you do not fully understand. The only reason a person gives up a study or becomes confused or unable to learn is because he or she has gone past a word that was not understood." There is an enormous amount of truth to this. Learn your words.

So, here we have three fundamental components that lead to effective studying: spaced repetition, practicing recall, and learning your words. Focusing on these three ingredients will get you prepared for the test. There are many other test taking tips readily available to anyone seeking guidance. Seek them out and note which you need to begin programming your mind to overcome.

The next element is to remain alert, poised, focused, deliberate, and appropriately calm during the test. Why not simply bring those words to mind? If you know your material, the next step is keeping psychologically cool. As a side note, I write "appropriately calm" because research indicates that being either too nonchalant or casual toward testing, or being too nervous about test taking are both detrimental. Ideally, one should be a bit stimulated and pumped up for a test; yet, not so much that it becomes a detriment to recalling information.

When I was applying to a doctoral program in psychology I had to take the Graduate Record Exam or GRE. I literally studied three nights a week for a couple of months. Several days before the exam I concluded that more study was of little benefit and that I had to focus on the psychological aspects of the test taking process. I knew I needed to focus on the specific task of test taking. I also knew I was prone to sloppy reading. Sloppy reading occurs when you scan through the words without deliberately reading each word. Sloppy reading is responsible for millions of communication errors. It is also what occurs when students do not learn their words. It is the kiss of death when taking tests. Students are notorious for sloppy reading multiple choice questions and, as a result, missing the answer. When their test is later returned they often comment that they misread the question. They then kick themselves for their sloppy reading.

With my awareness of this I began repeating to myself the following statement: "I read every word of every question and every word of every answer and my mind delivers the answer when recognized." I was very deliberate in placing this instruction in my mind in the days preceding the test. This was the perfect directive for the moment as it was the opposite of sloppy reading and the precise instruction needed to obtain a high score. It worked and I was later accepted into graduate school. I offer this story to present an example of the mental programming needed to manage the test taking process once the knowledge was acquired.

Putting the above thoughts together, below are some examples of mental programming dominant thoughts for managing these aspects of test taking.

I study across time.
I practice spaced repetition.
I practice recall.
I practice recalling every piece of information I study.
I learn, I recall, I break, I learn, I recall, I break.

I study, I break, I study, I break.
I learn my words.
I use the dictionary consistently.
I use the dictionary when needed.
I study with immediate access to the dictionary and I use it.
I use the dictionary.
The dictionary is my learning coach.
The dictionary is my learning guide.
I always learn the meaning of the words.
I am clear as to the meaning of the words.
I am a serious student.
I approach learning seriously.
I earnestly learn.
I earnestly practice effective study techniques.
I earnestly employ effective study habits.
I cultivate effective learning skills.
I am prepared, I am poised.
I am calm and focused.
I am poised and focused.
I am as focused as a bullet in flight.
I am prepared, relaxed, focused, alert.
I approach each question with deliberate, precise attention.
I recognize what I know and deliver it on tests.
I read every word of every question and every word of every answer and my mind delivers the answer when recognized.
I am prepared, calm, and focused.

Contentment and Self-Esteem

There are very few objectives that are as poorly understood and misguided in the affirmation world than issues of happiness, self-esteem and the like. Much of the public is also naïve to these emotional states. This is reflected in the everyday language regarding them. For example, when asked what they want, people often reply, "To be happy." Even worse, they refer to happiness as coming from someone else with comments like, "They make me happy." In the midst of such linguistic confusion and misunderstandings, I thought I would offer a bit of philosophical examination and then some ideas on mental programming relative to contentment and self-esteem.

I have been a bit hesitant to take on these issues. The reason for my hesitance is that neither can be accomplished directly with mental programming. They can be greatly aided with effective mental programming, but they are not appropriate goals in and of themselves. You cannot be happy just by repeating you are happy. You cannot really feel good about yourself just by saying you feel good about yourself.

The reason this does not work is that both of these states are secondary consequences. In this sense they are byproducts. They are secondary consequences and byproducts of doing what is truly meaningful to you. (To some degree, you could argue that all emotional states are byproducts.) Therefore, I will not offer any mental programming statements such as, "I am happy," or "I have good self-esteem." I do not believe such statements will work and I believe they are detrimental if not backed by meaningful actions. From the perspective of this book, the notion that you can simply think yourself happy is a flaw of the affirmation domain.

It is important to note that the states of being happy or joyous are actually temporary. While you can have an overall happiness about your life and experience joy from time to time, happiness and joy are, for the most part, temporary, passing emotions. They are by nature short-lived. We recognize this when we get suspicious of people who appear happy all the time. I know I am suspicious of people who constantly display happiness. I wonder if they are paying attention to the world around them.

That being said, what are legitimate goals within this realm? Legitimate, lasting states to be sought include objectives of contentment, being pleased, growing, and having a meaningful life. However again, these objectives are only accomplished as byproducts of doing meaningful endeavors. All mental programming to reach these ends must include activities and attention to the root origins of each—that is, meaningful action.

The question now becomes what things do you need to do to feed your self-esteem and to feel content with your life? This is everyone's personal life's quest. This is part of the discovering of the self. Some would say this is the ultimate goal of each individual. You may need to work on relationships, do service to others, build something, write something, tend to someone, grow something, nurture something, let go of something, organize something, serve your god, etc. Only you really know. You have to discover and decide what is meaningful to you.

Never let your self-image stop you from
taking steps to improve your self-image.
Author Unknown

Denis Waitley, a great motivational speaker and expert on the habits and attitudes of successful people, offers perhaps the best definition of happiness I have ever run across. After searching I cannot find the direct quote of his full definition; however, I remember his message very well because of the impact it had on my life. Dr. Waitley stated that happiness is a byproduct of winning your own self-respect and the respect of others by pursing activities and goals that you think are truly worthwhile. Thus, happiness can never be a goal and should not be approached as a goal. The goal should be the pursuit of meaningful activities of which happiness is a secondary consequence.

Happiness as a direct pursuit is doomed to fail. It usually ends up with self- indulgence, escapism, and hedonistic pleasure seeking which does not deliver the desired state in the end. Dr. Waitley goes on to say that you cannot buy happiness. You also cannot wear it, drive it, inhale it, drink it, swallow it, inject it, or travel to it. You will not find it at the mall or on Amazon or eBay. You can't marry it, sleep with it, or give birth to it. You cannot depend on another person to provide it to you. Happiness is a pure inside job.

Interestingly, truly meaningful behavior does not have to be complex or grandiose. It can be as simple as taking care of the neighbor's dog or cleaning the toilet if you view these as meaningful acts. You also do not necessarily have to be successful at the end goal. Happiness is a byproduct of the pursuit, not the outcome. You may be involved in a competitive sport or activity in which you love to participate. However, you could rarely win and, yet, receive much happiness from the pursuit and participation of the activity. You have probably seen interviews with people who have pursued something and failed. When asked if they would do it all again, many reply, "Yes." The pursuit was the root of the happiness, not the outcome.

To this end people often ask the question: What would you do if you knew you would not fail? Perhaps a better question is: **What would you do *even if you knew you would fail*?** Obviously, this second question draws attention to the pleasure of the pursuit and not the end goal.

The same ideas apply to matters of self-esteem, self-worth, self-regard, etc. It is difficult to feel genuinely good about yourself if you never pursue anything you really believe to be meaningfully worthwhile. It is worth mentioning here that the pursuit of meaningful activities requires a level of brutal honesty on the part of the pursuer. If you constantly conform to social expectations that you do not truly believe in and remain involved in situations you really do not feel are worthwhile, happiness is going to be difficult to achieve.

So, the mental programming regarding happiness and self-esteem will be centered on seeking meaningful activities. If you focus here, happiness and self-esteem issues will take care of themselves. By the way, byproducts are formally defined as "...secondary results, unintended but *inevitably produced* in doing or producing something else."

Another point that is foundational and frequently addressed in philosophical discussions of happiness deserves mentioning as it provides a basis for mental programming. There is no contentment, being pleased, meaningful growth and living without gratefulness and appreciation. These are the foundational psychological prerequisites to contentment, etc. I was once at a seminar where the speaker emphatically declared that the short cut to happiness is gratitude. What a profound life truth. If this strikes your interest, perhaps you should read about the foundational importance of gratitude when seeking meaning and contentment. This has been written about extensively. If you do not appreciate anything it will be hard to find happiness. The blogger and author Matt Furey promotes the proposition that before New Year's resolutions are listed, one should first list the things from the previous year for which one is grateful. This is a good topic to search on the internet. It is also a good place to focus and direct the mind.

Based on these ideas, below are suggestions for mental programming for those interested in their happiness and self-esteem.

I seek meaningful activities.
I do what is meaningful to me.
I am aware of what is meaningful.
I do one truly meaningful act each day.
I am alert to what produces contentment.
I am grounded in the reality of contentment.
I grow in doing what is important.
My time is used for the important.
My actions reflect what is truly important.
I set aside time each day for the truly important.
I expand my awareness of meaningful actions.
I assess the meaningfulness of my actions and act accordingly.
I see the importance of often perceived undersized actions.

I recognize those things for which I am grateful.
I recognize and state aloud those things for which I am grateful.
I tune into the things for which I am grateful.
I am ever aware of my gifts.
I am grateful.
I appreciate.
I appreciate and express my appreciation.
I expand my awareness of appreciation and gratefulness.
I send my gratefulness inward and outward.
I direct my gratefulness inward and outward.

Public Speaking

What's the number one fear in America today? Public speaking. It continually ranked higher than death, cancer, terrorists, AIDS, snakes, spiders, plane crashes, and a host of other fears. With such a high ranking, I guess I had better give it some attention.

It appears that the primary concern regarding public speaking is that others will be judging you negatively and that they will be hypercritical of mistakes. As someone who has done hundreds of trainings throughout the country and the world, I can tell you that, by and large, this is a highly unwarranted concern. The only speakers who get judged harshly in public statements most often don't really care about the audiences' needs. These are politicians who speak to constituents for whom they are not representing their concerns, or corporate leaders who double talk about concerns for employees who know the real focus is on profits and executives' large salaries. The average person who has to speak before a group is almost universally supported by their audience who is sitting there usually grateful that they do not have to do the speaking themselves.

Have you ever been in a setting with a nonprofessional speaker who was struggling and obviously nervous speaking before the group?

What were you thinking? Were you criticizing them or feeling sorry for them? By and large, audience members are supportive of their speaker. Audiences have much empathy for their speaker. Because so many have a fear of public speaking, the real bottom line fact is that the audience is supporting the speaker and concerned for them. If you make a mistake when speaking, I suggest you just stop, slow down, think, and correct your error. Audiences really don't care if you make a mistake if you correct it. They are much more patient and understanding than people give them credit.

The keys to public speaking are to be prepared and realize your audience is internally supporting you. The audience is thankful you are doing the job and not them. I am not going to discuss at length how to make a speech other than to make a couple of points.

First, know your audience and speak to them regarding their concerns. Remember everyone is always listening to radio station WIIFM—What's In It For Me. So, make certain that you are addressing the audience with an awareness of their concerns. Second, have your first minute of the presentation memorized cold. The first moments before an audience are typically the most difficult. To manage this, know and practice what you are going to say to the point it is automatic. Learn your opening to the point the subconscious is in control. This way you give yourself time to get comfortable as you move into the rest of your presentation.

Take a look at the mental programming statements below which are designed to have you in an appropriately aware mental state. Along these lines let me provide you with my favorite piece of mental programming I have used when speaking before large audiences. Here it is: "I love them and they love me." How's that for a mind set before going in front of a crowd and speaking? Send out your love and accept theirs.

I love them and they love me.
I recognize and accept my audience's support.

I am prepared and accepting of my audience's support.
I respect my audience, my audience supports me.
I am calm, I am relaxed, I am prepared.
I send and receive support.
I understand that my audience empathizes with me.
I empathize with my audience.
I prepare, I understand, I deliver.
I display all of my humanness when I speak.
I allow the genuine me to shine when I speak.
I understand my audiences' concerns.
I am prepared to address my audiences' concerns.
I correct my speaking mistakes with care.

Sports Programming

There are so many specific mental programming protocols for the various sports, I will address this area in general and then use golf as my principal example.

Before going into specifics, let's look at factors that separate the pros from the amateurs. I suggest that two overarching factors are strategic. Professionals act with full intention and recover from their errors immediately. That is, you must approach what you want to do with maximum commitment and with completely focused attention to its accomplishment. I hate to say the forthcoming words but I will to make this point. You must not be doubtful or reticent or tentative when you commit to do an action. Avoid such words and behaviors. You approach the move with absolute commitment. This is what the pros do every time over and over.

Next, you must cultivate the ability to recover from mistakes. Everyone makes mistakes in their game. The difference is that pros recover, amateurs don't. Once a mistake is made, the professional athlete isolates it from the rest of the game. The moment a mistake is concluded, it is, in essence, forgotten relative to the next move. The next move is approached again with the full intention of completing it successfully.

I believe these two abilities are universal throughout all sports and are the foundational, vital attributes that must be developed to advance. How do you develop them? The same way as everything else, through practice and spaced repetition. You become aware of developing these skills and you practice them across time until they become automatic. There is no proficient person in their respective sport that has not cultivated these skills to the point that they are automatically done by the subconscious. How do I know this? I see it all the time. In actual sports participation there is no time to stop and work through mistakes. You must move on immediately. Therefore, if you cannot move on with full intent toward your next move automatically, you will not succeed. The only way to do this is to cultivate the skill at the subconscious level. You must do it until it becomes automatic, without conscious thought.

That's it for the general goals and objectives regarding sports.

The key to creating effective mental programming for your particular sport endeavor is to very specifically define the actions and mental state that are necessary when you execute your sports motions correctly. I will use the one sport that I am familiar as our example, golf. When conducting trainings on dominant thought theory, I always like to throw in a golf example or two for the sportspeople in the audience. I will not address every aspect of golf, just a couple of key points.

The primary point I want to address with golf is contact with the ball. The entire game of golf is dependent on the moment the club head hits the ball. Every other nuance taught culminates at the moment the club head hits the ball. This is the point at which attention to the task must be maximal. Virtually all sports have similar moments.

Unfortunately, when people are initially taught golf they are given the instruction, "Keep your eye on the ball." This is, actually, ineffective and potentially detrimental. The reason this instruction is so ineffective is that it actually promotes moving your head before you make contact. The reason for this is that a golf ball is leaving the tee or ground at over

150 miles per hour. An extremely well-hit drive can be moving over 200 mph. So, when you focus on keeping "your eye on the ball," you are asking your brain to keep an eye on a ball getting ready to take off at 150 plus miles per hour. The brain instinctively knows the ball is going to go very fast. The only way you can actually *keep your eye on the ball* is to move your head early. You cannot move your head at 150 plus miles an hour. You cannot actually see a golf ball moving that fast from a close side angle. It is simply too fast. In order to follow your instruction, you would have to move your head *before you hit the ball* in anticipation of the speed it will be going!

And what happens when you try to keep your eye on the ball? You turn your head early taking your eye off the ball, and, as everyone who has attempted this treacherous game has learned, you either hit the ball in the wrong direction or miss it altogether!

Obviously, we need a better mental instruction.

Here are a few of my favorite instructions for hitting a golf ball.

See contact.

Watch the club head hit the ball.

Kiss your right shoulder. (Right handed players.)

Kiss your left shoulder. (Left handed players.)

Keep your head down.

Notice the difference in the instruction. These are much more specific and do not have the inherent flaw when you try to keep your eye on the ball.

This type of analysis and mental programming is similar to what is required to hone your focus in other sports. Define precisely as possible a clear, positively worded statement that includes the necessary focus for the game you play and then repeat. Look for flaws in your language that may stimulate the negative outcomes. If there are many moves for your game, such as in basketball, you have to generalize the statements. (As should be obvious by now, phrases such as "Don't lose," "Don't let them get past you," "Don't drop the ball," etc. should be removed from your vocabulary. Ugh!)

Here are some ideas from which to build.

I am as focused as a bullet in flight.
I act with full intention.
I watch the ball.
I see the ball.
I recover and refocus.
I mend and refocus.
I constantly move forward.
My mind is on the play at hand.
My mind is on the next move.
I support the focus of my team.
I immediately move toward recovery for my teammates.
I learn from my actions and act with full intention. (Notice what I do not say here!)
I constantly learn; I constantly progress.
I analyze issues after the game, learn, and move forward.

Finding Your Life's Direction

This section is for a very special group of people—those who do not know what they want. This lack of direction could be in numerous areas. It is most often related to career choice. However, it could also be related to hobbies, avocations, relationships, or any other life decisions, directions or interests. Such people feel lost, so to speak—without direction. Sometimes people have pursued a direction only to realize it is not for them. They are clear that the present direction is not right for them; but, they have no idea which direction to go. Also, there may be an important decision to be made and the options and answers are just not clear. Even the approach to making the decision could be a vague, muddled array of rambling thoughts.

I have been there and have known and still know those in this position. Blessed are those who are clear early in life regarding career choice and directions they want to pursue. The struggles of those seeking to find themselves can be extremely painful.

In such cases, the mind may need to be programmed around a number of themes. The programming may be such that it enhances self-awareness—awareness of talents and interests. The mind may need to be programmed to avoid biases that may have clouded a clear understanding of one's self or possibilities and, thus, be programmed toward truthfulness and the new. The programming may include themes of openness and honesty with oneself or others. Hence, the programming may need to increase awareness of subtle clues and insights delivered-up from the subconscious. Alternatively, one may need programming that increases awareness of any information that may be helpful in creating some direction or decision.

Also, the programming may likely include themes of going out and literally testing options as opposed to sitting there thinking. The enduring quote from Francis Bacon is so true: "Truth emerges more readily from error than from confusion." We learn more from attempting and being wrong than sitting around thinking in states of confusion. How deeply insightful. Here you can see how mental programming promoting experimentation and trying things could be essential to breaking through the unknowns of life.

Based on these thoughts, below are some mental programming statements that build from these themes. Because this particular area of mental programming is very broad and unspecific in nature, so are the mental programming statements. In a sense they could start sounding like some affirmations. However, if you are lost, these statements provide a starting point. Statement refinements will come to those who seriously pursue their life quests. Keep in mind I am just throwing out ideas that may or may not strike a chord relative to your particular situation. Chances are you will have a sense of the programming you need. If not, just grab one and try it. What have you got to lose?

I explore.
I explore things and learn.
I am aware of subtle clues that inform me about me.
I am aware of all information that guides me toward understanding myself.
I am open to new ideas and directions.
I seek guidance from those who are experienced.
I allow myself to experiment and learn.
I learn from the experience of myself and others.
I am aware of options.
I seek options.
I constantly learn about vocations.
I seek vocational guidance.
I try different things in order to learn about....
I experience to learn, I learn from experience.
I welcome new perspectives.
I embrace and welcome guiding information.
I test the new and different.
I am acutely aware of my strengths and talents.
I explore my talents.
I develop my talents.
I accept feedback regarding my strengths and talents.
I act on new knowledge of myself.
I accept confusion. (If you fight it, it gets worse. So perhaps you need to accept it first?)
I fumble forward toward understanding myself.
I am honest with myself about myself.
I study that which may guide me.
I investigate that which may guide me.
I learn from others.

Tips on Talking to Children

One of the places that I am most confident of the importance of understanding and applying dominant thought theory is in talking with children. I know this for two reasons. First, I watch and listen as parents talk with their children. I hear the dominant thoughts and I see the results. The evidence is before us everywhere. As a mental health professional I get even more opportunity to see the results of beneficial or damaging language parents use. It is a pervasive occurrence that clients enter therapy struggling with detrimental themes from their childhood programming.

The second reason I know that dominant thoughts have a significant impact on communications with children is because of the changes that are reported to me when parents learn to talk to their children after becoming aware of the dominant thoughts they are saying. A couple of instances stand out in particular.

A man heard one of my presentations years ago and decided to seriously test the theory. He went home and began speaking to his children with an acute awareness of the dominant thoughts he was planting in their minds. Needless to say, he reported that in a matter of weeks a significant change was clearly evident in his children's behavior. He became a fan of the theory and raved about the impact he had in his family through changing his language style. I know this because he was also the leader of a local professional group and, as a result of his personal experience, he brought me back to speak a number of times.

I once spoke to a lady who was divorced with three children and admitted that her household was chaos and confusion. After one of my trainings we talked briefly regarding what she was literally saying to her children. Needless to say, the ever-so-common phrases we hear were present. "Stop fighting," Stop yelling," "Stop hitting," to name a few. After a brief discussion regarding alternative phrasing she left. Two weeks later I received a letter telling me her household was changing rapidly. She was astounded by the new atmosphere that had developed as a result of delivering a completely new array of dominant thoughts to her children. My sense was she had been a bit skeptical regarding the efficacy of the approach and was now a believer. And here's the kicker. She was so impressed with the change in her children that, in the closing lines of her letter, she wrote she was now ready to start working on herself!

In order to be thorough in this discussion, I am going to present common statements spoken by parents and alternatives with much better dominant thoughts. With a little thought and practice, it is easy to learn the application of this approach. This list is short but the concepts are readily grasped.

Don't hit your little sister.	Keep your hands to yourself. Be kind.
Stop fighting.	Cooperate and get along.
Stop yelling, stop screaming.	Talk quietly.
Don't pick that up.	Only look. Keep your hand down.
Don't touch that.	Look and keep your hands by your side.
Don't you lie to me.	Tell me the truth now.
Don't give me a hard time.	Be cooperative. Be nice.
Don't bring the cell phone the table.	Leave the cell phone in to your room.

You're going to fall and your neck!	Get a good grip as you move from break branch to branch. Maintain your footing and balance at all times.
Be careful not to cut yourself.	Always cut away from yourself. Be aware of the direction the blade is going.
Don't ride your bike in the	Ride in the yard and driveway street. only.
Stop playing on the computer.	Focus on your homework.
You are not dumb.	You are smart and capable.
Don't be nervous.	Remain calm and relaxed.

Notes

Chapter 1

1. Denise C. Park, "Acts of Will," *American Psychologist* 54(7), (1999), 461.
2. John A. Bargh, Mark Chen, and Lara Burrows, "Automaticity of Social Behavior: Direct Effects of Trait Construct and Stereotype Activation on Action," *Journal of Personality and Social Psychology* 71(2), (1996), 230-244.
3. John A. Bargh and Tanya L. Chartrand, "The Unbearable Automaticity of Being," *American Psychologist,* 54(7), (1999), 462-479.
4. Susan M. Andersen, Gordon B. Moskowitz, Irene V. Blair, and Brian A. Nosek, "Automatic Thought," in E. Tory Higgins and Arie W. Kruglanski (eds.). *Social Psychology: Handbook of Basic Principles* (2nd. ed.) New York: The Guilford Press, 2007, 138-175.
5. John A. Bargh, "Automaticity in Social Psychology," in E. Tory Higgins and Arie W. Kruglanski (eds.). *Social Psychology: Handbook of Basic Principles*. New York: The Guilford Press, 1996, 169-183.
6. Jenny Hogan, "Would You Like Fries with That?" Available from: www.inspiringchampions.com/press/pages/publishedArticles/WouldYouLikeFriesWithThat-S&SN-08-09.html [Accessed Aug. 2016]
7. Southwest Sydney Business Enterprise Centres, Biztips, "Up Selling and Cross Selling – Would You Like Fries with That?" Available from: https://www.swsydneybec.com.au/up-selling/ [Accessed Aug. 2016]
8. Rob W. Holland, Merel Hendriks, and Henk Aarts, "Smells Like Clean Spirit: Nonconscious Effects of Scent on Cognition and Behavior." *Psychological Science* 16(9), (2005), 689-693. doi:10.1111/j.1467-9280.2005.01597.x
9. Lawrence E. Williams and John A. Bargh, "Experiencing Physical Warmth Promotes Interpersonal Warmth," *Science* 322, (2008), 606-607.
10. Hans IJzerman and Gun R. Semin, "The Thermometer of Social Relations: Mapping Social Proximity on Temperature," *Psychological Science* 20(10), (2009), 1214-1220.
11. Charles S. Carver, Ronald J. Ganellen, William J. Froming, and William Chambersand, "Modeling: An Analysis in Terms of Category Accessibility," *Journal of Experimental Social Psychology* 19(5), (1983), 403-421.
12. Aaron C. Kay and Lee Ross, "The Perceptual Push: The Interplay of Implicit Cues and Explicit Situational Construals on Behavioral Intentions in the Prisoner's Dilemma." *Journal of Experimental Social Psychology* 39, (2003), 634–643.

13. Nicholas Epley and Thomas Gilovich, "Just Going Along: Nonconscious Priming and Conformity to Social Pressure," *Journal of Experimental Social Psychology* 35, (1999), 578–589.
14. Aaron C. Kay, S. Christian Wheeler, John A. Bargh, and Lee Rossa, "Material Priming: The Influence of Mundane Physical Objects on Situational Construal and Competitive Behavioral Choice," *Organizational Behavior and Human Decision Processes 95,* (2004), 83–96.
15. Jens Forster and Nira Liberman, "Knowledge Activation," in E. Tory Higgins and Arie W. Kruglanski (eds.). *Social Psychology: Handbook of Basic Principles* (2nd. ed.) New York: The Guilford Press, 2007, 201-231.
16. Harriet Over and Malinda Carpenter, "Eighteen-Month-Old Infants Show Increased Helping Following Priming with Affiliation," *Psychological Science* 20(10), (2009), 1189-1193.
17. Tanya L. Chartrand and John A. Bargh, "The Chameleon Effect: The Perception- Behavior Link and Social Interaction," *Journal of Personality and Social Psychology* 76, (1999), 893-910.
18. John A. Bargh, Peter M. Gollwitzer, Annette Lee-Chai, Kimberly Barndollar, and Roman Trötschel, "The Automated Will: Nonconscious Activation and Pursuit of Behavioral Goals." *Journal of Personality and Social Psychology* 81, (2001), 1014–1027.
19. Stéphane Doyen, Olivier Klein, Cora-Lise Pichon, and Axel Cleeremans, "Behavioral Priming: It's all in the Mind, but Whose Mind?" *PLoS ONE* 7(1), (2012), e29081.doi:10.1371/journal.pone. 0029081
20. John A. Bargh, "Priming Effects Replicate Just Fine, Thanks," *Psychology Today,* (May, 2012). https://www.psychologytoday. com/blog/the-natural-unconscious/201205/priming-effects-replicate-just-fine-thanks
21. Jay G. Hull, Laurie B. Slone, Karen B. Meteyer, & Amanda R. Matthews, "The Nonconsciousness of Self-Consciousness," *Journal of Personality and Social Psychology* 83(2), (2002). 406-424. http://dx.doi.org/10.1037/0022-3514.83.2.406
22. Joseph Cesario, Jason E. Plaks, E. Tory Higgins, "Automatic Social Behavior as Motivated Preparation to Interact," *Journal of Personality and Social Psychology* 90(6), (2006), 893-910. DOI:10.1037/0022-3514.90.6.893.
23. Jamie Decoster and Heather M. Claypool, "A Meta-analysis of Priming Effects on Impression Formation Supporting a General Model of Informational Biases," *Personality and Social Psychology Review* 8, (2004), 2-27. doi:10.1207/S15327957PSPR0801_1

24. C. Daryl Cameron, Jazmin L. Brown-Iannuzzi, and B. Keith Payne, "Sequential Priming Measures of Implicit Social Cognition: A Meta-Analysis of Associations with Behavior and Explicit Attitudes," *Personality and Social Psychology Review* (published online 5 April 2012). doi:0.1177/1088868312440047

Chapter 2

1. Susan M. Andersen, Gordon B. Moskowitz, Irene V. Blair, and Brian A. Nosek, "Automatic Thought," in E. Tory Higgins and Arie W. Kruglanski (eds.). *Social Psychology: Handbook of Basic Principles* (2nd. ed.) New York: The Guilford Press, 2007, 138-175.
2. Christina Merrick, Melika Farnia, Tiffany K. Jantz, Adam Gazzaley, and Ezequiel Morsella. "External Control of the Stream of Consciousness: Stimulus-Based Effects on Involuntary Thought Sequences," *Consciousness and Cognition* 33 (2015), 217-225.
3. Allison K. Allen, Kevin Wilkins, Adam Gazzaley, and Ezequiel Morsella, "Conscious Thoughts from Reflex-Like Processes: A New Experimental Paradigm for Consciousness Research," *Consciousness and Cognition* 22, (2013), 1318–1331.
4. John A. Bargh and Tanya L. Chartrand, "The Unbearable Automaticity of Being," *American Psychologist*, 54(7), (1999), 462-479.
5. Jens Forster & Nira Liberman, "Knowledge Activation," in E. Tory Higgins and Arie W. Kruglanski (eds.). *Social Psychology: Handbook of Basic Principles* (2nd. ed.) New York: The Guilford Press, 2007, 201-231.
6. E. Tory Higgins, "Knowledge Activation: Accessibility, Applicability, and Salience," in E. Tory Higgins and Arie W. Kruglanski (eds.). *Social Psychology: Handbook of Basic Principles.* New York: The Guilford Press, 1996, 133-168.
7. Davidson, Richard J., and Bruce S. McEwen. "Social Influences on Neuroplasticity: Stress and Interventions to Promote Well-Being." *Nature neuroscience* 15.5 (2012), 689–695. doi:10.1038/nn.3093.
8. University Health News Staff. "Neuroplasticity: Your Brain's Marvelous Ability to Reengineer Itself." *University Health News*, January 15, 2016. https://universityhealthnews.com/daily/memory/ neuroplasticity-your-brains-marvelous-ability-to-reengineer-itself/
9. John A. Bargh, Mark Chen, and Lara Burrows, "Automaticity of Social Behavior: Direct Effects of Trait Construct and Stereotype Activation on Action," *Journal of Personality and Social Psychology* 71(2), (1996), 230-244.

10. John A. Bargh, "Automaticity in Social Psychology," in E. Tory Higgins and Arie W. Kruglanski (eds.). *Social Psychology: Handbook of Basic Principles.* New York: The Guilford Press, 1996, 169-183.
11. S. Schmitt, "Implementation Intention Effects in Schizophrenic Patients," unpublished Master's thesis in Peter M. Gollwitzer, "Implementation Intentions," *American Psychologist* 54(7), (1999), 493-503.

Chapter 3

1. Jens Forster and Nira Liberman, "Knowledge Activation," in E. Tory Higgins and Arie W. Kruglanski (eds.). *Social Psychology: Handbook of Basic Principles* (2nd. ed.) New York: The Guilford Press, 2007, 201-231.
2. Daniel, M. Wegner, "Ironic Processes of Mental Control, "*Psychological Review* 101(1), (1994), 34-52.
3. Daniel M. Wegner, Matthew Ansfield, and Daniel Pilloff, "The Putt and the Pendulum: Ironic Effects of the Mental Control of Action," *Psychological Science* 9(3), (1998), 196-199.
4. Tim Woodman and Paul A. Davis, "The Role of Repression in the Incidence of Ironic Errors," *The Sport Psychologist* 22, (2008), 183-196.
5. Sian L. Bellock, James A. Afremow, Amy L. Rabe, and Thomas H. Carr, "'Don't Miss!' The Debilitating Effects of Suppressive Imagery on Golf Putting Performance," *Journal of Sport and Exercise Psychology* 23, (2001), 200-221.
6. Matthew Ansfield, Daniel M. Wegner, and Robin Bowser, "Ironic Effects of Sleep Urgency." *Behaviour Research and Therapy* 34(7), (1996), 523-531.
7. Daniel M. Wegner, David J. Schneider, Samuel R. Carter, and Teri L. White, "Paradoxical Effects of Thought Suppression" *Journal of Personality and Social Psychology* 52(1), (1987), 5-13.
8. Christina Merrick, Melika Farnia, Tiffany K. Jantz, Adam Gazzaley, and Ezequiel Morsella. "External Control of the Stream of Consciousness: Stimulus-Based Effects on Involuntary Thought Sequences," *Consciousness and Cognition* 33 (2015), 217-225.
9. Mihály Csíkszentmihályi, *Flow: The Psychology of Optimal Experience,* 1990, New York: Harper & Row.

Chapter 4

1. Aldous Huxley, *The Education of an Amphibian* in John A. Bargh, Peter M. Gollwitzer, Annette Lee-Chai, Kimberly Barndollar, and Roman Trötschel, The Automated Will: Nonconscious Activation and Pursuit of Behavioral Goals. *Journal of Personality and Social Psychology* 81, (2001), 1014–1027.

2. John A. Bargh and Tanya L. Chartrand, "The Unbearable Automaticity of Being," *American Psychologist* 54(7), (1999), 462-479.
3. Suzana Herculano-Houzel, "The Human Brain in Numbers: A Linearly Scaled-Up Primate Brain." *Frontiers in Human Neuroscience.* 2009; 3(31):doi: 10.3389/neuro.09.031.2009.
4. Stanford University Medical Center, "Stunning Details of Brain Connections Revealed," *Science Daily,* (November 2010), <www.sciencedaily.com/releases/2010/11/101117121803.htm>.
5. AI Impacts, "Scale of the Human Brain," http://aiimpacts.org/scale-of-the-human-brain/.
6. Riken Research, "Largest Neuronal Network Simulation Achieved Using K Computer," Press Release, (August 2, 2013), http://www.riken.jp/en/pr/press/2013/20130802_1/
7. Roy F. Baumeister and John Tierney, *Willpower: Rediscovering the Greatest Human Strength,* 2012, New York: Penguin Books.
8. S. J. Scott, *Habit Stacking: 127 Small Changes to Improve Your Health, Wealth, and Happiness,* (2nd ed.), 2017, Oldtown Publishing LLC.
9. A. N. Whitehead, *An Introduction to Mathematics,* New York, Holt in John A. Bargh and Tanya L. Chartrand, "The Unbearable Automaticity of Being," *American Psychologist* 54(7), (1999), 462-479.
10. Susan M. Andersen, Gordon B. Moskowitz, Irene V. Blair, and Brian A. Nosek, "Automatic Thought," in E. Tory Higgins and Arie W. Kruglanski (eds.). *Social Psychology: Handbook of Basic Principles* (2nd. ed.) New York: The Guilford Press, 2007, 138-175.
11. Michael Shermer, "The Pattern of Self Deception," YouTube, https://www.ted.com/talks/michael_shermer_the_pattern_behind_self_deception#t-10878, (accessed 6-12-16).
12. Leslie A. Hart, *Human Brain and Human Learning,* (1983), Longman Publishing Group.
13. Christina Merrick, Melika Farnia, Tiffany K. Jantz, Adam Gazzaley, and Ezequiel Morsella. "External Control of the Stream of Consciousness: Stimulus-Based Effects on Involuntary Thought Sequences," *Consciousness and Cognition* 33 (2015), 217-225.
14. Sian L. Bellock, James A. Afremow, Amy L. Rabe, and Thomas H. Carr, "'Don't Miss!' The Debilitating Effects of Suppressive Imagery on Golf Putting Performance," *Journal of Sport and Exercise Psychology* 23, (2001), 200-221.
15. Leonard Mlodinow, *Subliminal: How the Unconscious Mind Rules Your Behavior,* (2012), New York: Vintage Books.

16. John Bargh, *Before You Know It: The Unconscious Reasons We Do What We Do*, (2017), New York: Touchstone.
17. Anthony R. Pratkanis, Jay Eskenazi, and Anthony G. Greenwald, "What You Expect Is What You Believe (But Not Necessarily What You Get): A Test of the Effectiveness of Subliminal Self-Help Audiotapes," *Basic and Applied Social Psychology* 15, (1994) 251-276. 10.1207/s15324834basp1503_3.
18. Clifton W. Mitchell, "Effects of Subliminally Presented Auditory Suggestions of Itching on Scratching Behavior," *Perceptual and Motor Skills* 80, (1994), 87-96.

Chapter 5

1. Tim Woodman and Paul A. Davis, "The Role of Repression in the Incidence of Ironic Errors," *The Sport Psychologist* 22, (2008), 183-196.
2. Sian L. Bellock, James A. Afremow, Amy L. Rabe, and Thomas H. Carr, "'Don't Miss!' The Debilitating Effects of Suppressive Imagery on Golf Putting Performance." *Journal of Sport and Exercise Psychology* 23, (2001), 200-221.
3. Susan M. Andersen, Gordon B. Moskowitz, Irene V. Blair, and Brian A. Nosek, "Automatic Thought," in E. Tory Higgins and Arie W. Kruglanski (eds.). *Social Psychology: Handbook of Basic Principles* (2nd. ed.) New York: The Guilford Press, 2007, 138-175.
4. Jens Forster and Nira Liberman, "Knowledge Activation," in E. Tory Higgins and Arie W. Kruglanski (eds.). *Social Psychology: Handbook of Basic Principles* (2nd. ed.) New York: The Guilford Press, 2007, 201-231.

Chapter 6

1. Davidson, Richard J., and Bruce S. McEwen. "Social Influences on Neuroplasticity: Stress and Interventions to Promote Well-Being." *Nature neuroscience* 15.5 (2012), 689–695. doi:10.1038/nn.3093.
2. John A. Bargh and Tanya L. Chartrand, "The Unbearable Automaticity of Being," *American Psychologist* 54(7), (1999), 462-479.
3. Phillippa Lally, Cornelia H. M. van Jaarsveld, Henry W. W. Potts, and Jane Wardle, "How are Habits Formed: Modelling Habit Formation in the Real World," *European Journal of Social Psychology* 40(6), (2010), 881-1094. DOI: 10.1002/ejsp.674
4. Susan M. Andersen, Gordon B. Moskowitz, Irene V. Blair, and Brian A. Nosek, "Automatic Thought," in E. Tory Higgins and Arie W. Kruglanski (eds.). *Social Psychology: Handbook of Basic Principles* (2nd. ed.) New York: The Guilford Press, 2007, 138-175.

5. Maxwell Maltz, *Psycho-Cybernetics* (1960), New York: Simon & Schuster.
6. Bogdan Draganski, Christian Gaser, Gerd Kempermann, H. Georg Kuhn, Jürgen Winkler, Christian Büchel and Arne May, "Temporal and Spatial Dynamics of Brain Structure Changes during Extensive Learning," Journal of Neuroscience 26(23), 2006, 6314-6317; DOI: https://doi.org/10.1523/JNEUROSCI.4628-05.2006
7. Tang, Y. Y., Hölzel, B. K., & Posner, M. I. "The neuroscience of mindfulness meditation." *Nature Reviews Neuroscience 16*(4), (2015), 213-225.
8. Neuroplasticity Explained. Everything Explained Today. http://everything.explained.today/Neuroplasticity
9. Rick Hanson, *Hardwiring Happiness: The New Brain Science of Contentment, Calm, and Confidence,* (2016), New York: Harmony, and *Buddha's Brain: The Practical Neuroscience of Happiness, Love, and Wisdom,* (2009), Oakland, CA: New Harbinger Publications.

Chapter 7

1. Sian L. Bellock, James A. Afremow, Amy L. Rabe, and Thomas H. Carr, "'Don't Miss!' The Debilitating Effects of Suppressive Imagery on Golf Putting Performance," *Journal of Sport and Exercise Psychology* 23, (2001), 200-221.
2. Susan M. Andersen, Gordon B. Moskowitz, Irene V. Blair, and Brian A. Nosek, "Automatic Thought," in E. Tory Higgins and Arie W. Kruglanski (eds.). *Social Psychology: Handbook of Basic Principles* (2nd. ed.) New York: The Guilford Press, 2007, 138-175.
3. Joanne V. Wood, W.Q. Elaine Perunovic, and John W. Lee, "Positive Self-Statements Power for Some, Peril for Others," *Psychological Science* 20(7), (2009), 860-866.
4. John A. Bargh, Mark Chen, and Lara Burrows, "Automaticity of Social Behavior: Direct Effects of Trait Construct and Stereotype Activation on Action," *Journal of Personality and Social Psychology* 71(2), (1996), 230-244.
5. Matthew A. Killingsworth and Daniel T. Gilbert, "A Wandering Mind Is an Unhappy Mind," *Science*, 330(6006), (Nov, 2010), 932. DOI: 10.1126/science.1192439
6. Gary Lupyan and Daniel Swingley, "Self-Directed Speech Affects Visual Search Performance," *The Quarterly Journal of Experimental Psychology* 65(6), (2012), 1068-1085. http://dx.doi.org/10.1080/17470218.2011.647039

7. Alexander James Kirkham, Julian Michael Breeze, and Paloma Mari-Beffa, "The Impact of Verbal Instructions on Goal-Directed Behaviour," *Acta Psychologica,* 139(1), (2012), 212-219. https://doi.org/10.1016/j.actpsy.2011.09.016

Chapter 8

1. Jens Forster and Nira Liberman, "Knowledge Activation," in E. Tory Higgins and Arie W. Kruglanski (eds.). *Social Psychology: Handbook of Basic Principles* (2nd. ed.) New York: The Guilford Press, 2007, 201-231.
2. E. Tory Higgins, "Knowledge Activation: Accessibility, Applicability, and Salience," in E. Tory Higgins and Arie W. Kruglanski (eds.). *Social Psychology: Handbook of Basic Principles.* New York: The Guilford Press, 1996, 133-168.
3. Susan M. Andersen, Gordon B. Moskowitz, Irene V. Blair, and Brian A. Nosek, "Automatic Thought," in E. Tory Higgins and Arie W. Kruglanski (eds.). *Social Psychology: Handbook of Basic Principles* (2nd. ed.) New York: The Guilford Press, 2007, 138-175.
4. Davidson, Richard J., and Bruce S. McEwen. "Social Influences on Neuroplasticity: Stress and Interventions to Promote Well-Being." *Nature neuroscience* 15.5 (2012), 689–695. doi:10.1038/nn.3093.
5. University Health News Staff. "Neuroplasticity: Your Brain's Marvelous Ability to Reengineer Itself." *University Health News,* January 15, 2016. https://universityhealthnews.com/daily/memory/neuroplasticity-your-brains-marvelous-ability-to-reengineer-itself/
6. John A. Bargh, "Automaticity in Social Psychology," in E. Tory Higgins and Arie W. Kruglanski (eds.). *Social Psychology: Handbook of Basic Principles.* New York: The Guilford Press, 1996, 169-183.
7. Peter M. Gollwitzer, "Implementation Intentions," *American Psychologist* 54(7), (1999), 493-503.
8. S. Schmitt, "Implementation Intention Effects in Schizophrenic patients" Unpublished Master's Thesis, (1997), in Peter M. Gollwitzer, Implementation Intentions," *American Psychologist* 54(7), (1999), 493-503.
9. Phillippa Lally, Cornelia H. M. van Jaarsveld, Henry W. W. Potts, and Jane Wardle, "How are Habits Formed: Modelling Habit Formation in the Real World," *European Journal of Social Psychology* 40(6), (2010), 881-1094. DOI: 10.1002/ejsp.674

10. S. J. Scott, *Habit Stacking: 127 Small Changes to Improve Your Health, Wealth, and Happiness*, Kindle Edition, (April 14, 2017), Oldtown Publishing LLC; 2 edition.
11. Julie K. Norem, *The Positive Power of Negative Thinking,* (2001), Cambridge, MA: Basic Books.
12. Roy F. Baumeister, Ellen Bratslavsky, Catrin Finkenauer, and Kathleen D. Vohs, "Bad is Stronger than Good." *Review of General Psychology* 5(4), (2001), 323-370.

Chapter 9

1. Clifton W. Mitchell, *Effective Techniques for Dealing with Highly Resistant Clients,* (2007), Johnson City, TN.: Clifton Mitchell Publishing,
2. Susan M. Andersen, Gordon B. Moskowitz, Irene V. Blair, and Brian A. Nosek, "Automatic Thought," in E. Tory Higgins and Arie W. Kruglanski (eds.). *Social Psychology: Handbook of Basic Principles* (2nd. ed.) New York: The Guilford Press, 2007, 138-175.
3. Jens Forster and Nira Liberman, "Knowledge Activation," in E. Tory Higgins and Arie W. Kruglanski (eds.). *Social Psychology: Handbook of Basic Principles* (2nd. ed.) New York: The Guilford Press, 2007, 201-231.
4 Ted P. Asay and Michael J. Lambert, "The Empirical Case for the Common Factors in Therapy: Quantitative Findings," in Mark A. Hubble, Barry L. Duncan, and Scott D. Miller (eds.) *The Heart and Soul of Change: What Works in Therapy*, Washington, D. C.: American Psychological Association, 1999, 23-55.

Chapter 10

1. William James, *The Principles of Psychology, (1890),* New York: Holt, as cited in John A. Bargh and Tanya L. Chartrand, "The Unbearable Automaticity of Being," *American Psychologist* 54(7), (1999), 462-479.
2. Maxwell Maltz, *Psycho-Cybernetics* (1960), New York: Simon & Schuster.
3. Shakti Gawain, *Creative Visualization: Use the Power of Your Imagination to Create What You Want in Your Life,* (1978), California: New World Library.
4. Joseph Murphy, *The Power of Your Subconscious Mind,* (1963), Englewood Cliffs, N J: Prentice-Hall Inc.
5. Norman Vincent Peale, *The Power of Positive Thinking,* (1952), New York: Prentice Hall.
6. Joe Karbo, *The Lazy Man's Way to Riches,* (1973), Sunset Beach, CA: Joe Karbo.

7. Shad Helmstettler, *What to Say When You Talk to Your Self,* (1986), Scottsdale, AZ: Grindle Press.
8. Rhonda Byrne, *The Secret,* (2006), Atria Books/Beyond Words.

Chapter 11

1. David Zinczenko and Matt Goulding, *Eat This Not That! Thousands of Simple Food Swaps that Can Save You 10, 20, 30 Pounds--or More,* (2007), New York: Rodale Books.
2. David Zinczenko and Matt Goulding, *Cook This Not That! Kitchen Survival Guide* (2010), New York: Rodale Books.
3. Anthony Robbins, *Unlimited Power: The New Science Of Personal Achievement* (1986) New York: Simon and Schuster.
4. Rick Hanson, *Hardwiring Happiness: The New Brain Science of Contentment, Calm, and Confidence,* (2016), New York: Harmony.
5. Nasim Taleb, *Fooled by Randomness: The Hidden Role of Chance in Life and in the Markets,* (2005), New York: Textere.
6. Nasim Taleb, *The Black Swan: The Impact of the Highly Improbable,* (2007), New York: Random House.

The future is the summation of the decisions
you are presently making.

About the Author

Clifton Mitchell Ph.D., is a professor emeritus and retired Licensed Psychologist who has a love for teaching and over 30 years' experience as an international clinical trainer and keynote speaker. He delivers practical information in a uniquely entertaining, fast-paced style filled with humor. As a keynote speaker at mental health conferences, businesses, and leadership organizations he has taught techniques for improving communications and for creating personal change through the precise use of language.

His primary areas of interest include the management of resistance in therapy as well as legal and ethical issues within the field of mental health. In his book, *Effective Techniques for Dealing with Highly Resistant Clients,* he presents cutting-edge approaches for managing psychological resistance, many of which incorporate priming and dominant thought theory presented here. His legal and ethical training is conducted in a fun, dynamic game show format.

He is published in numerous professional journals including the *Psychotherapy Networker, Psychotherapy in Australia, Journal of Personality Assessment, Perceptual and Motor Skills, Psychology and Education, Journal of Psychological Type, The Professional School Counselor, Vistas,* and *The Advocate.* His ideas and writings have also been published in *Men's Health Today* and *Barron's Financial Weekly.* Dr. Mitchell retired from East Tennessee State University where he received the Teacher of the Year award in 2002. For more information please visit: www.cliftonmitchell.com.